BEOWULF
on the
BEACH

ALSO BY JACK MURNIGHAN

*The Naughty Bits: The Steamiest and Most Scandalous
Sex Scenes from the World's Great Books*

*Classic Nasty: More Naughty Bits: A Rollicking Guide to
Hot Sex in Great Books, from* The Iliad *to* The Corrections

Full Frontal Fiction: The Best of Nerve.com (coeditor)

BEOWULF
on the
BEACH

WHAT to LOVE
and WHAT to SKIP in
LITERATURE'S
50 GREATEST HITS

Jack Murnighan

THREE RIVERS PRESS
NEW YORK

For my grandpa Walter Becker (d. 2006),
who didn't read a word of literature in his life.

If only still to have your hand in mine.

Copyright © 2009 by Jack Murnighan

Published in the United States by Three Rivers Press, an imprint of the
Crown Publishing Group, a division of Random House, Inc., New York.
www.crownpublishing.com

Three Rivers Press and the Tugboat design are registered trademarks of
Random House, Inc.

Library of Congress Cataloging-in-Publication Data
Murnighan, Jack.
Beowulf on the beach / Jack Murnighan.—1st ed.
p. cm.
ISBN 978-0-307-40957-7
1. Literature—History and criticism. 2. Best books. I. Title.
PN524.M87 2009
809—dc22
2008050484

Printed in the United States of America

Design by Helene Berinsky

10 9 8 7 6 5 4 3 2 1

First Edition

Contents

Contents

And Philip ran thither to him . . . and said,
Understandest thou what thou readest?
And he said, How can I, except some man
should guide me?

—Acts of the Apostles 8:31–32

Preface

What, you weren't planning on packing *Beowulf* with your flip-flops and sunscreen? How about *Ulysses, Don Quixote,* or *The Iliad*? But you still feel bad about not reading them, right? Or maybe you lumped your way through the required readings in college but weren't exactly head over heels. No surprise there; how many college classes did you take where the point was to *like* literature? And did anyone tell you that *Moby Dick* is funny, that Dante will make you cry, that Jesus tells a joke, that *Anna Karenina* is a beach read, or that Joyce can be great, especially if he's talking about booze, sex, or organ meats? These books are dazzling, but that's not how they're normally taught or perceived. And if you don't go back to the classics as an adult, you might never know how much better they are when they're read for pleasure, not for a test. As long as the so-called great books stay locked in the ivory tower, people don't see how gripping and meaningful they can be, and their kaleidoscopic glories get squandered.

I propose a simple fix: let's give literature another look, but this time we'll enjoy ourselves. And I don't just mean above the ears; I want you to *feel* these books in your heart, in your soul, and maybe even below the waist. I myself am a recovering academic (it's a tough twelve-step program), but since the day I took off my tweed, I've been on a mission to appreciate the classics for their deep humanity and wonder. And trust me, if you read any or all

1

of the books I'm championing here, you'll be shocked at what you find. Dollars to doughnuts, you'll laugh out loud, well up some droplets, get a little turned-on, be awestruck, impressed, and deeply, pivotally affected. Once you open yourself to the humor, drama, adventure, sex, poignancy, elegance, tragedy, and beauty of the great books, you'll see why they've long been considered among the most inspiring and engaging things ever written.

This book will be your field guide, helping you read and relish fifty of the biggest woulda-coulda-shoulda classics of all time. I've included some tips on reading good books in general (Go slowly! Use a pen! Reread!), and for each of the individual titles, an easy-access introduction that emphasizes the stuff you'll relate to most and how to corral it. And though I *know* you're going to run out and read all the original tomes, each chapter also has the following cheat sheet (including, because not every classic is perfect, the all-important What to Skip):

The Buzz—your cocktail party Ph.D.

What People Don't Know (But Should)—less hype, more substance

Best Line—to dip your toe in the water . . .

What's Sexy—. . . or into the hot tub

Quirky Fact—this you won't forget

What to Skip—and you can skip *lots*

This isn't Cliff's Notes telling you what you'd need for school; it's an attempt to show you what's in the great books that makes them really matter. It's tragic how many of us think back on what we read in college and feel, like T. S. Eliot wrote in *Four Quartets*, that we "had the experience but missed the meaning." But if I have my way, you'll soon be adding some classics to the books you love the most.

HOMER
(c. 900 B.C.)

∽∾∾∽

The Iliad

Because the gods of irony still rule the firmament, Homer happens to be the name of both the *pater familias* Simpson, cartoon mainstay of the living room box, and the acknowledged father of Western literature, oft called greatest writer of all time. Origins are a funny thing, of course, and while we point all our literature back to Homer, we neither know the exact time when he wrote (most modern scholars think between the 10th and 8th century B.C.) nor even whether the same person necessarily wrote *The Iliad* and *The Odyssey* (the latter of which is sometimes argued to have been written by a woman). Then there's the fact that this other guy named Hesiod might be even older than Homer and wrote a book called the *Theogony* where, among other things, the world is created and the gods come to be—one from hacked-off genitals floating in the ocean. You can see why most people prefer to leave him out of the conversation. . . .

But somehow or other, Western literature got itself going, whether by Homer, Hesiod, or someone else long forgotten or never recorded. As founding stories for a whole civilization go, however, *The Iliad* and *Odyssey* are pretty well suited, at least at first blush. Each appears to be a supremely heroic tale with a super-macho protagonist—Achilles in *The Iliad,* Odysseus in *The*

Odyssey—offing his fair share of flunkies and weenie men. Most founding myths are based on just such triumphs at someone else's expense. The only problem is that anyone who reads *The Iliad* or *The Odyssey* closely will see that the heroes themselves are barely responsible for their actions; the gods interfere with nearly everything, handing out victories and failures whimsically and petulantly like demented children throwing bread to geese. It's a bit sad and bracing, actually, to find out that Achilles the great warrior really wins his battles less because of the strength of his arm or the trueness of his spear and more because higher forces come to his aid. In what many people think is the greatest tale of heroism and unmitigated studliness, it turns out that humans are just Cabbage Patch Kids tossed around by bratty, vindictive gods that hardly deserve the name.

That said, *The Iliad* is still as riveting and potent as anything you'll ever read. The story is familiar: scads of Greek troops have sailed to Troy (a possibly fictitious city in what is now Turkey) to take back Helen, the West's first great beauty, whom the fair-haired Trojan prettyboy Paris swiped away from her husband, the trollish Greek prince Menelaus. But the siege isn't going so well; it's already lasted ten years and the Greeks' best fighter, Achilles, is pouting in his ship because he wasn't given the slave girl he wanted. We follow the give-and-take of the battle until Achilles finally gets off his sulking heinie, and then the proverbial hits the proverbial.

The Iliad is action at its best, and whoever Homer was, he knew how to tell a story. Its taut dialogue and vivid narration make *The Iliad* unfold in your mind in Hollywood Technicolor (and it's a lot better than the big-screen *Troy*, the blockfizzler adaptation from 2004). When you think about *The Iliad* that way, you won't believe how much it reads like a screenplay: set piece after set piece, great characters, killer action, and the approaching thunderstorm tension as we wait for Achilles to pick up his weapon. But to make sure you feel all the bone-jarring power of Western literature's first masterpiece, I'll give you some selling points.

Here are a few surefire ways to love *The Iliad*:

1. Because you hear the sound of drums, the relentless booming drums of war, pounding pounding pounding. The poem itself has incredible rhythm (even in translation; see "Best Line" on page 8), and once you let yourself slide into its cadence, you can feel the battle building, the battle raging, the concatenated roar of the wounded dying beneath your feet. As you read, imagine the scene, imagine all those years of unsuccessful assault, of a city surrounded and assailed by an enormous unyielding force, day after day after day. No one goes anywhere; they just keep fighting. The drama only builds ("Here in the night that will break our army or else will preserve it") and everywhere there are bodies "lying along the ground, to delight no longer their wives, but the vultures." This is a war poem, and you have to feel it from within.

2. For the gore. How many world-class books contain scenes with decapitated heads still speaking; decapitated heads being bowled; pierced-through hearts still beating and shaking the spears that transfix them; spears stabbing through eyes, cheeks, tongues, teeth, jaws, and genitals; spears going in one ear and out the other; brains, entrails, eyeballs, noses, and blood strewn across the ground; eyes mounted on spears; men trying to hold in their spilling entrails; marrow gushing from neck bones; and other such delights?

3. For the macho taunts, as when an effeminate archer (i.e., not a hand-to-hand warrior) is mocked: "Foul fighter, lovely in

your locks, eyer of young girls . . . Now you have scratched my foot and even boast of this" or when the Greeks are heckled: "Wretches . . . was it your fate then far from your friends and the land of your fathers, to glut with your shining fat the running dogs?" There are a couple dozen such disses to savor.

4. For the riveting monologues, like the Greek leader Agamemnon's renunciation speech to his soldiers and its trenchant "This shall be a thing of shame." Or that of Hector, the great Trojan hope, berating Paris: "Stand up against warlike Menelaus? . . . The lyre would not help you then, nor the favors of Aphrodite, nor your locks, when you rolled in the dust." These are two early ones, but as *The Iliad* progresses, the speeches get more and more blistering.

5. For the similes: the incredible description in Book II of the Greek warriors streaming from the ships like bees from a stone; the same men as grain, shifting from one sentiment to another; the sound of the battle being joined like rivers crashing into one another, etc. Keep an eye out for long sentences that begin with "as"; these are Homer's great similes, the moments when he really swings his stylistic ax.

There are also a few other things to keep in mind:

1. Don't get confused by the multiple names for everything: Ilion = Troy; Paris = Alexandros; Danaans = Achaians = Greeks; Achilles = Aiakides; etc. Good editions will have a glossary in the back to help with the confusion.

2. Enjoy the word repetition—or at least don't let it drive you crazy. Athena will be referred to as "grey-eyed" and Hera as "ox-eyed" about nine trillion times. That's just the way they did it back then; think of it as the Homeric tic. Bummer for Hera.

3. Read the Lattimore translation, even though he spells the names funny. Many have translated *The Iliad*, but no one has rendered the stark supreme majesty of its language like Lattimore.

Now that we've got that all sorted out, you should have no trouble relishing the origin and apex of virility lit. Hollywood can send out its Stallone and Schwarzenegger myths of all-meat masculinity, but if you want it rough, tough, and literate, Homer has the first and last word.

The Buzz: It was all for a woman—no surprise there, right? When the Trojan prince Paris decided to leave Greece with a rather pleasant souvenir, namely Helen, he kind of ticked off a few folks. This is why Helen—whom we call Helen of Troy though she was originally Helen of Sparta—is referred to as "the face that launched a thousand ships"; because of her, the Greeks sent their entire fleet in pursuit. Historians now tell us that if this invasion actually took place—and it might have—the Greeks didn't have anywhere near that many vessels to assail Troy's walls. Still. Her cuckolded husband and his homeboys came to get her back, didn't take no for an answer, and thus we have our story.

What People Don't Know (But Should): We all have heard how Troy fell: the Greeks left the Trojans a "present" of a giant wooden horse that they allowed into the city—the only problem was that it was filled with Greek soldiers who then opened the gates. But none of that actually happens in *The Iliad,* and it's only briefly alluded to in *The Odyssey* (we know the story from later retellings, especially in *The Aeneid* a millennium later). No, *The Iliad* is Achilles' tale, culminating in his eventual mano-a-mano encounter with Hector—good stuff. Pretty amazing, though, that the hero can wait almost three-quarters of the book before he straps on his armor. Yes, he's literature's great tough guy, but he sure had a bee in his bonnet about not getting that slave girl.

Best Line: As mentioned, note the rhythm and buildup in this quote (and, yes, Lattimore spells Hector with a "k"): "But the Trojans, gathered into a pack, like a flame, like a storm cloud, came on after Hektor the son of Priam, raging relentless, roaring and crying as one, and their hopes ran high of capturing the ships of the Achaians, and killing the best men beside them, all of them" (XIII, 39–43).

What's Sexy: Instead of going to fight Menelaus when he's challenged, ladies' man Paris asks Helen to go to bed with him, saying that he was never as turned on as then. (I guess when the hubbie comes back to eighty-six you and take back his wife, that can be something of an aphrodisiac.) There's also an impressive sex scene between Zeus and Hera, making it clear how much it helps one's game to be all-powerful: Zeus first causes crocuses and hyacinths to grow so high and thick as to make a bed, then he "drew about them a golden wonderful cloud, and from it a glimmering dew descended" (XIV, 349–50). Oh my . . .

Quirky Fact: In Plato's dialogue *Ion,* the title character is what was called a rhapsode, a traveling performer who could recite the entirety of *The Iliad* or *The Odyssey* from memory. That's about a few days of recitation to memorize—and rhapsodes could start up from any point in the story. A lot of people use this to argue that, with the rise of technology, our ability to remember things has faded. But thinking of how many rock songs most of us can sing, I'm more convinced that there was simply less to keep in one's brain back then, and today we just don't realize how much we know.

What to Skip: By and large *The Iliad* makes for a brisk, white-knuckle read, but there are a few passages that lag. Don't worry if you jump ahead at II, 494–759 (a list of warriors and where they came from) and IX, 529–99 (story of an unrelated side battle). You won't miss anything.

HOMER
(c. 900 B.C.)

∽∾∽

The Odyssey

So you've just composed the poem that 2,800 years later will still be considered the greatest action story ever; where do you go from there? It's hard not to feel for Homer—talk about being set up for a sophomore slump. But assuming he is the one who wrote *The Odyssey,* Greece's greatest poet triumphed again his second time around, managing to come up with one of the better follow-up plots this side of *The Empire Strikes Back.*

Having already chronicled the ultra-manly warrior Achilles, this time Homer gives us a hero of a very different stripe. Odysseus is studly, sure, but he's more famous for being finagling and wily (he is sometimes called Polytropos—a Greek way of saying "he of the honeyed tongue"). *The Odyssey* tells of Odysseus' struggle to get back from Troy to his home in Ithaca (Greece, not upstate New York). It's the archetypal tale of wandering, of trials and tribulations, detours and deferrals, menacing sea monsters and horndog goddesses who just won't let him out of their bowers of bliss. We follow the crafty one (called Ulysses by the Romans, giving Joyce his title), who, having already spent ten years away from his wife and son in the sacking of Troy, loses another ten being buffeted around isles mythic and real, all because he managed to tick off the sea god Poseidon—

clearly not a good idea when you're trying to sail back to your fatherland.

All the while, dozens of suitors are assailing Odysseus' wife, Penelope, and more or less turning Odysseus' house into a Cornell frat: eating up his livestock, guzzling down his cellar, and being insolent and cavalier in the extreme. But their day is coming; oh, is it coming. Time and again we're told that there will be some serious reckoning when the big O gets back; in fact, one of the great joys of *The Odyssey* is reading the various lines describing what the suitors are in for ("If they ever see that man return to Ithaca, they will pray they are nimbler on their feet"; "They do not know the black fate that is near them, to destroy them in a single day," etc.). As with Achilles' wrath in *The Iliad,* we know there's an ass-whupping on the horizon, but Homer makes us wait, letting the bloodthirsty anticipation build and build in the minds of what's now almost three millennia of readers. In Achilles' tale, it takes him a full 17 books (of 24) before he goes and puts the smackdown on the Trojans; in *The Odyssey,* it takes Odysseus 21 books (again out of 24) before he makes it home and begins waxing those pesky suitors. In both cases, even though the grim results have long since been announced, we still turn Homer's pages, getting more and more antsy for the "heroes" to show us their chops.

Beyond salivating for the suitors' comeuppance, the other key to enjoying *The Odyssey* is to read it like you're watching a movie. Like its big brother, *The Iliad,* it's exceptionally cinematic (it has been adapted, in part or whole, numerous times. The best—though the connections are pretty thin—is the Coen brothers' *O Brother Where Art Thou?*). Although Odysseus is forever recounting his tribulations, he's a pretty efficient storyteller; the dialogue tends toward the spare and the action speedy, so it's important that you let the reel run on your cerebral scrim as you read. To get the most out of *The Odyssey,* you really have to imagine the suitors sloshing honeyed wine and gnawing sheep joints, not knowing Odysseus is coming home to settle the bill; you have to see the alluring nymph Calypso and her fair braids and smell the citron and cedar in the air; you have to imagine the bewitching enchantress Circe and her handmaidens bathing and oiling poor Odysseus; you have to shudder as Cyclops splatters the heads of Odysseus' men on the ground then devours them whole, bones and all; and you have to visualize Odysseus in Hades, the land of the dead, pouring out a pool of blood to attract the spirits of the deceased so they will come and speak to him. Translations and historical texts use language that typically has less force than things written in our time and mother tongues, so it's that much more important to help them along by visualizing. That said, the plot of *The Odyssey* is eminently palpable, so it should make for easy mental staging (maybe imagine Christian Bale as Señor Honey-Tongue; I think he's got the right combo of machismo and seeming wiliness, plus the dubious likability I'm about to tell you about . . .).

The tough part about *The Odyssey* is that Odysseus comes off much of the time as an annoying blowhard, always bragging but rarely accomplishing anything without help from his protectress, Athena, the goddess of war. Even his supposed craftiness and cunning tends to play out in pretty lame ways. But that's the thing with these Greeks: their gods weren't especially heroic or moral, so how could their mortals be? To me the best way to enjoy *The Odyssey* is to minimize the role of Odysseus; let him simply be the central figure who sets the action in motion, and let the action be the story. As you'll see in "The Buzz" on page 13, the important parts of the story have little to do with him. He is the title character of one of the most famous tales in world history, but he might also be among literature's most disappointing heroes.

The Buzz: Many of Odysseus' adventures aren't particularly interesting in themselves, but they are iconic. Here's the list of the significant gods and monsters he comes across and what you need to know about them:

Aeolus: God of winds. Gives a bag filled with breezes to Odysseus; his men think it will have gold in it and open it prematurely, blowing them off course. It's a classic parable of greed.

Calypso: Called "the nymph of the fair braids," she offers the earliest recorded feminist speech in Western lit, arguing that goddesses should be able to sleep with men as freely as gods do with women. For her reward, nymphomania is named after her. Odysseus is "stuck" with her for seven years.

Circe: The other of Odysseus' seductresses, she casts magic spells over men to turn them into animals (no, beer is not involved).

Cyclops: Our famous one-eyed friend is actually named Polyphemus and only one of a whole island of cyclopses. And he doesn't seem like that bad a guy, at least until he starts grabbing two of Odysseus' men at a time and eating them alive.

Oxen of the sun god: Don't touch those cows! Another parable of that which should be left alone. Odysseus' men were warned against killing them but did so anyway and got their collective butts handed to them. When will they learn?

Penelope: Odysseus' wife is a symbol of constancy, holding out the twenty years her hubby's away, despite the myriad suitors trying to get some of dat.

Proteus: A god who can take any shape; thus the adjective *protean,* meaning like a chameleon or changeable in any situation.

Scylla and Charybdis: These two incarnate the dilemma of having to pick the lesser of two evils. Charybdis is a whirlpool that will probably kill your whole crew, Scylla a sea monster that will eat a six-pack of your men as you pass. You have to go by one or the other on the trip from Troy to Greece (through the Strait of Messina); which do you choose? Odysseus picks Scylla, pays the six-man toll (he knew he wouldn't be one of them), and moves on.

The Sirens: Their singing is irresistible and leads men to their graves. Odysseus' shipmates plug their ears with wax, but *el capitan* has himself tied to the mast of the ship so he can hear what the singing sounds like without diving into the water after them. Sadly, Homer doesn't describe it. I'm thinking Maria Callas.

Tiresias: A soothsayer, one of the souls of the dead in Hades that Odysseus calls forth to tell him of the future. In life, Tiresias was turned into a woman for smacking a pair of snakes with a stick while they were getting it on (don't mess with nature's way!). Having been a woman for a while, he was then asked who receives more sexual pleasure, men or women. He said that women receive ten times as much. Zeus' wife, Hera, got mad that he revealed women's secret and blinded him. Later he is turned back to a man. None of this is recounted in *The Odyssey,* however (he comes up in various Greek tragedies); here he simply tells Odysseus how to make it home easier.

What People Don't Know (But Should): As I mention above, there are scholars who think *The Odyssey* was written by a woman. It would be great if it was, because the only ancient Greek woman writer who currently gets any regard is Sappho, and sadly she's most famed for the lesbian overtones of her poems instead of their stately lyric beauty (and few of them have come down to us in their entirety). Let's hope a little more evidence surfaces; it would be great to know just how active women were as writers in the earliest years of our culture.

Best Line: In one of the side stories where we learn more of Odysseus' travails, the changeling Proteus is captured by Menelaus and asked for news of what happened to the other Greeks returning from Troy. Before spilling the bitter beans, the god tells him, "You will not long be tearless when you have found it all out" (IV, 493–94, Cook translation). What truer words regarding life have we ever heard?

What's Sexy: In Book V, we hear of Odysseus' imprisonment by Calypso—part of his almost decade of dallying. Apparently Odysseus only sleeps with her "by necessity . . . an unwilling man with a willing woman" (154–55), as when they go "into a nook of the hollow cave / And took pleasure of love, abiding with one another" (226–27). Not so sure I buy the innocent-Odysseus thing, though, especially since Homer later describes how he "went like a mountain-bred lion . . . /To try for sheep to go into their thick fold—/ So was Odysseus about to mingle with the fair-braided girls" (VI, 130–35). *That's* not innocent.

Quirky Fact: To escape from the cyclops, the Greeks tied themselves to the bellies of thick-fleeced sheep—bound three together per man—and Odysseus hid himself under a giant ram. When the blinded Polyphemus gropes the animals, he feels nothing and sends them out of the cave to forage, allowing the men escape. When in danger, hide under sheep!

What to Skip: You can safely skip all of Books III (a side story by the king Nestor on the death of Agamemnon) and VII (a lot of unnecessary court ceremony); then Books XI, 230–319 (references to many of the dead that Odysseus sees, none of which are vital to the story); XIV, 184–364 (Odysseus' false tale to the swineherd Eumaeus—gratuitous); XIX, 395–466 (more court ceremony); and XXIV to line 205 (the god Hermes leading the dead suitors to Hades).

THE BIBLE

❧

The Old Testament
(c. 15th- to 2nd-century B.C.)

"What a book it is, and what lessons are in it! What a book the Bible is, what a miracle, what strength is given it to man."

—Dostoevsky

It helped to found both Christianity and Judaism, the two most popular religions of the West; you would think that on this half of the globe no book would evoke more curiosity. But the collection of (scholars think) 15th- to 2nd-century B.C. scriptural writings—ostensibly by Moses and others—that have come to be called the Old Testament or the Hebrew Bible remain woefully under-read. Even the Jewish tradition focuses almost exclusively on the Torah (the story of Moses in the first five books), leaving the rest of the dense, difficult, inconsistent but often extraordinary collage pretty unknown. It's true that the New Testament has a lot of advantages over its predecessor: It's shorter, easier to read, and much kinder and gentler; it has a central hero to drive things along, and doesn't break into quite as many page-long lists of who begat whom. But what the Old Testament lacks in conventional reader-friendliness it more than makes up for in diversity and sheer, fascinating, almost incalculable weirdness. Page after page you're blindsided by things you'd never think you'd see in a religious book: mother-child cannibalism, daughter-initiated incest, gang rape, murder of spouses and children, torture, and genocide. Like contemporary Judaism, it condones divorce (see Deuteronomy 24:1, retracted in Matthew in the New Testament)—there are various resurrections (no need to wait for Christ to bring back the dead, right?); virgin daughters are offered up to angry mobs; a son of God is promised (but said to be named Immanuel); frogs are sent as a scourge (what do they do, exactly?); prophets come and go, perform miracles, admonish the heathen, but the man in the sky—despite being all-powerful—still can't seem to get people to stop worshiping in the pagan groves of Baal.

In other words, it's wackier than wacky, not short on plot, and I can guarantee you'll never read anything like it. But think about it: how nutzo is it that this is some of the most influential writing *in the history of man* and yet its violence is staggering (the prophet Elisha has bears kill forty-two children because they called him "bald-head"—do they cover that at Sunday school?), its sexiness undeniable ("Blow upon my garden, that the spices thereof may flow out," Song of Solomon 4:16), its writing often exquisite ("In wisdom is much grief, and he who increaseth knowledge increaseth sorrow," Ecclesiastes 1:18), and its penchant for list-making clearly infectious (sorry about that). It's the major document of the last two-thousand-plus years of Western civilization, but if you tried to start a religion with it now, you'd probably get in more trouble than our friends down in Waco.

Reading the Old Testament again, you'll clearly be struck by many things, but perhaps none more repeatedly than how "stiff-necked" the Israelites are (meaning how stubbornly they defy, generation after generation, the relatively simple laws of Moses— no golden calves, people!), even after they've seen a variety of miracles demonstrating that there's only one God in town, and he's got a short fuse. Even Solomon, said to be the wisest man

who ever lived or will live, finds himself breaking the commandments and worshiping idols (spurred on by the "strange
women" that he married—and he married 700 of them!). What
gives? If the Lord came to you as he did to Solomon and said,
"Reader, ask what I shall give thee," and, like Solomon, you had
your wish granted (he asked for "an understanding heart . . . that
I may discern between good and bad"), wouldn't that be enough
to convince you who's living in the apartment upstairs? Or if
you're Pharaoh (in the Old Testament, he's just called Pharaoh,
not *the* Pharaoh) and you refuse to release the Israelites you've
been keeping as slaves even though the Lord is sending you
plague after plague after plague, wouldn't you finally relent and
believe in him before he kills all your firstborn too? (Now the
raw deal for Pharaoh is that at a certain point the Bible says, "But
the Lord hardened Pharaoh's heart," so in fact it wasn't really
Pharaoh's fault. Sucks to be the bibilical Pharaoh.)

Here's what I think is going on: in reading the Old Testament
stories, every time we think, "Why is he sinning? Doesn't he know
that the Lord will punish him?" we are probably supposed to pose
ourselves similar questions. *Oh, crap, fornication this morning;
what was I thinking?* That kind of subtle lesson would account
for the constant backsliding and repetition in the Old Testament,
which does, I admit, get rather exasperating.

So, yes, trying to plow your way through the whole thing—
especially at the loris pace required—can make the Old Testament as annoying as any book ever written. But the keys to
enjoying it are pretty simple: read it for the quotes and stories
you recognize, read it for crossword answers (What land is Job
from? Uz) and for Scrabble words (a "hin" of oil), skip liberally
(and judiciously—see below), read the best books for their sheer
literary splendor (especially Job and the Song of Solomon), read
it for its profound wisdoms (primarily in Proverbs and Ecclesiastes), read it for the Lord's bombast (at its most imperial in

Isaiah and Jeremiah—think Samuel Jackson in *Pulp Fiction*: "And you will know MY NAME IS THE LORD!"), read it to see all the craziness that the local pastor would stutter to explain (Why in Genesis does Abraham keep pretending his wife Sarah is his sister and letting her get abducted?), read it to appreciate how different the New Testament is and how strange that they can be part of the same religion, and read it because on nearly every page you will be moved, shocked, perplexed, or amused. You can't read much of the Old Testament and not be flabbergasted, and how many books can you say that about?

One final reason for reading either the Old and New Testaments is that, like Proust's *Remembrance of Things Past* but even more so, you get a tutorial in slow reading. Slow reading doesn't get quite the press that speed-reading does, but there are certain books (say, all the ones discussed in the volume you're holding now) that give more fruit the slower you go. With the Bible, it's an absolute necessity, conditioning you to read in a way you probably don't read anytime else. I always say that reading the good book is like looking for nudity in the scrambled Playboy channel: you know there's a lot there, but if your attention deviates even for a second, you're likely to miss it. Of course, since the Old Testament runs to over 700 pages, you'll probably want to consult "What to Skip" on pages 23–31. Please do; I read the whole thing twice just so you don't have to.

I also recommend reading the King James version (the early 17th-century translation commissioned by the king of England), not only because the archaic language lends an appropriate gravitas to it all, but also because so many phrases that we toss about (like "my cup runneth over") come from that translation and sound funny in modern-English versions. If you're confused by a passage in the King James, though, or want to check the accu-

racy of the translation, I'm in favor of the New Oxford Annotated edition. The notes aren't always as helpful as you'd like them
to be, but they're better than winging it alone or asking the Lord
to visit your dreams.

The Buzz: The Old Testament is often called the Hebrew Bible,
since that's the language most of it was written in. The Jewish religion calls the first five books (Genesis through Deuteronomy)
the Torah, whereas Christians call that section the Pentateuch.
In Christian terms, the Old Testament is famous for the severity
of the Lord—we all have heard "an eye for an eye," but I prefer the
concentrated thunder behind "I will wipe Jerusalem as a man
wipeth a dish, wiping it, and turning it upside down" (2 Kings
21:13). Yes, the Old Testament Lord is punitive and vindictive,
forever smiting and plaguing, but when you reread the commandments, he's really not asking for that much (granted, my
neighbor's wife is not that covetable . . .). Think of the Old Testament Lord as a 1950s dad with especially unruly kids who's
maybe a little quick to the strop.

What People Don't Know (But Should): Reading the Old Testament is a sustained exercise in realizing what you didn't know
about the bigger half of the Christian Bible. Trying to isolate one
thing feels pretty arbitrary, but let's take this: for two millennia,
Christians have been trying to find (or attribute) signs in the Old
Testament that point to the coming of Christ (I already mentioned the rather embarrassing Immanuel announcement that
the New Testament evangelist Matthew just glosses over in 1:23).
What you hear less about is how much of Christ and how many
of Christ's actions were already contained in characters and
scenes in the Old Testament: Elijah and Elisha raising people
from the dead, a small number of loaves feeding all the people, lepers being cured, etc. As much of a deviation as the New

Testament can feel from the Old, it's clear that the Christian writers tried to connect the two. *"Listen, we can get a lot more traction if we just lighten the big guy up a little bit . . ."*

Best Line: There are literally hundreds of world-class lines in the Old Testament, but the greatest concentration is in the book of Job. My favorite passage is this lament, especially the end:

> Why died I not from the womb? Why did I not give up the ghost when I came out of the belly? . . . There the wicked cease from troubling; and there the weary be at rest. There the prisoners rest together; they hear not the voice of the oppressor. The small and great are there; and the servant is free from his master. Wherefore is light given to him that is in misery, and life unto the bitter in soul; Which long for death, but it cometh not; and dig for it more than for hid treasures; Which rejoice exceedingly, and are glad, when they can find the grave? Why is light given to a man whose way is hid, and whom God hath hedged in? For my sighing cometh before I eat, and my roarings are poured out like the waters. [3:11–24]

What's Sexy: Yes, this is the Bible, but apart from David giving two hundred Philistine foreskins for the hand of Michal—oops, maybe that's not sexy—there's actually a lot more hanky panking than you'd think. And it gets started early. In Genesis 2:18 God says, "It is not good that the man should be alone" (a belief I've long subscribed to), so he makes the animals as company for Adam, then he makes Eve. Setting aside the order of these events, it's still marked how Adam gets a partner in Eden faster than most of us would at Hedonism V. Then there's Lot, the guy who was ready to turn his virgin daughters out to the crowd in Sodom. Thankfully angels intervene, because that wouldn't have gone well. Then, after God's killed off seemingly everyone else (bad Sodomites!), the same daughters get Lot drunk so he'll impregnate them without knowing who they are. Oh my! And we haven't even left Genesis yet, much less gotten to the Song of Solomon, the sexiest part of the Bible (discussed below).

Quirky Fact: The Old Testament is probably the greatest compendium of quirky bits this side of *Ripley's* (the 450 sq. ft. flying scroll in Zechariah, anyone?), but one of the primary stories struck me as odd in a larger and more significant sense. We are told that Israel means "he who has wrestled with God" and was the name given to Jacob (he of the ladder) after he wrestled with an angel. What's strange, though, is that at an earlier point, Israel (still called Jacob at that point) agreed to give his brother Esau—who was dying of hunger—a bowl of soup, but only if Esau surrendered his inheritance to him. Damn, bro! Then he tricks Esau out of their blind father's blessing by wearing goatskins to simulate Esau's he-man hairiness. Am I the only one who thinks that's a strange and rather shady history for someone who has a nation and a people named after him? Who says the antihero is a modern invention?

What to Skip: I'm tempted this time around to call this section What Not to Skip. There's a lot of forgettable material in the Old Testament, so unless you're locked in an otherwise bookless hotel room for a month (thank you, Gideons), are a serious religious diehard, or want to be reminded of all the plagues and disasters visited upon the Israelites, you can probably skip around. To me, the best books by far are Job and the Song of Solomon. If you only read those two, you'll get the Bible at its most literary. If you want a clearer sense of the whole in the shortest amount of time, add Genesis (note the beginning of the universe but skip the lists) and Exodus (focus on the tale of Moses, but skip all the particulars of the tabernacle and the consecration of the priests).

From there I'd say that you can and probably should skip Leviticus and Numbers' tales of the Israelites "murmuring" that maybe it was a bad idea to leave Egypt—even though they were Pharaoh's slaves. They sure were hard-hearted, because they keep questioning whether the Lord is going to take care of them, despite the miraculous parting of the Red Sea and the falling of manna to feed them in the desert *for forty years.* Talk about a bunch of doubting Thomases (oh, wait, he's in the New Testament . . .).

Deuteronomy has some crazy rules as to who will be among the elect ("He who is wounded in the stones or hath his privy member cut off shall not enter into the congregation of the Lord"—sorry, eunuchs) and has Moses' death (uneventful) but can be skipped.

In Joshua, the eponymous hero kicks a lot of Hittite and Amorite ass—with the Lord's help, big whup. Skip.

Judges contains the stories of Gideon (another 300-against-the-rest tale, minus the abs) and Samson (much weirder than you think; did you remember that he caught 300—yes, again—foxes and set all their tails on fire?), but you can skip the rest.

Ruth is a short, sweet story of faithfulness in a daughter-in-law—only a few pages, and moving to some people. To me not so much.

The First Book of Samuel contains Saul and his misadventures and then David, the shepherd boy and slayer of Goliath (much better story than you probably remember), who eventually becomes a great king of Israel. Read this one.

The Second Book of Samuel contains David's son Absalom's rape of his sister and his rise to power, the birth of Solomon, and, to my mind, the most moving passage to that point, David's lament at Absalom's death (18:32–33). It also contains the story of another little guy named Elhanan slaying the equally large brother of Goliath (21:19), but somehow he's never gotten the ink that David has.

David ends up being the hero not only of this book but of the Old Testament as a whole. In the next book, God will keep his covenant with the people of Israel only because David did "that which was right in the eyes of the Lord . . . save only in the matter of Uriah"—the guy David had killed so he could marry Uriah's wife, Bathsheba (1 Kings 15:5). Just that—otherwise he's dreamy.

The First Book of Kings has the death of David and the rise and fall of Solomon—very good, but skip the temple specifics again—but then descends into some pretty repetitive tales of various kings who don't follow the commandments and get punished. Skim through these till you get to that famed bad-girl, Jezebel, Ahab's wife (16:31), and the prophet Elijah, the closest thing in the Old Testament to a prefiguration of Christ (he raises a widow's dead son at 17:22), beginning in Chapter 17.

The Second Book of Kings has the death of Elijah and the rise of Elisha, the sweetheart who had the kids killed for calling him baldy, mentioned above (2:23–24). Elisha performs a lot of miracles (the most to date) but is entirely uncompelling. This book also contains the mother-child cannibalism aforesaid (6:28–29) but should probably be skipped whole-cloth.

Skip Chronicles I and II, Ezra, and Nehemiah. They repeat stuff that's come before and then have interminable lists.

Esther contains her and Mordecai's tale, not unlike a Boccaccio story where cleverness and subterfuge win the day (though in Boccaccio it doesn't result in a massacre of non-Jews, that I recall . . .). Not bad but easily skipped.

Job of course is a must, as I've already said, though it does get a little repetitive, so you can skip Chapters 18, 20–21, 36, and 39.

The Psalms (songs written mostly by David) are very repetitive but include a few beautiful prayers and are some of the most

famous parts in the Bible, especially Psalm 23, "The Lord is my
shepherd . . . though I walk through the valley of the shadow of
death . . ." Psalm 123 contains a line my brother I took as our
motto: "O Lord, have mercy upon us, for we are exceedingly filled
with contempt." Another says to the "daughter of Babylon,"
"Happy shall he be, that taketh and dasheth thy little ones against
the stones" (137)—eeks. If you read these straight through, as
opposed to hearing a few sung, they're pretty hard going; I'd
recommend that you not bother unless you find the prayers
evocative and meaningful—or have a lot of enemies you want
cast down.

The Proverbs (of Solomon) don't really give you evidence
that he was the wisest man of all time (I'd throw Gandhi and
Dostoevsky's names into the mix), but they do have some incredible lines ("Lean not unto thine own understanding . . . Be
not wise in thy own eyes." [3:5–7]) and some pot-calling-the-
kettle advice against succumbing to "strange women" (22 and
23). Chapter 8, where he describes how we were part of God even
before creation, is majestic in the extreme. There are emphatic
cases made for silence and for child-beating. Chapter 30, not
Solomon's but that of a cameo wise guy named Agur, is refreshing and has a great surprise at the end of the things he finds wonderful but can't understand (I won't spoil it). In general, the
Proverbs are occasionally profound, often confusing, and highly
repetitive. My advice to you: browse liberally and mull long.

With Ecclesiastes (meaning "The Preacher") the Old Testament takes a turn to the yet darker. He's famous for two things:
providing lyrics to the Byrds' song "Turn! Turn! Turn!" and
for saying, "All is vanity." But Ecclesiastes doesn't mean fake-tan
vanity; he means pointlessness, as in "all in vain," so you can
imagine how upbeat his no-point-in-this/no-point-in-that philosophy sounds. That said, the writing here (and moving forward) is significantly more literary ("the race is not to the swift,

nor the battle to the strong") and profound than any of the previous books (barring Job), so this is actually one of my faves.

The Song of Solomon is among literature's all-time erotic treats and is utterly shocking in a biblical context (many Christian commentators try to say that the figure of the lover represents the Church; don't believe it for a minute). Read the whole thing—it's short and sexy the whole way through—but pay special attention to 5:4; never will you read a stranger reaction to love feelings.

If you thought that the Lord had been going easy on all those stiff-necked Israelites, well, welcome to Isaiah. Here we are told that every man shall eat "the flesh of his own arm" (9:20), that "all the merry-hearted shall sigh" (24:7) as they are put in "the furnace of affliction" (48:10), and that the Lord will smite girls down and "discover their secret parts" (3:17) for walking with tinkling bangles. Cheery all around. The virgin birth of Immanuel is announced (7:14); and he will "take on our sins" (53:5–12). Lucifer is mentioned for the first time (14:12). We see that the Lord is making the Egyptians rebel (19:14). Isaiah walks around naked and barefoot for three years—it's tough to be a prophet—and, waiting for God, says the plangently beautiful "mine eyes fail with looking upward" (38:14). From Chapter 40 through to the end of the book we get great stuff on God's might: "Who hath measured the waters in the hollow of his hand" (40:12) and "saith to the deep, Be dry" (44:27)—I really can't get enough of that. Then there's the lone joke in the Old Testament: The Lord says of eunuchs, "I will give them an everlasting name, that shall not be cut off" (56:5)—now that's below the belt! Finally Isaiah asks God where is "the sounding of thy bowels and of thy mercies toward me?" (63:15)—hope that's nothing more than thunder.

Jeremiah advises to "take away the foreskins of your heart" (4:4), otherwise bad things, very bad things, are going to happen. The Lord makes some good-natured declarations such as "I will melt them" (9:7) and "Women . . . teach your daughters wailing"—9:20). And because "everyone neighed after his neighbor's wife" (5:8)—sexy!—he will "shew them the back, and not the face, in the day of calamity" (18:17) Also contains the beautiful line "the way of man is not in himself: it is not in man that walketh to direct his steps" (10:23), the incredible 5:22 ("Fear ye not me . . . which have placed the sand?") and lots more berating and brimstone, thus the word *jeremiad*.

Lamentations is for you if you didn't already get enough of Jeremiah's ranting and whining, especially about Jerusalem being like a dirty-skirted, defiled, seen-naked, menstruating woman. And how could you?

Ezekiel is officially (according to me) the most loopy of the Old Testament books. In Chapter 1 he sees a truly whacked-out vision of the Lord—don't make me explain all the heads, wings, wheels, colors, and whatnot. Then in 4:12 he's told to bake and eat cakes of human dung (like I said, it's tough to be a prophet), but thankfully God commutes it to cow dung in 4:15. In Chapter 8 he's given another intricate vision and more lines like "Son of man, eat thy bread with quaking" (12:18) and still more whoring and menstruating Jerusalem. This is the book that Samuel Jackson is supposedly quoting from in *Pulp Fiction* (25:17). Sadly, most of the quote is made up, but at least he got the idea across. Much of the second half of this book should be skipped (29–31, 41–42, 45–end).

Daniel is one of the more interesting books throughout. It starts with the story of Nebuchadnezzar forgetting his dream and then having all his magicians and astrologers chopped into pieces for not being able to get it back for him. The devout Daniel, though, miraculously can recall and interpret it (a kingdom will come, etc.). Still that's not enough to convince the 'Nezzar to follow the commandments, so he sets up a golden image (no!), God speaks to him and takes away his kingdom, then Beshazzar becomes king, has a feast, and a ghostly hand comes and writes some cryptic and very creepy words on a wall: MENE MENE TEKEL UPHARSIN. Daniel translates: MENE: "God hath numbered thy kingdom, and finished it" (5:26). TEKEL: "Thou art weighed in the balances, and art found wanting" (5:27): UPHARSIN: "Thy kingdom is divided" (5:28)—kind of anticlimactic, but those first two are awesome (I write "Tekel" on the board when my students turn in crummy papers). Daniel then has some very trippy allegorical dreams and visions (7–10) including one of a goat that grows a horn that throws down the stars and stamps on them (8:9–10). Some horn . . .

The rest of the Old Testament books are all short, and, with the exception of Amos and Jonah, don't have much to recommend them.

Skip Hosea though it contains the famous "reap the whirlwind" (8:7).

Joel is skippable, but I love "away, ye drunkards, and weep" (1:5).

Amos has a few things to note: First, there's another account of evil being the Lord's, not men's, fault: "Shall there be evil in a city and the Lord hath not done it?" (3:2). Then there's my favorite simile in all of the Bible: "As the shepherd taketh out of the mouth of the lion two legs, or a piece of an ear, so shall the children of Israel be taken out that dwell in Samaria in the corner of a bed, and in Damascus in a couch" (Ask your local priest about that one . . .). Finally, it has a great the-Lord-is-a-serious-mo-fo quote at 4:13: "He that formeth the mountains, and createth the wind, and declareth unto man what is his thought, that maketh the morning darkness, and treadeth upon the high places of the earth, The LORD, The God of hosts, is his name." Awesome.

Obadiah has more unaccountable Esau bashing—"For thy violence against thy brother" (1:10). What violence? My oh my. Skip.

The book of Jonah is only two pages long, and though you might think you know the story of him and the whale, it's weirder than you remember. The Lord tells him to go to Nineveh but instead he flees to Tarshish. Now if the Lord told you expressly to go to A, why would you possibly go anywhere else? I really don't understand these guys. So the Lord plagues Jonah's ship, Jonah agrees to be cast into the sea, he gets swallowed up, spends three days in an undersea Radisson, and gets vomited back on land. Now, the Lord tells him *again* to go to Nineveh, and, lo and behold, this time he does it—clearly Jonah's a quicker study than Nebuchadnezzar or Pharaoh. When he gets there, he prophesies the townspeople's doom for their sins. But they repent and change their ways, so Jonah gets upset because his prophecy won't be fulfilled and he *begs to die*! What? Talk about a putz. Nonetheless, God makes a gourd to shadow Jonah's head and comfort him (a gourd?), but then sends a worm to smite the gourd so it withers, and it ends with an equally unintelligible discussion between Jonah and God. This is definitely the most inexplicable book of the Old Testament, page for page.

In Micah it is foretold that a ruler of Israel will come from Bethlehem (5), but the brimstone of the rest can be skipped. Nahum has more making naked of women and dashing of children against stones—skip. Habakkuk has the awesomely foreboding "Write the vision . . . that he may run who readeth it" (2:3) and advises against getting your neighbor drunk so you can look on his nakedness (2:15) but still says to "let thy foreskin be uncovered" (2:16). Skip.

In Zephaniah, the Lord says, "I will utterly consume all things from off the Land" (1:2) and in Haggai, "I will shake the heavens and the earth" (2:21). I think we already knew that—skip.

Zechariah should be skipped but has one of my favorite Bible bits: a twenty cubit by ten (450 sq. ft.) flying object that goes over the earth, destroying the houses of thieves, which the King James (and a few other translations) calls a "roll" (5:1–4). Would that be a kaiser or a hoagie? Actually it's a scroll, but before I looked it up in the Oxford Annotated, I was really enjoying the image of a giant airborne bun. . . .

In Malachi (which you can skip) the Old Testament concludes: "Behold, I will send you Elijah the prophet before the coming of the great and dreadful day of the LORD: And he shall turn the heart of the fathers to the children, and the heart of the children to their fathers, lest I come and smite the earth with a curse." Well, then. And a good day to you too.

THE BIBLE

≈≈≈

The New Testament
(1st–2nd century)

What a difference a revision can make! It's not often that a religion gets to take a mulligan on its founding scripture, but that's exactly what happened with Christianity. Wanting to amend the old eye-for-an-eye, scourges-visited-on-the-Israelites, they-will-know-my-name-is-the-LORD vibe of the Old Testament, the writers of the New added God's mercy, took some vague hints from the previous scripture as portents of a new prophet, called him Jesus, and wham! They had themselves a new religion—and a holy book a lot easier to comprehend (most of the time) than the first.

Now, any Fiction 101 student would see that the Old Testament could have used a charismatic leading man—Moses wasn't as gripping as you'd have him be, Jacob's unpleasantness I discussed in the last chapter, David was okay (if you're not Uriah or Goliath) but doesn't hang around the whole time, and Elijah was pretty impressive but died off early—you hear what I'm saying. Of course I don't want to suggest that Jesus wasn't an actual historical figure and the son of God from an immaculate birth—only that it was rather convenient for the religion that he was those things, considering how much better they make the narrative.

The rest of the story of Christ makes for pretty good copy too. Told in four slightly different ways in the respective gospels of his disciples Matthew, Mark, Luke, and John, the Savior-to-be is born without the help of nookie, he's given some nice gifts by three wise men, he grows older and gets baptized (at which point the sky opens up and the Holy Spirit comes down—pretty good sign), goes into the wilderness and is tempted by the devil (no dice), comes back, gives his famous Sermon on the Mount (the heart of his message), performs some miracles, attracts his posse but is betrayed by one of them (Judas), gets hung out to dry, dies, and comes back from the dead so some people can go to Heaven despite their bad behavior. After the four gospels, the New Testament has a series of sermony letters that can pretty much be skipped (see below) and ends with the apocalyptic Book of Revelation (can't miss that), but virtually everything that we think of as Christianity is contained in these four short stories.

Now, considering what a cool guy Christ is, I was still at times a little disappointed with His Shagginess. I had remembered Jesus as the loving, accepting, mild Agnus Dei (Lamb of God), preaching tolerance and forgiveness and generally standing for a lot of stuff that most people would endorse, even if they're not so convinced he's the son of God. And there are myriad quotes that exhibit the messiah to be just such a Mensch, as this one demonstrates: "I say unto you, Love your enemies, bless them that curse you, do good to them that hate you, and pray for them which despitefully use you, and persecute you" (Matthew 5:44). Wouldn't that be great if we all (or any of us) did that? Makes you really love the guy.

The problem, though, is that are a lot of other times when he doesn't seem quite so pleasant. What are we supposed to do with quotes like: "Think not that I am come to send peace on earth: I came not to send peace, but a sword" (Matthew 10:34); "I am come to send fire on the earth" (Luke 12:49); "Suppose ye that I am come to give peace on earth? I tell you, Nay; but rather division" (Luke 12:51); "As many as I love, I rebuke and chasten" (Revelation 3:19); or "I pray not for the world, but for them which thou hast given me; for they are thine" (John 17:9)? None of these bodes so well for us little people. Even the oft-quoted "He that is not with me is against me" (Matthew 12:30) or "Give not that which is holy unto the dogs, neither cast ye your pearls before swine, lest they trample them under their feet, and turn again and rend you" (Matthew 7:6) make me a little suspicious. Aren't we all supposed to be friends here?

Then there are two episodes that also give pause: first, the parable of the wedding (Matthew 22:2–14), where a king can't get anyone to come to the party (not sure why; he *is* the king). He decides to bring men from "the highway," but one isn't dressed for a wedding, and for that he is cast into "outer darkness" (22:13). Christ concludes: "Many are called, but few are chosen" (22:14). I realize that it's the same point as with Esau in the Old Testament, but damn, who walks the highway dressed for a wedding?

Second, in Matthew 26 and John 12 there's the story of the woman who poured expensive ointment on Christ. The disciples took offense, saying the pricey stuff should have been sold and the money given to the poor. Christ's response is: "Why trouble ye the woman? for she hath wrought a good work upon me. For ye have the poor always with you; but me ye have not always" (Matthew 26:10–11; John 12:3–8). The poor you have always? Aren't we supposed to be working on that? And, as the son of God, do you really care if it's La Mer? Isn't Nivea good enough?

All these things made me a bit more circumspect about my man-crush on Jesus. At times he seemed just a little severe, as when he says: "If any man come to me, and hate not his father, and mother, and wife, and children, and brethren, and sisters, yea, and his own life also, he cannot be my disciple" (Luke 14:26). I know this is how they do enrollment in the CIA, but is this WJWD? Then when he says, "Ye are my friends, if ye do whatsoever I command you" (John 15:14)—I tried that with my roommates in college, but it didn't go so well. . . .

The most perplexing moment, however, is in Matthew 22:31, when the joy of man's desiring protects Peter from the devil, but later doesn't stop Satan entering Judas (Luke 22:3; John 13:2). Of course, Judas then betrays his idol and commits suicide from the guilt. But what was he supposed to do? And why does he get such a bad rap if Satan was the one pulling the strings and Christ didn't interfere?

So maybe the New Testament isn't as consistently touchy-feely as we hoped it would be, but then what religion is? I once saw a Buddhist monk refuse to move his bag to allow a pregnant lady to have a seat on the bus. But as religions and religious texts go, there's much more in the New Testament to love than hate, and all nit-picking aside, Christ's compassionate message really is beautiful. "Love thy neighbor as thyself"—that's about as good as it gets, right?

Nota bene: For book-by-book breakdowns, see "What to Skip" below.

The Buzz: Buzz? What buzz?

What People Don't Know (But Should): First of all, Pilate tried very hard to get Christ off, saying repeatedly that he was innocent and should be let go. It's only because the mob outside wanted the criminal Barabbas released instead that Christ didn't go free.

Second, most of us say "kill the fatted calf" to speak of a bad thing, but the father of the Prodigal Son kills it out of joy at his son's return—it's a good thing (Luke 15:27), especially at a tailgate for homecoming.

Finally, it seems at times like Christ doesn't really have a sense of his own power. At one point the exasperated Savior kvetches, "O faithless and perverse generation, how long shall I be with you? how long shall I suffer you?" (Matthew 17:17). Then, while on the cross, he says the famous, "My God, my God, why hast thou forsaken me?" (Matthew 27:46) as if he wasn't in on the whole plan, you know, to take on our sins with his death and rise from the grave. And earlier, having moved the stone in front of Lazarus' grave, he said, "Father I thank thee that thou hast heard me," as if it was only by God's paying him mind that he was able to do it. But if you can bring yourself and another guy back from the dead, what's so tough about moving a rock?

Best Line: "Consider the lilies of the field, how they grow; they toil not, neither do they spin: And yet I say unto you, that even Solomon in all his glory was not arrayed like one of these" (Matthew 6:28–29). That's exquisite.

I also love the various epithets Christ gives to himself over the course of the gospels. See, when you're the son of God, you really know how to do things, like make an entrance.

This is he, of whom it is written.

A greater man than Solomon is here.

A greater than Jonas is here.

I am the living bread.

I am the bread of life.

I have meat to eat that ye know not of.

I am the light of the world.

I am the door of the sheep.

I am the good shepherd.

I and my Father are one.

I am the resurrection and the life.

I am come a light into this world.

I am the way, the truth, and the life.

I am the true vine.

I am the vine, ye are the branches.

I have overcome the world.

I am Alpha and Omega, the first and the last.

I am he that liveth and was dead.

I am he which searcheth the reins and the hearts.

What's Sexy: There's not much that's technically sexy in the New Testament, but since so many people's chances for eternal happiness could be at stake, I'm going to give you all the sex-related stuff:

On cheating: "Whosoever looketh on a woman to lust after her hath committed adultery with her already in his heart" (Matthew 5:28). In this regard, the New Testament is harsher than the Old—pity.

On homosexuality: "Vile affections . . . Women did change the natural use into that which is against nature: And likewise also the men, leaving the natural use of the woman, burned in their lust one toward another . . . to do those things which are not convenient" (Romans 1:26–28). Based on what I've seen in the Greyhound men's room, it's not that inconvenient.

That there's not much hope: "Know ye not that the unrighteous shall not inherit the kingdom of God? Be not deceived: neither fornicators, nor idolaters, nor adulterers, nor effeminate, nor abusers of themselves with mankind" (1 Corinthians 6:9).

Euphemism of the week: "Let us walk honestly . . . not in chambering and wantonness" (Romans 1:13). Chambering!

As Chaucer's Wife of Bath said: "Let the husband render unto the wife due benevolence: and likewise also the wife unto the husband" (1 Corinthians 7:3).

And as she did: "If they cannot contain, let them marry: for it is better to marry than to burn" (1 Corinthians 7:9).

For George Costanza: "For this is the will of God, even your sanctification, that ye should abstain from fornication: That every one of you should know how to possess his vessel in sanctification and honour" (1 Thessalonians 4:3–4).

But can I keep the non-superfluous part? "Lay apart all filthiness and superfluity of naughtiness" (James 1:21).

All in all, more than you'd expect from the Christian rulebook, right?

Quirky Fact: I have to give you a few. First, there's a joke in the New Testament—just as there was one and only one joke in the Old—but mind you, it's anti-Semitic. John 1:47 reads, "Jesus saw

Nathanael coming to him, and saith of him, Behold an Israelite indeed, in whom is no guile!"

Then, were you aware that the Virgin Mary was a lush? Me neither until John 2 where she goes to Christ and makes him perform a miracle *because there's no wine at a wedding she's attending.* Jesus, honey, we're out of booze again!

On a rather more serious note, in Matthew 16:18–19 Christ says to Peter, "Thou art this rock upon which I will build my church . . . and I will give unto thee the keys of the kingdom of heaven," then tells the disciples that he has to go to Jerusalem where he will be killed and raised again. Peter says, "Be it far from thee, Lord: this shall not be unto thee" (16:22), and Christ turns on him, saying, "Get thee behind me, Satan"—the same thing he said to the actual devil during the temptations—and then "thou are an offense unto me: for thou savourest not the things that be of God, but those that be of men" (16:23). That's a pretty short fuse for the Lamb of God, no? And why call Peter Satan? It's true that the disciple will later take some tribute money (in 17:24) and eventually will lie and claim he wasn't with Christ when the ca-ca hits the fan (26:69–74), but still. And if he's so bad, why is he the rock you're building the church on?

Then there's the problem of inconsistency (which plagues both the Old and New Testaments). Take this example: Matthew 1:23 points out that the Old Testament says a virgin will bear a son and they will name him Emmanuel (*sic*—it's spelled with an "I" in Isaiah; I know it's being transliterated from the Hebrew, but it's the Bible; shouldn't they proofread?). The other problem is that an angel just told Mary that the son would be named Jesus (1:21). It seems to me that if you are trying to coordinate the two testaments, why not just go with Immanuel, by either spelling? It means "God is with us"; that's got a nice ring to it, right?

One more quickie: in Matthew's gospel, Christ's first words coming back from the grave are "All hail" (Matthew 28:9)—that seems fair. Whereas in Luke he asks some people why they're sad (Luke 24:17) and then if they have any meat (24:41). Any *meat*? Is he the Savior returning or a grizzly coming out of hibernation?

What to Skip: The gospels are, of course, can't-miss world-historical texts and should be read not only for all the greatness of Christ (despite my teasing above) but for the currency of so many of the stories in our everyday lives and language. They're also surprisingly short. Matthew goes by pretty quickly and is very familiar; Mark tells the same stories again so you don't have to read it; Luke is almost gratuitous but tells the stories differently enough from Matthew to make it worth it; and John is considerably different and decidedly worthwhile.

Apart from the Book of Revelation, the remaining parts of the New Testament (Acts and the twenty-one Epistles) are optional, so I've given them the standard breakdown and quoted my favorite lines. Revelation gets special treatment because it's so unbelievably crazy, and I'm big into eschatology—aren't you?

Acts recounts how an anti-Christian guy named Saul got converted and became the Apostle Paul, the author of most of the Epistles. Saul/Paul's story is among the more surprising conversion stories in the Bible, but isn't indispensable (nor anywhere near as good as Saint Augustine's in his *Confessions*).

From that point, it's epistle after epistle until you get to John's Book of Revelation. Paul wrote thirteen (fourteen if you attribute the perhaps-anonymous Epistle to the Hebrews to him), the saints Jude and James each wrote one, Peter wrote two, and John three. Paul's Epistles are all named for the audience they were written for; the others are named after their authors. Each of them is pretty much just a mishmash of sermony stuff, and they're much better taken in bits than as wholes. For that reason,

I'll summarize the stuff that's new and especially important and then point out my favorite elements. Speed Bible!

Paul's Epistle to the Romans argues that everything's predestined (8:29) and that we're all sinners and can be saved only by God's mercy, summed up with the cheery "There is none righteous, no, not one" (3:10). But it also has Paul's incredible confession of his failure to live up to his own morality: "That which I do, I allow not: for what I would, that do I not; but what I hate, that do I" (7:15). Ouch.

The First Letter to Corinthians has more great lines than any of the other letters, like this reminder to us all of how much we should be thankful for (and humbled by): "For who maketh thee to differ from another? and what hast thou that thou didst not receive? now if thou didst receive it, why dost thou glory, as if thou hadst not received it?" (4:7) or this sobering (but true) bit of epistemology: "If any man think that he knoweth any thing, he knoweth nothing yet as he ought to know" (8:2). There are also the famous quotes: "When I was a child, I spake as a child, I understood as a child, I thought as a child: but when I became a man, I put away childish things" (13:11–12); "O death, where is they sting?" (15:55), and my all-time favorite (expressing the suffering of he who wants terribly to be united with God but is stuck, for the time being at least, in the world's confusion and suffering): "For now we see through a glass, darkly; but then face to face: now I know in part; but then shall I know even as also I am known" (13:12). Sadly, it also contains some idiotic misogyny; search it for "woman" if you want to get ticked off.

The Second Letter to Corinthians has the well-known "the letter killeth, but the spirit giveth life" (3:6). Paul also disses the Old Testament, calling it a "veil" taken away by Christ (2:14). He's much harsher toward the OT than any of the other apostles. But he does call mortal life "our light affliction which is but for a moment" (4:17)—that's gorgeous.

The Epistles to Galatians and Ephesians have more damning and negativity, but Philippians has the lovely "I know both how to be abased, and I know how to abound: everywhere and in all things I am instructed both to be full and to be hungry, both to abound and to suffer need" (4:12).

Colossians has the elegant incitement to "walk in wisdom toward them who are without, redeeming the time" (4:5).

The Second Epistle to Thessalonians has another perplexing, whose-fault-is-it-anyway line: "God shall send them strong delusion, that they should believe a lie: That they all might be damned" (2:11–12).

Timothy 1 humorously says that a bishop should not be a "striker" or a "brawler" (3:3)—no mention of kiddie porn? It also takes most of the fun out of things, saying that "she that liveth in pleasure is dead while she liveth" (5:6). It does, however, have the famous maxim: "The love of money is the root of all evil" (6:10).

You might want to ask about this line in Philemon: "The bowels of the saints are refreshed by thee, brother" (1:7).

Hebrews is not exactly my favorite, saying first, "What son is he whom the father chasteneth not?" (12:7) then later blaming Esau "who for one morsel of meat sold his birthright" (12:16). He was starving! His brother put the gun to his head! I'm sorry, but Esau's okay in my book; I'll take the consequences. It also contains the ultimate bumper-sticker quote: "Jesus Christ, the same yesterday, and today, and forever" (13:8).

The General Epistle of James has some good advice: "Be swift to hear, slow to speak, slow to wrath" (1:19). It also has this exquisite passage: "From whence come wars and fightings among you? come they not hence, even of your lusts that war in your members? Ye lust, and have not: ye kill, and desire to have, and cannot obtain: ye fight and war, yet ye have not, because ye ask not" (James 4:1–2) and this humbler, "What is your life? It is even a vapour?" (4:14).

The First Epistle of Peter infamously calls women the "weaker vessel" (3:7), and the Second has the Bible's great recipe: "Add to your faith virtue; and to virtue knowledge; And to knowledge temperance; and to temperance patience; and to patience godliness; And to godliness brotherly kindness; and to brotherly kindness charity" (1:5–7). Bake at 350°F and you might get saved.

The First Epistle General of John has two stand-out lines: "If any man love the world, the love of the Father is not in him" (2:15) and "Let us love one another: for love is of God; and every one that loveth is born of God, and knoweth God. He that loveth not knoweth not God; for God is love" (4:7–8).

The unpleasant General Epistle of Jude contains a bubbly prognostication for sinners: that they will be as "trees whose fruit withereth, without fruit, twice dead, plucked up by the roots; Raging waves of the sea, foaming out their own shame; wandering stars, to whom is reserved the blackness of darkness for ever" (1:12–13). That's me!

Finally we get to the end: the psychotic, psychedelic, harrowing, last-days celestial uh-oh, that is, the Revelation of St. John the Divine. This you have to read. I mean, it's the end of the world and everything. You don't want to miss that.

John's vision begins with Christ as a man with eyes of flame and a sword coming out of his mouth (helps with grapefruit). The Savior allows John to see the throne of heaven, complete with twenty-four supplicating elders, four bizarro beasts, and God sitting there shining like some crazy diamond (oh wait, that was Syd Barrett . . .). In God's hand is a book with seven seals, and for a minute John thinks no one will be able to open the book, but then 100 million angels start singing (later we find out that only 144,000 people will be saved, so where are all these goody-goodies coming from?) and the Lamb comes to open the thing.

With the first four seals, the horses of the apocalypse start riding, and by the sixth the sun turns black and the moon turns to blood, the stars fall (no horn this time), "and the heaven departed as a scroll when it is rolled together" (6:14)—whoa. Not surprisingly, "Every free man hid . . . and said to the mountains and rocks, Fall on us, and hide us from the face of him that sitteth on the throne and from the wrath of the Lamb" (6:16–17). Of the Lamb? It's beginning to sound like the rabbit in *Monty Python and the Holy Grail.*

Then John writes, "I saw another angel ascending . . . to whom it was given to hurt the earth and the sea" (7:2)—somehow I suspect he's going to do a good job. Angels mark the heads of the 144,000 predestined elect, but for everyone else things are about to get rather less cozy *(I'm afraid, Professor Murnighan, your name does not seem to be on my list . . .).*

With the opening of the seventh seal "there was silence in heaven about the space of half an hour" (8:1). That *can't* be good. And then we have this to look forward to: "Men [shall] seek death, and shall not find it, and shall desire to die, and death shall flee them."

Then a bottomless pit opens and out flies a horde of scorpion-tailed locusts shaped like horses with the faces of men—no joke (9:2–10)—but still men "repented not" (9:20). What are they waiting for, exactly, horse-faced scorpions with human asses?

Then the thunder speaks (giving T. S. Eliot one of his section titles for "The Waste Land"), but John is told not to write what it says. My best guess is that it sounded something like what the house said in *The Amityville Horror*: "GET . . . OUT!"

"And the angel which I saw stand upon the sea and upon the earth, lifted up his hand to heaven, and sware . . . that there should be time no longer" (10:5–6). Houston, we have a problem.

After that, John writes down a lot of shit that even God couldn't explain (13). The Holy Spirit was chewing some interesting leaves when he dictated that chapter.

In 14, we find out that Babylon "made all nations drink the wine of the wrath of her fornication," which I suspect is the most mixed metaphor in the history of script (14:8). Christ then comes bearing a sickle and reaps the earth (14:14–16), but then an angel goes and does the same three verses later (Christ is clearly a pretty shoddy earth-reaper), and from the winepress of God's wrath comes blood (14:20). No surprise there.

Angels pour out the seven golden vials of God's wrath, creating sores, killing all life in the sea, turning rivers to blood, scorching men with fire, making everything dark, and causing men to gnaw their tongues for pain—but still men repented not. Then frogs assemble all the sinners in Armageddon and the seventh vial releases a voice, saying, "It is done" (16:17), and an earthquake hits "such as was not since men were upon the earth . . . and every island fled away, and the mountains were not found" (16:18–20).

Next up is the whore of Babylon, who has quite the impressive tattoo on her forehead—you really have to check it out (17:5). The fall of her city is prophesied.

Then a white horse comes down from heaven, ridden by the Word of God, who had "on his vesture and on his thigh a name written, KING OF KINGS AND LORD OF LORDS" (19:16)— that makes his clothes easy to identify at the laundromat. He casts Satan into a lake of fire, from which he is cast into a bottomless pit by an angel (why do they have to keep redoing Christ's work?), though he will be released a thousand years later "for a little season" (20:3). *Springtime on Parole for Satan*? I see a musical here. . . .

Now things get serious. The dead are brought before the heavenly throne, the book of life is opened, and "whosoever was not found written in the book of life was cast into the lake of fire" (20:13). Yeah, I'll see you there.

John then gets to see a new heaven on earth, the new Jerusalem, bride to Christ (that'll be some honeymoon), and says, "And I heard a great voice out of heaven saying, Behold . . . God shall wipe away all tears from their eyes; and there shall be no more death, neither sorrow, nor crying, neither shall there be any more pain: for the former things are passed away. And he that sat upon the throne said, Behold, I make all things new. And he said unto me, Write: for these words are true and faithful. And he said unto me, It is done" (21:3–6). All very nice for the chosen 144,000.

"And the Spirit and the bride say, Come. And let him that heareth say, Come. And let him that is athirst come. And whosoever will, let him take the water of life freely" (22:17). I'll be feeling rather thirsty in the lake of fire by then.

Christ's last words: "Surely I come quickly" (22:20). Take your time, really.

VIRGIL
(70–19 B.C.)

⤳⤳

The Aeneid
(19 B.C.)

In all the rereading I did for this book, of all the times I stood tiptoed on a dining room chair risking life to gravity and lung to dust, reaching for some old title off my least used, topmost shelves, nothing I took down surprised me more than *The Aeneid*. In retrospect, I had never given it much of a chance. I didn't read it in high school (rube that I am, where I grew up there was no classical education and you couldn't have found a Latin class within 150 miles) and didn't have to read it in college—so clearly didn't. Thus I only got around to the great Roman epic as a grad student, slogging through because I knew how esteemed Virgil was by the medievals I was ostensibly scrutinizing. But returning to it this time, having trained my eye to move slowly, to linger and luxuriate line by line, the two-millennium hubbub about *The Aeneid* started to make sense. I had been expecting Virgil's 1st-century B.C. retelling of the Troy story to be a stiff, antiseptic, jingoist account of the founding of Rome, but what I discovered was sustained majesty, poetic and narrative delicacy, and consummate grandeur. If Homer is the lion of poets, the most fearsome, roaring loudest, carrying furthest; Virgil is the cheetah, sleekest, fastest, most dynamic, and most elegant (and, by extension, Dante would be the kingfisher, flying high and diving deep; and Milton the bald eagle, soaring highest, seeing all, alone in his eyrie. Okay, I'll shut up now . . .).

As long as you take your time and either have great Latin or read it in the Mandelbaum translation (I've compared it to all other readily available ones and it's far, far more poetic), *The Aeneid* will probably be, cover to cover, the most gratifying book written before Shakespeare that you'll ever read. When I read, I'm an underliner, and reading *The Aeneid* (as with *Moby Dick* or *One Hundred Years of Solitude*), I struggled not to underline half of the book. Page after page (barring Books VII and VIII—see below), I was breathless, rapt. My ex-girlfriend, who endured years of the barnyard noises I apparently make while reading, said she had never heard me gasp, shudder, and wow more than I did reading the Virgil. I'm sure she's right; I was entranced.

If you've already read your Homer, the plot of *The Aeneid* will be somewhat familiar. Virgil combines the story lines of both *The Iliad* and *The Odyssey,* taking one of Homer's minor characters, the Trojan general Aeneas, as his hero, and retelling the city's fall (especially the Trojan horse component only alluded to by Homer) and then Aeneas' journey home (where he encounters many of the same obstacles as Odysseus). Of course much of the material is new—the invasion and burning of Troy; Aeneas' plangent and tragic romantic encounter with Dido, the queen of Carthage; his arrival in Italy and battle with the local king, Turnus, etc.—but storywise there's nothing in it you can't imagine Homer writing.

So the secret to Virgil's glory doesn't lie in the plot, but neither does it lie in the main character. Aeneas, repeatedly called pious Aeneas (that in the British accent of my grad school mentor made a nice little rhyme) because of his devotion to his father, proves to be almost as cold and unsympathetic as Odysseus in *The Odyssey.* Fleeing Troy's flames, Aeneas carries his father out on his back, but he makes his wife walk behind him and then manages to lose track of her in their flight, never to see her again. (Sure he goes back and looks for her, but by then most readers will already have him shitlisted.) A few pages later he seduces Dido and then walks out on her, trying to escape at night with no good-bye. When she takes him to task (in an exceptionally moving, protofeminist jeremiad; see the "Best Line" on page 51) his only defense is that the gods have called on him to go found a city, not to dally among the pillows. Dido ultimately kills herself from grief, but Aeneas barely gives her another thought. Pious he may be, but he isn't pitying. And in subsequent adventures, each time a vanquished enemy squirms on the battlefield under Aeneas' dripping blade, entreating the general to spare him, his famous furor defeats philanthropy, and "pious" Aeneas separates the supplicating head from its pedestal.

If *The Aeneid*'s story is pretty familiar and its hero hard to love, how does Virgil beguile us so? The answer is in the writing, entirely in the writing. His poetry is mesmerizing; it's as if he took the double-bass drumming of *The Iliad* and added violins, layering and nuancing till he witched all of music's register. *The Aeneid*'s "high style" (as it was called) is utterly without parallel until certain passages in Dante (who esteemed Virgil above all others and clearly mimicked him as best he could). Virgil's epic can boom thunderclaps, echo the nightingale, and soothe like a purling brook. In toto, *The Aeneid* achieves the highest level of poetic grace the world has ever known. (And Virgil earned it; methodical in the extreme, he spent twelve years writing two short books of poems and the last eleven years of his life writing *The Aeneid* and even then considered it unfinished.)

I really believe you'll have no trouble finding and feeling the wonder of Virgil's verse, as long as you commit yourself to looking for it. No matter how skeptical you are, no matter how scarred by your high school Latin teacher, go back and read Book II at least (again, in the Mandelbaum translation), and you'll be convinced. Virgil left behind the stateliest document the world has ever produced.

The Buzz: Every great empire mythologizes its own origins— or so the thinking goes. We Americans have all our grade-school notions of the Pilgrims and the founding fathers, and it proba- bly serves us well not to press the veracity of those too deeply. The Brits would have us forget that English takes its name from the Engles (a people more Scandinavian than limey) and Britain from Breton (a region of France) and that if not for a few hun- dred years of French-speaking on their isle, they'd be cockneying a Germanicized Icelandic. So small surprise that a people as self- obsessed as Emperor Augustus' Romans would want an ass- kicking story of their city's founding. Thus: "Yours will be the rulership of nations; remember, Romans, these will be your arts: to teach the ways of peace to those you conquer, to spare defeated peoples, tame the proud." Teach the ways of peace to those you *conquer*? Now *that* is self-righteous! And trust me, Virgil was being fully deadpan. The glory that was Rome: *ecce Virgilius*.

What People Don't Know (But Should): In their master works, both Dante and Milton wrote that they were going to attempt (in Milton's phrase) "things unattempted yet in prose or rhyme," and, yes, they both scaled some untouched ladders. But while neither author drew much (if anything) from other writers in their respective mother tongues, both are massively indebted to *The Aeneid* for their style and gravitas. (Dante acknowledges this openly by making Virgil his guide through *Inferno* and referring to him as the "highest" poet.) Reading them, you sense Virgil lurking behind their words, like a concerned if proud dad watch- ing his sons learn to bicycle. Dante and Milton scanned and re- scanned Virgil's lines till they were the very stuff of their veins; if you open yourself to Virgil's sublime prestidigitation, you'll want to as well.

Best Line: Although there are literally hundreds of incredible lines to choose from, I'm going to pick a short and not-at-all-sweet passage that happens to be one of the great F-you, post-breakup send-offs in history, compliments of Dido when she catches Aeneas trying to sneak away in his ships:

> ". . . I do not
> refute your words. I do not keep you back.
> Go then, before the winds, to Italy.
> Seek out your kingdom overseas; indeed,
> if there be pious powers still, I hope
> that you will drink your torments to the lees
> among sea rocks and, drowning, often cry
> the name of Dido." [IV, 519–526]

What's Sexy: In Book IV, there is a nice euphemism for sex: "the soft rewards of Venus" (41–42). It comes just before Dido and Aeneas get it on in a cave while Juno fires lightning and nymphs ululate (221–23). Sadly, the next line is: "That was the first day of her death and ruin." Ouch. Before it all goes wrong, however, Dido "deigned to join herself to him / that now, in lust, forgetful of her kingdom, / they take long pleasure, fondling through the winter, / the slaves of squalid craving." I guess Virgil didn't approve.

Quirky Fact: I have to mention two. A little one first: In passing, Virgil mentions an army "that keeps their left foot naked as they march" but on the right wear "a rawhide boot" (VII, 908–9). Okay . . .

Of perhaps greater historical and literary interest, in Book V, Virgil describes a boxing match in language Norman Mailer could have only dreamed of penning. With gloves sewn with lead and iron inside, one of Aeneas' men, Dares, takes on the old, enormous warrior Entellus. They fight, but Aeneas has to end the bout when Dares "spits thick gore out of his mouth, and teeth that mingle with the blood." Entellus the victor taunts them, saying, "Learn what strength was once in my young body, and from what a death you have just rescued and recalled your young Dares," then turns to the ox he received for winning the battle, punches it between the horns (!)—splattering its brains everywhere—and says to his king, "O Eryx, unto you I offer up this better life, instead of Dares." That's about as bad-ass—and psychotic—as it gets, right? Who would have guessed that Virgil was the best boxing writer ever?

What to Skip: As ecstatic as I am about the work as a whole (especially Book II, which ranks among the finest poetry ever written, start to finish), Books VII and VIII are less compelling than the rest and aren't necessary to the plot (they mostly contain some prehistory of Italy and an introduction to Turnus, whom Aeneas will have to face). You won't miss them. Also, the lists of things sacrificed to the gods are repetitive and can drag on; once you get the idea from one or two, skim or skip the rest.

OVID
(43 B.C.–A.D. 18)

✿

Metamorphoses
(A.D. 17)

The Roman poet Ovid, whose full name, Publius Ovidius
Naso, sounds rather like an unfortunate respiratory condition, is to his countryman Virgil rather as *The Odyssey* is to *The
Iliad*: he comes soon after, he knew he was nowhere near as good
(but had plenty of interesting stuff), he makes up for in variety
what he doesn't have in depth, he is consistently lively, and he
has remained popular for over two millennia. Epochal little-
brother syndrome can sting rather acutely (as anyone who's tried
to write a novel since *One Hundred Years of Solitude* can tell you),
so you have to feel a little bad for all those Romans versifying in
the generation that followed *The Aeneid*. But maybe because the
Virgilian mini-me Ovid did write in that generation he has always been mentioned in the same breath as Virgil, and that might
be a principal reason that he's still read. Literary history is a big
fan of twos: *The Iliad* and *Odyssey,* Old and New Testaments,
Dante and Boccaccio, Tolstoy and Dostoevsky—if two books or
two countrymen can be linked, it seems they are. Ovid might
well have snuck into literary history inside Virgil's Trojan horse.

I'm speculating on the reasons behind Ovid's popularity in
part because most of *Metamorphoses'* tales aren't that compelling
in themselves. Of the classics I've covered so far, this is the first

one that might disappoint you if you were just to pick it up and give it a try. Yes, his characters have become part of our basic cultural vocabulary (Narcissus who fell in love with his own reflection, Adonis the beauty, Icarus who flew too close to the sun, etc.), and yes they influenced some of the great writers of the Middle Ages (notably Chaucer and Boccaccio), but to my mind the rewards of the *Metamorphoses* are minimal compared to most other books of equal notoriety. The key to enjoying it is to read the few really good tales and a few of the famous ones and to skip the rest. Don't worry; you can do it in good conscience.

But why then has Ovid been so popular for so long? I think the answer might be a little scandalous. You know the unifying theme of all the stories is transformation, but it turns out that the driving motivation behind a considerable chunk of the stories is rape. We're not talking rape in the Jodie Foster in *The Accused* sense—thankfully—but more in the superficially more palatable river-god-envelopes-the-comely-bather kind of way. Still. Just as I always suspected that nudity in classical sculpture and painting has had a lot more erotic piquancy to viewers than people want to admit (am I the only one who gets turned on by Titian's *Venus of Urbino*?), my guess is that the gods' perpetual desire to seduce or ravish human females and nymphs in the *Metàmorphoses* had a similar effect on its readership. By my tally, the *Metamorphoses* recounts well over a dozen rapes plus a dozen or so attempts. Somebody was clearly enjoying the idea of being a god and getting to have your way with mortals—or being mortal and the gods having their way with you.

I have to confess that my own fantasies of sneaking up on women as a shower of golden rain wore out when I started going on actual dates, and even my afternoon daydreams about seeing the mythic Diana bathing must have faded sometime in my thirties. So hearing about Jupiter (Zeus to the Greeks) turning into this or that or the other to get with some sylvan hottie—all the while trying to keep his wife Juno from finding out—seems more yawn- than tingle-inducing (though I will admit that it's not often that the king of gods is represented as a bumbling philanderer). And Juno (Hera) forever getting angry and punishing the innocent girls comes off as both lame and wrong. So unless you're reading the *Metamorphoses* under the strict supervision of some parochial school nuns, I doubt you'll get much from the book on the arousal front.

Instead, the intriguing part of the sex in the *Metamorphoses* is its resemblance to the turn-of-the-twentieth-century classic encyclopedia of sexual deviance, Krafft-Ebing's *Psychopathia Sexualis*. Seen as a whole, the *Metamorphoses* can appear to be Ovid's attempt to catalog the aberrations of his day, including bestiality, fetishism, lesbianism, Elektra-complex incest, brother/sister incest, Pygmalionism, hermaphroditism, and mutilation. It's admirably thorough, but, like any inventory of sexual proclivities, its joys will be sporadic. The stories might strike us because we wouldn't expect them in a Lit 101 text, but in terms of actual pleasure to read—not so much. The best ones (coincidentally all in Books IX and X) detail Byblis and her passion for her brother, Iphis' same-sex love for Icanthe, Pygmalion's falling for his statue, and Myrrha's love for her father; each of these is psychologically deep and somewhat emotionally moving. But apart from these and the select tales listed below, the *Metamorphoses* isn't likely to be much more gratifying than an encyclopedia of Greek and Roman mythology. Considering how short, easy, and racy most of its stories are, however, if you do happen to have an interest in classical lore (or a pronounced enthusiasm for divine/mortal couplings), you might find Ovid's chef d'oeuvre a perfect highbrow addition to your bathroom literature.

The Buzz: Ovid's *Metamorphoses* is a compendium of myths, many of which remain iconic to this day. The best tales I'll list below in "What to Skip," the most famous—though not the most compelling—ones are (in alphabetical order): Arachne who challenged Pallas (Athena) to a weaving contest (never a good idea to compete with the higher-ups), Medea and her tragic love for Jason of the Golden Fleece, Midas and his disastrous wish, Niobe and her tears, the hero Perseus and his triumphs, Proserpine's seduction by Pluto, and Venus falling for Adonis.

What People Don't Know (But Should): How about the prevalence of rape in the tales, as noted above? And they give this book to kids?

Best Line: Yes, there's a lot of dross in the *Metamorphoses,* but there are also a lot of great lines. Procne, seeking words to describe her sister Philomena's rape and mutilation "could find none bitter enough"; the rapist Tereus, having unknowingly dined on his offspring, calling himself "the wretched tomb of my son"; Medea confessing, "I see clearly what I am doing: love, not ignorance of the truth, will lead me astray"; the king Aeacus' stately "Men of Athens, ask not my help, but take it"; and, my favorite, the lovelorn Iphis' incredible "I shall thirst in the midst of waters." Sounds like something from the Bible, no?

What's Sexy: If you're looking for consensual sex, you'll be hard-pressed to find any; the lovers tend to meet their maker before they meet their partners. But as to the less-savory kind, see above.

Quirky Fact: Despite being a celibate, Ovid wrote a sex and seduction manual called *The Art of Love* that was banned in Rome during his lifetime.

What to Skip: Skip lots. The best tales are, in order of appearance (and indexed in most volumes): Daphne and Apollo, Phaeton,

Apollo and Coronis, Battus, Cadmus and the serpent, Actaeton and Diana, Juno and Semele, Tiresias, Echo and Narcissus (who doesn't drown in this telling), Pyramus and Thisbe, Venus and Vulcan, Hermaphroditus and Salmacis, Cadmus (again), Arachne, Philomela (very gruesome), Atalanta and the boar, Athena and Meleager, Philomenon and Baucis, Byblis and her brother, Iphis and Icanthe, Orpheus and Eurydice, Phoebus and Hyancinthus, Pygmalion, Cinyrus and Myrrha, Alcyone and Ceyx, Ajax's speech at the beginning of Book XIII, Polyxena, Pythagoras and his blistering argument for vegetarianism, Cipers who sacrifices all for the republic, and, if you can handle it, Ovid's full-face suck-up to the emperor Augustus in the last few pages of Book XV (apparently it didn't work, as he was exiled in A.D. 8).

Apart from those, I really don't think you'll miss a thing if you forgo the rest. But if you do read everything, be prepared for a couple dozen people to turn into birds and a few dozen more to turn into trees. Egads.

ANONYMOUS

Beowulf
(10th century)

Beowulf is a badass, and to appreciate the poem named after him, you need simply squeeze the bicep of the second biggest stud in literary history (after Achilles). If there's such a thing as Man Lit, this is it: a plot-driven, action-brimming, hero-of-heroes story line, man vs. monster, battle to the death—just the thing to get your blood flowing and make you feel a little like a rampaging medieval Viking.

The setup, in a nutshell, is this: a group of Dark-Aged Scandinavian warriors are being assailed night after night by a monster called Grendel. Each morning they wake to find men (called thanes) dead in the mead hall. Eventually Beowulf comes from a neighboring tribe to fight Grendel and then later his gorgon-like mom—yes, his mom (more on this later)—en route to a few more heroic deeds, including a death-duel with a dragon. It's among the first literary works composed on Britain's green isle, and it's still the most macho.

Literary, yes, but let there be no mistake: this is no *Pride and Prejudice;* the only significant female character in the poem is Grendel's mom, and Beowulf has to go whup up on her. This is no *Remembrance of Things Past;* psychology in *Beowulf* runs about as deep as the pools of blood Grendel leaves on the floor of the alehouse. And this is no *Iliad* even; it's like a shotglass-sized, white-lightning distillate of the action, machismo, and inexorable all-consuming Fate of its great forebear (which the author of *Beowulf* couldn't have known), a single barroom roundhouse to the jaw compared to *The Iliad*'s floating like a butterfly and stinging like a bee.

Did I say it was short? The whole thing amounts to only seventy or so pages, so it can easily be read during a baseball rain delay (I told you it's Man Lit . . .). So if you have any desire to check some world classics off your to-do list (and that's probably why you're reading this book), *Beowulf* is definitely among the quickest and easiest.

That's not to say, though, that we can read it in the original. Although it was written in the place that in the year 927 came to be called England, the action takes place in Scandinavia, and the "Old English" it was composed in is actually Anglo-Saxon, a Germanic/Scandinavian precursor even to the precursors of what we now call our mother tongue. I'm a trained medievalist and can read Chaucer's 14th-century Middle English pretty effortlessly, but even so, I still can't make heads or tails of the language of *Beowulf* (though if I spoke Icelandic or Danish I'd have a better shot).

So clearly almost everyone has no choice but to read it in translation, and, as always, which translation you pick makes all the difference. The edition I like best is E. Talbot Donaldson's prose version—much better in my opinion than Seamus Heaney's verse rendering. Donaldson is regarded as one of the foremost English medievalists, and I feel very safe in his hands. (Yes, Heaney owns a Nobel Prize for poetry, but somehow I suspect he's been too busy attending award ceremonies to have developed Donaldson's Anglo-Saxon chops.) What the Donaldson translation manages to capture that Heaney doesn't is the staccato rhythms of *Beowulf*'s language, a kind of thudding, working-the-heavy-bag tattoo that matches perfectly with the subject matter. By trying to beautify the language, Heaney loses some of its clipped, rough, cut-knuckled charm. Donaldson was capable of hearing the testosterone in the cadence of the original and does an incredible job of delivering it in his translation.

Once you can hear how *Beowulf*'s poetry works, there are only a few more things you need to get the full effect of England's first and fiercest lit. One is to get a clear sense of the milieu being described and how we learn in passing that it's, well, not quite as touchy-feely as the one we live in today. When Beowulf is being praised, we hear that "drunk, he slew no hearth-companions." *Drunk, he slew no hearth-companions?* Well, he really is quite the fine fellow. Clearly here's a culture where evenings are spent with the guys sitting around the alehouse swilling mead and occasionally offing each other. Nor is this all; over and over we are reminded of the austerity and severity of *Beowulf*'s Dark Ages Scandinavia: "The one whom death takes can trust the Lord's judgment"; "Fate always goes as it must"; "Afterwards, he will walk who may," etc. It's a warriors' world, and much of the enjoyment of Beowulf consists in shouting, "Holy shit!" after every Y-chromosome jaw-dropper (and nowhere more so than in the "Best Line" quoted on page 61).

The other stylistic element you need to recognize and savor is the recurring locution "That was a good _____" (insert "king" or "nation")—more evidence of the mentality of *Beowulf*'s author and the stud culture that he was part of. *Beowulf* sets up this construction (or its negative) to describe some bellicose, merciless, dominant power, as in: "It was their custom to always be ready for war whether at home or in the field, in any case at any time that need should befall their liege lord: that was a good nation." And, my friends, *that* is the way to write Man Lit.

There is a minor apology one has to make on behalf of the

great *Beowulf*: it has a rather odd, highly anticlimactic plot structure. The best monster is Grendel, and the most gripping (as it were) scenes are when he and Beowulf fight. But Grendel comes at the beginning, and from then on the action sort of goes downhill (see "What to Skip" on page 62).

Apart from that, love *Beowulf* for what it is: the first major literary work in the English tradition, and a highbrow, 1,000-year-old precursor to *The Predator*.

The Buzz: *Beowulf* is generally considered to be the earliest extant English literary work, but that's not quite true. There are fragments of a poem called "The Dream of the Rood" on an 8th-century cross, but *Beowulf* is the earliest "complete" poem (only a little bit of it is missing) and is by far the most literary and compelling of the Anglo-Saxon works that have come down to us.

What People Don't Know (But Should): Although your professor probably didn't want to admit it, there are parts of the language of *Beowulf* that nobody understands. So next time someone tries to call it Old English, you're better off ignoring the English part and thinking Anglo-Saxon.

Best Line: How's this for manly? "Now for a time there is glory in your might; yet soon it shall be that sickness or sword will diminish your strength, or fire's fangs, or flood's surge, or sword's swing, or spear's flight, or appalling age; brightness of eyes will fail and grow dark; then it shall be that death will overcome you, warrior."

Quirky Fact: In my understanding of action adventures, this is the only one where the hero, having vanquished his ferocious enemy, then has to go and fight the enemy's mom. That's a twist that doesn't seem to have caught on.

What's Sexy: Despite Angelina Jolie being cast as Grendel's mom in the 2007 film version, in the poem itself, the dam's a terrifying old hag-monster. Nor is there a whole lot of sex in *Beowulf*, for, as you'll notice, it's a little bit of a boy's club around the old mead-house.

What to Skip: A number of sections can be skipped to no ill effect: the second half of XIII (an unimportant description of another warrior), all of XVI and XVII (the side story of the warrior Finn), and the confusing and unnecessary XXVII.

DANTE ALIGHIERI
(1265–1321)

∽∾∾∾

Inferno
(1308)

> *... I am one who, when*
> *love breathes inside of me, takes note, and in the manner*
> *which it is expressed within, I seek to express it without.*
> —*Purgatorio* (XXIV, 52–54)

In the early years of the fourteenth century, the Florentine poet Dante Alighieri sat down to what was a rather ambitious project: a three-part poem, in which he's the main character and is taken on tours of Hell, Purgatory, and Heaven. The result is what is collectively called the *Commedia* or, in English, *The Divine Comedy*—"comedy" back then simply meant that it had a happy ending. The first part, *Inferno* (Hell), you probably had to read in school; the last, *Paradiso* (Heaven), I'm going to try to get you to read in the next chapter; and the middle, *Purgatorio* (Purgatory), can be skipped, apart from the incredible lines above (some of my all-time favorites).

Inferno is far and away the easiest to read of the three canticles (as they're called) and contains two of the best set-scenes in the entire history of Western literature. Rightfully famous, the tales Dante hears from two of Hell's tenants, Francesca and Ugolino (in Books V and XXXIII, respectively), are as moving and beautiful as anything you'll read in literature anywhere. With Francesca, you cry at the glory of two people loving each other forever—in Hell as in life, always. With Ugolino, hearing how he's locked in a prison with his little sons, watching them starve to death, you simply cry at the worst tragedy you can imagine befalling a person, the most heart-shredding, excruciating misery. The two stories bookend perhaps the greatest span of human feeling—from the joy and love of togetherness to the despair and agony of loss—and each of them is capable of touching us in the deepest of all emotional places.

Romantic as Francesca's story is, it goes by quickly and can be hard to appreciate if you don't take your time. We meet her and her lover, Paolo, in the second circle of Hell, the final restless place for those undone by lust. She tells Dante where she's from, then begins her next three stanzas with the word "love"—which we know from the epigraph was one of Dante's favorite themes: "Love, that quickly seizes the noble heart" (100), "Love, that lets no lover not love" (103), "Love led us to one death" (106). But not until line 121 does she really begin to tell Dante her story. This is the closest I can get it to the original (and yes, poets, I've ignored the rhyme and meter to try to make it more reader-friendly).

> And she to me: "There is no greater sorrow
> than to think of happy times
> while in misery—and this your teacher knows
>
> But if you have such strong desire
> to know the first root of our love,
> I will tell you, as one who weeps as she speaks.
>
> One day we were reading, for pleasure,
> of Lancelot, how love had him enveloped.
> We were alone and without suspicion.

Again and again, while reading,
our eyes would meet and our faces redden,
but it was a single moment that defeated us.

When we had read how the desired smile
was kissed by a lover such as he,
this one, who from my side will never be taken,

his body all a-tremble, kissed me on the mouth.
A *Gallehault* that book and he who wrote it!
And no more did we read that day."

While Francesca was speaking, Paolo was weeping (139–40),
and Dante, overcome with pity, "fell as a dead body falls" (142).
And thus ends the canto.

This line affects me the most: "this one, who from my side
will never be taken." I want you to imagine Francesca pointing
to the sobbing Paolo; they are in Hell, but they're together.
They suffer, but they know that they will never be separated—
and somehow that seems worth it. Maybe it's my dating history,
maybe it's the current divorce rate, but the love behind the
"this one" and the assurance that he'll never leave her feels
sublimely poignant. Dante too, feeling their love, is so moved
that he faints, dropping like a sandbag. His response helps you
feel how beautiful their union must have been; it dramatizes
the emotions of the moment and magnifies them to a higher
level.

With Ugolino, one need not worry about being unaffected;
hearing his tale, you wonder if the writers of the *Saw* films
didn't go back in time and give Dante a hand. In brief, Ugolino
tells how he was betrayed in life by a politician he had been
scheming with (and whose head he ends up gnawing on in Hell)
and was locked in the notorious "Hunger Tower" with his four

young sons. Then he delivers these lines that tear me apart every time:

> "How cruel you must be, if you don't already suffer,
> Thinking what my heart knew was coming;
> And if not at this, at what do you cry?" [40–42]

He hears them nail shut the tower door and knows that none of them will ever be fed again.

> "I didn't cry; I had turned myself to stone.
> But they wept, and my little Anselm
> said, 'Papa, how you look . . . What is it?' " [49–51]

> . . . .

> "and from my grief, I bit my hands;
> and they, thinking that I did it from a desire to eat,
>   rose up

> "and said, 'Father, it would hurt us less if you ate us
>   instead. You dressed us in this miserable flesh, and
>   you can undress us.' " [58–63]

> . . . .

> "Then, after we had reached the fourth day,
> Gaddo threw himself outstretched at my feet,
> Saying, 'Father, why do you not help me?'

> "And then he died; and just as you see me,
> I saw the other three fall one by one
> between the fifth day and the sixth." [67–72]

By this point, droplets have been hitting my page for quite a few lines, but Dante has one last twist in store.

> "Now, blind, I started groping over each;
> I called to them for two days; but
> the fasting had more force than the grief." [73–75]

Poor Ugolino gives way to his hunger, only making his eternity in Hell that much more painful for the memory and the shame. His capitulation is subtle, but clearly the final twist of the screw of the most moving—to my mind—lines ever penned.

By themselves, these scenes would make *Inferno* an all-time classic, but there's quite a bit more to enjoy. For a complete, canto-by-canto breakdown, see "What to Skip" on page 69.

The Buzz: A lot of people, especially native Italians, will quote the first lines of *Inferno* to you (*"Nel mezzo del cammin di nostra vita / mi ritrovai per una selva oscura"*—In the middle of the path of our life, I found myself in a dark forest) and then not know anything else about the poem. If that's as far as you got, what happens next is that Dante will be led on a tour of Hell by the poet Virgil so he can see what happens to sinners and amend his wicked ways. Dante's Hell has nine layers (circles), each designated for a particular type of sinner (the first circle for infidels; the second for adulterers and the lascivious; third for gluttons; fourth for misers and prodigals; fifth for the wrathful; sixth for heretics; seventh for the violent; eighth for the fraudulent, panderers, and seducers; and ninth for traitors). Within these circles, the wicked receive appropriate (or what we now call "Dantesque") punishments, suited to their crimes. Flatterers find themselves in a lake of shit, for example, because on earth they were full of it.

What People Don't Know (But Should): Dante is generally considered the father of Italian poetry, despite the fact that there were other quality poets in his native Tuscany who predated him (some of whom appear in the *Commedia*). It is true, however, that his Florentine dialect became the Italian spoken everywhere because of his fame. But there was a long-standing tradition of poetry in Sicily as well, and had any of their poets taken off, everyone in Italy might well be speaking Sicilian, and the Italian that Dante helped legitimate would now be considered just a regional language.

Best Line: My favorite of Dante's lines occur either in the Francesca or Ugolino scenes discussed above, but there's another incredible moment that I have yet to mention. In the Middle Ages, the poets Homer, Ovid, Horace, and Lucan were held in the kind of esteem that nowadays we reserve for Shakespeare. Thus, in Canto IV, Dante gives them all the title "highest." But then, in Canto XXV, after he's described the transformation of a man into a snake, knowing that he's beaten Ovid and Lucan at their own metamorphosizing game, he defiantly says, in Mandelbaum's translation:

> Let Lucan now be silent, where he sings
> of sad Sabellus and Nasidius,
> and wait to hear what flies off from my bow. [94–96]

> Let Ovid now be silent, where he tells
> of Cadmus, Arethusa; if his verse
> has made of one a serpent, one a fountain,
> I do not envy him. [97–99]

In the original, the first lines say, "Taccia Lucano" and "Taccia . . . Ovidio," which are actually forceful commands, along the lines of "Lucan, shut the f—— up! Ovid, enough!" Considering how esteemed the recipients of these shut-its were, Dante's might be the most audacious lines in the history of literature. (For a contemporary parallel, it would be akin to me saying, "Harold Bloom, silence! You thought *you* could convince people to read classics!" Oh, wait, that is what I'm saying.)

What's Sexy: Francesca concludes her speech saying that Lancelot's kiss jazzed them up so much that they put down their book "and no more did we read that day." Nice.

Quirky Fact: When Boccaccio gave public lectures on the *Commedia* a generation after Dante's death, he tried to explain the deep theological and moral allegories running throughout the poem but was consistently shouted down by the people of Florence, who demanded that he simply say what real-life people some of the characters were based on and why they got the punishments they did. What's world-class literary merit next to quality gossip, anyway?

What to Skip: It seems crazy to me that in literature surveys, some college students are asked to read *Inferno* in its entirety. Even to a mature, erudite reader, its joys are sporadic (about half of the book, in my opinion, can actually be skipped—see below), much of it is cryptic, many of its themes are simply no longer relevant (do we care about 14th-century Florentine political conflicts?), and no translation retains the elegance and grace of the original (though I'd go with Mandelbaum's over the others).

That said, the Francesca and Ugolino scenes obviously number among my favorite bits of writing of all time (see above), so there's an argument for reading (or assigning) just those if you want a one-hour Dante. But truthfully, *Inferno* is pretty great at both ends, and some of the middle is okay too. Here are my recommendations, plus the highlights of the better cantos, so you can decide for yourself:

I: Read for the setup. Dante is sent to Hell, meets Virgil (67).

II: Dante says he's "not Aeneas, not Paul" (32) so why should he be going to Hell and have to come back to speak of it (as they did)? We also hear about how Beatrice came to Virgil and asked him to go and guide Dante (53).

III: The gateway to Hell with the famous inscription "Abandon all hope, Ye who enter here" (9).

IV: The first level of Hell—for infidels. Here Dante calls Virgil "altissimo" (highest) (80) but the same honor is given to four other famous pagan poets: Homer, Horace, Ovid, and Lucan (88–93)—so much for the superlative. Then they agree to make Dante one of their band (101)—not lacking ego, our poet. Ovid and Lucan don't know he's going to diss them twenty-one cantos later.

V: Contains Francesca's monologue (begins 88), discussed above. Can't miss, especially 121–38.

VI–IX: Punishment of gluttons, prodigals, misers, and wrathful. Easily skipped.

X: Contains the noble Farinata (23), who identifies Dante by his Tuscan accent and seems, like many of the true tough guys in *Inferno*, "as if he had tremendous scorn for Hell" (36). Dante also meets the poet Guido Cavalcanti's father (52), who asks, "If it is your great intellect that allows you to journey here . . . where is my son? Why is he not with you?" (58–60)—nice compliment for a dad to pay his child. Dante accidentally reveals that Guido's dead, prompting some moving lines from the father (68–69).

XI: Explanation of the system of Hell.

XII–XIV: Punishment of murderers and thieves, suicides, and blasphemers. Nothing too great.

XV: Dante recognized by his homeboy Brunetto Latini (22), who foretells that Dante would be exiled from Florence (which he was) but would eventually receive his due honor (70).

XVI–XXIII: Punishment of sodomites, usurers, panderers, flatterers, prostitutes, cheating priests and monks, ersatz magicians, and corrupt politicians. Easily skipped.

XXIV: Now begin the more interesting punishments, like sinners wrapped in snakes (85).

XXV: The incredible transformation of man to snake and Dante telling Ovid and Lucan to go whistle (94)—see "Best Line" above.

XXVI: Ulysses, in Hell for lying and malice, appears (79) and tells his story.

XXVII: More punishment of fraudulent counselors (seems pretty far down, right? Apparently it's really bad to give crappy advice)—skip.

XXVIII: Great beginning, plus Muhammad appears, split down the middle "from the chin to where we fart" (23). I guess he bet on the wrong god.

XXIX: Punishment of sowers of discord. Skip—though auditory and olfactory tortures are added to the sufferings of the sinners.

XXX: Alchemists and counterfeiters get their rewards—skip.

XXXI: Here Dante first sees the giants, which he mistakes for towers (20)—pretty incredible. From this point on it's all amazing.

XXXII: Outstanding beginning, saying that "it's not a task to take lightly, to show the base of the universe, not for a tongue that once cried 'mama' and 'papa' " (7–9). Then he says he will attempt what every reporter strives for, never more tersely expressed: "That from the fact the telling not differ" (12). Meets Ugolino (124).

XXXIII: Ugolino's tale in earnest: 1–9, 38 ff. Perhaps the most poignant piece of writing ever—see discussion above. And then this exquisite detail: The sinners are trapped in ice, exposed to frigid winds that freeze their tears, such that "their very weeping there won't let them weep" (94–96). That's poetry at its most sublime.

XXXIV: At last, the ultimate bad-boy, Lucifer (28), portrayed with three heads, each of which munches on an arch-sinner (55): Judas, Brutus, and Cassius. Brutus, like Farinata in Canto X, is too proud to exhibit any pain (66)—even Virgil is impressed. Note: this is the only of the three canticles that has a thirty-fourth canto (the other two have thirty-three each, thus making 100 total), but it ends, as they all do, with the word *stelle* (stars).

DANTE ALIGHIERI
(1265–1321)

∽∼∾

Paradiso
(1321)

In *Paradiso,* Dante posed for himself as great a challenge as any writer could possibly have: to describe being in Heaven, face-to-face with God. And we're not just talking about any old god, for Dante's Lord was the "get-medieval-on-your-ass," ineffable, unknowable, all-powerful Christian god of the 14th century: as superhuman and daunting a deity as human pen ever aimed to represent. If you are at all interested in how he managed the business, or in the various poetic and imagistic devices that he had to push to their absolute utmost trying to do so, then you have a decent chance of enjoying *Paradiso.* If, however, you don't think an encounter with our dread creator, as imagined by one of Europe's finest poets, will fluff your fancy, at least consider this conundrum: How do you write about the thing that's most important to you, that centers your and everyone else's life and world, that is the supreme of all that is good and beautiful and true but that is entirely beyond human comprehension? That's what Dante set out to do, and with the proper gaze, one can see in his attempt a poetry unlike any other.

Paradiso begins, and immediately Dante puts his chips on the table: "In the Heaven that takes the most of His light / was I, and saw things that to retell / one neither knows how to nor can when he descends / because, as we try to re-approach Him / our intellect falls so deeply inward that the memory cannot follow" (I, 4–9). It's nice when the author tells us that the story is not a tellable one, right? Clearly, things are not as they normally are with this book *Paradiso.* Reading it for the things we tend to enjoy—plot, character, psychology, suspense, or even arousal—you're probably going to stay thumbs-down (like pretty much all Italians who are forced to read it in school). No, this one has a purely poetic and theological agenda, as we watch Dante negotiate the exact problem he set forth in the first few lines: how to tell what can't be told, how to speak of Heaven and its ineffable king.

Now, however, I grudgingly have to confess that *Paradiso,* unlike almost every other book I talk about here, is pretty hard to enjoy without a little academic horsepower under your hood. The problem is, if you're not used to reading allegorical poetry, *Paradiso* ain't gonna work. In *Inferno* and even *Purgatorio,* understanding Dante's use of allegory isn't that important to enjoying what you're reading. Once we're in Heaven, however, there's some reckoning to be done. But take heart, dear reader, for I am about to offer you the quickest of all possible tutorials in reading Dante's allegory—don't say I never did anything for you.

Allegory has been said to mean a lot of different things at different times, but for Dante it meant that his poetic images could have a number of different meanings—and he wants you to look for them. So far this is pretty normal, as are most of the images he uses. Many are exquisitely beautiful, if a bit predictable, and not too hard to decipher: concentric rings, unbearably bright lights, the celestial choir, angels in flame, and finally the culminating "eternal rose" composed of all the angels and the blessed shining together—all stuff you might expect to find in the upper room.

But Dante also employs another kind of allegory that's much more sophisticated, as he tries to represent the unrepresentability of Heaven to mortal minds. These kinds of images are Dante's real advancement: the ability to create signs that tell you that they can't properly signify and that the words they are using no longer correspond to the things they used to stand for. Take the image of light, which, with vision (and to a lesser extent sound and hearing), is the most important of all of Dante's rewritten concepts. If you monitor the modulation of light in *Paradiso,* you'll see how intricately Dante tries to weave the symbolic tapestry of his Heaven. First the lights are so bright that Dante can barely stand them; then they become too bright, and eventually he is actually blinded; then he is weaned to be able to "see" a higher "light"—but we are told this isn't seeing at all; then we find that there's a "living light," but of course that isn't actually a light at all, and it's *alive.* After that comes another "light" that God allows the angels to "see" to make himself more and more visible, and so forth. Dante keeps using the words "light" and "see," but he hasn't been talking about what any of us know by those terms for a long time.

That's why I have to keep putting everything in quotes, not because I want to annoy you, but because Dante wants us to understand that the words have been separated from their original meanings, and that to think that we know what he's talking about is an error. But Dante's great point is this: that we can't help but keep committing that error as he keeps using the words—that is, the fact that we keep thinking in our minds that the light is a light—and that he has no choice but to employ human words (how else could he say it?) are both signs of the feebleness of the mortal mind and its unreadiness to bear witness to the glory of the One above. The word "light" doesn't signify what it says, but the fact that he's forced to use it, and forces us to make the mistake of thinking it, signifies that we can't and couldn't understand what was really going on. That's pretty intricate, no?

Even if all of this sounds like gobbledygook—and I suspect it just might—at least go into reading *Paradiso* knowing that it's as sophisticated a linguistic and epistemological inquiry into its subject as you will ever find. Dante is trying to reach the Unknowable, and he tried to make his poetry an asymptote moving closer and closer to the axis it knows it can never touch.

The Buzz: If you're going to talk about *Paradiso*, you have to talk about Beatrice. Beatrice Portinari was a girl in Florence whom Dante met briefly when he was nine and she eight, then in passing nine years later, but never again as she died at age twenty-four—before too much reality could intrude on Dante's idealized image of her. She is the one who first takes him to Virgil in *Inferno* and then becomes his guide near the end of the *Purgatorio* and through most of *Paradiso*. As they move closer and closer to God, she gets brighter, more beautiful, and happier, mirroring in herself the increasing beatitude of *Paradiso*'s spheres.

What People Don't Know (But Should): Dante might well have been the most arrogant poet in recorded history (with Milton a close second). See some astounding hubris in II, 7–18 ("not so amazed as you shall be"); XVII, 127–35 (his "voice . . . will leave behind vital nourishment"; XIX, 7–10 ("what I now relate, no voice has ever reported") and the quote in the next section.

Best Line: Here is my translation of Dante trying to describe Beatrice's smile in Heaven, both lamenting his mortal inabilities and backhandedly complimenting himself on having nonetheless taken on such a task (and, again, I've not tried to reproduce the meter and rhyme):

> If all those tongues should sound together
>
> .   .   .   .
>
> To aid me, still not the thousandth part of the truth

Would be reached, singing of the heavenly smile
And how it lit her sacred face.
For in depicting Paradise,
The divine Poem needs take a leap,
Like one who finds a block in his path.
But considering the heaviness of my matter,
And the mortal shoulder trying to carry it,
None would blame should I tremble beneath.
No waters for a little boat are these
Through which my audacious prow doth cut,
Nor for a pilot who would have care for himself.
    [XXIII, 55–69]

What's Sexy: Beatrice is an attractive guide and all, but Dante's Heaven seems to be missing a few things I'd like to find if I ever make it to the promised land. Heaven in the Bible sounds a little more promising; why else would Deuteronomy insist that every male elect must have his frank and beans?

Quirky Fact: Dante spent the last two decades of his life in exile from his home in Florence (which at the time was an independent city-state), so when Cacciaguida, his great-great-grandfather (see below), foretells Dante's future, he says Dante will "taste how salty another's bread is." That's because Florentine bread didn't contain salt—and doesn't to this day.

What to Skip: If you're reading *Paradiso* as I've advised you to—for a sense of how Heaven works and why Dante as a human is unfit to understand the celestial happenings—by the end of the first twelve or so lines of Canto V, you'll get the point. From then on, unless there are religious figures you're interested in, I'd skip everything but the openings to each canto (normally the first ten or fifteen lines are the best) until you get to XXIII. But, to do a little goody-goody celeb head-count, Aquinas, Boethius, and King Solomon (among others) appear in Canto X; St. Francis in XI; St. Dominic and others in XII; XIII has Aquinas back and a discussion of Solomon; XV–XVII have Cacciaguida discussing Florence and Dante's futures (including, in XVII, some moving lines prognosticating Dante's exile—see "Quirky Fact"); XVIII briefly mentions the great conquerors Joshua, Charlemagne, Roland, and William; XXI has Peter Damian; and XXII has St. Benedict and Jacob's ladder.

At Canto XXIII, you really start to get to the good stuff. It begins with an all-time crazy simile (twelve lines long!) about Beatrice being like a bird on a tree limb (much better than it sounds), then moves on to the quote in "Best Line" above, then Mary appears, who for the time being Dante can only see as a "living star" circled in fire and heavenly melody—no longer the oenophile we saw in the New Testament.

From there, it's pretty much a Who's Who of biblical greats: St. Peter in XXIV, who questions Dante on his theological understanding (sadly, their dialogue is a little academic—skim); St. James (actually, both St. Jameses conflated in one) in XXV; St. John in XXVI and then this fellow called Adam whom you might have heard of; St. Peter again in XXVII, and the structure and creation of Heaven in XXVII–IX.

In XXX comes God. Dante can't see Him yet, but he can see the Eternal Rose of angels, which he continues to describe in XXXI. Here Beatrice leaves Dante, and St. Bernard takes his hand. In XXXII, Dante sees Mary as preparation for his final encounter. Then in XXXIII, the hundredth and last canto of the last canticle of Dante's great trilogy, the pilgrim meets his maker. I'm sure you want to know what Dante found "at the end of all desires" but don't even think I'm going to give it away. Let's just say that I've already given you a hint of how he'll "describe" Him.

GIOVANNI BOCCACCIO
(1313–75)

∽∽∽

The Decameron
(1353)

"Just as folly often destroys men's happiness and casts them into deepest misery, so prudence extricates the wise."

You want to live in Boccaccio's world. Okay, not 14th-century Italy per se (perhaps a bit too much plague, among other inconveniences), but rather in a mental meritocracy like that which obtains in *The Decameron,* where quick thinking and a barbed tongue will take you to the top—or someone's bottom, if that's what you're after.

The Decameron consists of 100 tales (10 told each day for 10 days by 10 Florentine nobles who were hiding out from the plague in 1348), and almost all involve someone outsmarting someone else and thereby getting out of a jam—or a debt, a dispute, or a disheveled bed. It's a world of trickery and deception, yes, but even the tricked, if they're smart enough, get their due revenge—and tend to add a little interest to the principal. When we think of the Middle Ages, we imagine that God must be ordering the universe; in *The Decameron,* however, it seems like intelligence did, and that's a cosmology we can all endorse.

Crafty as Boccaccio's characters are, in most of the stories their brainy machinations work in service of messages sent from a decidedly different part of the body. It's a sexed-up world, Boccaccio's, where adultery, if we are to believe him, is *cosi fan tutti*, (practiced by everyone everywhere), and "all other pleasures . . . are mere trifles by comparison with the one experienced by a woman when she goes with a man." In *The Decameron*, even the wives who want to remain chaste seem to get tricked into sleeping with their suitors, to the point where the cloth caps that men wore in that era would have to have been fitted with holes to accommodate the horns each of them was sporting. (I guess you could take this as another knock on the Boccaccian universe.)

Sex—adulterous and otherwise—is so rampant in *The Decameron*, one has a harder time finding a tale that doesn't involve some nook-nook than finding one that does. But the most striking element in all this hanky-panky is the degree to which Boccaccio focuses on women's pleasure. Some literary scholars would have you believe that sex in premodern literature was invariably concerned with the male point—of view and otherwise—but time and again Boccaccio says that sex is what women "enjoy doing most" and is both "the greatest pleasure that Love can supply" and "the one thing that gives young women their greatest pleasure." He even exonerates cheating wives if they weren't getting the good stuff at home. Despite some moments of severe misogyny in a few of its tales, *The Decameron* is in a certain sense a progressive document, suggesting that women were entitled to a right that still isn't inalienable in many cultures.

Read Boccaccio, then, for the cleverness, the randiness, the verbal play, and the general *gioia di vivere*. Skip a lot (see pages 82–85), give yourself over to the general mirth, and know that there might not be a six-century-old bestseller quite as light and playful as *The Decameron*—nor one with as much illicit sex, adultery, and religious figures doing naughty things.

The Buzz: As I said above and will reiterate when discussing Chaucer's *Canterbury Tales,* people tend to forget how bawdy the writers of the Middle Ages could be. Boccaccio, however, has always been known for his raunch. He's had a rake's reputation for centuries, but it's actually pretty exaggerated. Though Boccaccio is Italy's preeminent writer this side of Dante (and only one generation his junior), most of his work has been woefully neglected, primarily because his lowest-brow, poppiest, most jazzed-up work is the one he's come to be famous for. Like Dr. Alex Comfort, the British scientist, poet, and novelist who authored fifty-odd books but is famous for only one (*The Joy of Sex*), Boccaccio got pigeonholed for his most scandalous work, causing people to forget his many other contributions to literature and letters (some of Italian literature's high points, actually). Boccaccio didn't intend *The Decameron* to be taken seriously; he calls it a mere "diversion for ladies in love" (and, yes, there were women readers back then—and a few writers too). But it's the one that stuck.

What People Don't Know (But Should): Boccaccio's introduction to *The Decameron* contains a first-person account of life during the Black Death (bubonic plague), movingly describing how people were afflicted and deserted, and how society and morality were turned upside down ("People behaved as though their days were numbered, and treated their belongings and their own persons with equal abandon."). It's gripping history, told in an elegant and serious tone you don't find elsewhere in *The Decameron*—good stuff.

Best Line: "No mortal being who is without experience of love can ever lay claim to true excellence" (IV, 4).

What's Sexy: What isn't? *The Decameron* has as much sex as any Best American Erotica collection—and many more priests.

The sexiest tales are II, 10 (the lover is better than the husband); III, 1 (naughty nuns!); III, 10 ("putting the devil back in Hell"); IV, 2 (hickey reference, see below); V, 4 (how many times will the "nightingale" sing?); V, 10 (gays! horny wives! threesomes!); the intro to Book VI (no virgins in the neighborhood); VII, 2 (the original tale of the tub); VII, 9 (some pear tree!); VII, 10 ("tilling" the garden); VIII, 2 (the "grinder's art"); VIII, 8 (wife-swapping!); IX, 6 ("tacked hard to windward again and again"); IX, 10 (pin the tail on the . . .). The conclusion to Book V also contains a bunch of salacious puns that, sadly, are considerably more funny in Italian.

Quirky Fact: *The Decameron* has perhaps the first high-literature reference to a hickey: "Take a look under your left breast, where I gave the Angel such an enormous kiss that it will leave a mark there for the best part of a week." (IV, 2) Five centuries later, Swinburne will become the great poet of the osculatory bruise, but Boccaccio might well be Europe's first to make that particular mark (I couldn't resist).

What to Skip: All ten days' introductions and conclusions can be skipped or skimmed (though the songs are pretty good at the end of each day). Apart from those, here's a tale-by-tale breakdown. Note: the ones I don't describe and advise you to skip are all pretty lame and repetitive somebody-tricking-somebody stories. You won't miss anything.

> I: Tale 1 is great (an archsinner "confesses" on his deathbed and is sainted); 5 is okay (a noblewoman resisting the king of France); the rest are skippable.

> II: Skip 1–6; 7 has the story of a woman with eight lovers taken to be a virgin; skip 8; 9 is skippable but begins with

an argument about women's constancy; 10 is great (about a wife choosing to get what she wants).

III: Tale 1 has a young buck pretending to be dumb so that he can get hired by some naughty nuns—funny and sexy; 2, 3, and 4 are okay (all have decent tricks); skip 5; 6 celebrates a woman suckered into having sex—not so kosher; skip 7 unless you want to read a long critique of the friars of the time; skip 8 and 9; 10 is straight-out vulgar, convincing a pious girl to "put the devil back in Hell"—you can imagine.

IV: Tale 1 is gruesome—a woman's lover's heart is sent to her in a chalice—but has the first real emotion in the book in Ghismonda's monologue; 2 is okay and has the hickey line mentioned in Quirky Fact (opposite page); 3 and 4 can be skipped, though the latter contains the "Best Line" above; 5 has the famous story of the basil plant growing madly with a head buried in its pot—still rather skippable; 6–10 can all be skipped.

V: Tales 1–3 can be skipped; 4 is funny and sexy, a crafty response to being caught sleeping in the wrong bed; 5–8 can be skipped; 9 is okay—a man sacrificing everything for a woman's love—and has some more feeling; 10 is among the raciest of the tales, with the wife complaining that since the husband deserts her "to go trudging through the dry stuff with clogs on"—he's gay—she'll "get someone to come aboard for the wet" and arguing that "women exist for no other purpose but to do this and to bear children." It ends with what might be a threesome—or at least a husband and wife passing a boy back and forth.

VI: Tales 1–4 can be skipped; 5 also, though it contains interesting comments on the early Renaissance painter Giotto; 6 is good—with a very novel way of insulting an old family; 7 and 8 should be skipped; 9 discusses the poet Guido Cavalcanti (a contemporary of Dante's whose father appears in *Inferno*) but can be skipped; and 10 can be skipped too.

VII: Skip 1; 2 is funny and sexy ("honey, go outside for a while; I think there's a werewolf"); 3 and 4 stink; 5 is good and has one of the best-thought-out tricks ("It's an edifying sight, I must say, when a mere woman leads an intelligent man by the nose"); 6–8 can be skipped; 9 is clever and sexy (again the wife outsmarts the jealous husband); 10 reveals that in Hell, everyone's had sex with someone they weren't supposed to. Sums up Boccaccio's worldview.

VIII: Tale 1 is okay (how to sleep with a man's wife for free); 2 has a randy priest—again—but is pretty funny; 3–5 should be skipped; 6 is funny—and contains candies made out of dog shit; 7 recommends that one never try to get the better of a scholar (a sentiment I'd like to endorse, but I fear we academics have fallen off a bit since the fourteenth century) but should still be skipped; 8 is okay, especially if you're into polyamory; 9 has some decent slapstick verbal humor but can be skipped; and skip 10.

IX: Skip 1; 2 is okay—more naughty nuns; 3 has a man tricked into thinking *he's* pregnant because his wife was on top during sex—not quite sure what to say about that—but is otherwise skippable; 4 and 5 can be skipped; 6 is the source of Chaucer's Miller's Tale—very funny; 7 is okay (variation on never cry wolf); 8 can be skipped; 9 is ultramisogynistic, told by one of the ladies but recommending that all women be beaten by their husbands—not to my taste; 10 brings it back a little with a bawdy tale of the adult version of pin the tail on the donkey.

X: Skip 1 and 2—and 3 as well, unless you're an anthropologist studying potlatch ceremonies; skip 4 unless you like necrophilial feel-ups; skip 5 and 6 but read 7 with its sweet and good older man (a rarity, at least here); skip the boring academic sophism of 8 and the straightforward, *Arabian Nights*-y 9; then, with 10, decide if you want to read the famous tale of Griselda, the peasant girl picked to marry a nobleman but forced to endure horrific tests of her submissiveness and resiliency. It's a highly misogynistic tale and not one I'd recommend. But it is famous.

Author's Epilogue: Pretty cute, tongue-in-cheek defense against various things *The Decameron* could be criticized for, including having "taken too many liberties." My favorite line is one that perhaps applies to this book as well: "The lady who is forever saying her prayers, or baking pies and cakes for her father confessor, may leave my stories alone." The very last line, by the way, where Boccaccio says *The Decameron* is "otherwise known as Prince Galahalt" is a reference to a famous panderer, cited by Francesca in *Inferno* as well, suggesting that he hopes *The Decameron* will help get some couples two-backing. And it probably did.

GEOFFREY CHAUCER
(1340–1400)

❧

The Canterbury Tales
(1400)

Chaucer gets a bad rap. English professors (at both college and high school), wanting their students to get a morsel of Chaucer's 14th-century English, often insist that they memorize the opening lines of *The Canterbury Tales'* General Prologue, concerning, of all potentially fascinating topics beneath God's vault, the time of year when people decide to go on religious pilgrimages. Who cares? How many students, now accustomed to the pace of instant-messaging and Halo III, are going to respond well to spending class time learning to enunciate "Whan that Aprill with his shoures soote/The droghte of March hath perced to the roote" and sixteen more lines of the same? With this as their first exposure to Chaucer, how could they possibly think that there'd be something in there worth knowing, much less that they might actually enjoy? April's showers sweet have washed away almost all potential for readerly enthusiasm.

The situation is easily rectified. Let students learn these lines of *The Canterbury Tales* instead, from the Wife of Bath's Prologue:

> Venus me yaf my lust, my likerousnesse,
> (*Venus gave me my lust, my lecherousness*)

And mars yaf me my sturdy hardynesse;
(And Mars gave me my sturdy hardiness)
Myn ascendent was taur, and mars therinne.
(My ascendent was Taurus, and Mars therein)
Allas! allas! that ever love was synne!
(Alas! Alas! That ever love was sin!)
I folwed ay myn inclinacioun
(I followed all my inclination)
By vertu of my constellacioun;
(By virtue of my constellation)
That made me I koude noght withdrawe
(That made me, I could not withdraw)
My chambre of venus from a good felawe.
(My chamber of Venus from a good fellow)
Yet have I martes mark upon my face,
(Yet I have Mars's mark upon my face)
And also in another privee place.
(And in another private place)
For God so wys be my savacioun,
(For God so wise be my salvation)
I ne loved nevere by no discrecioun,
(I never loved by no discretion)
But evere folwede myn appetit,
(But ever followed my appetite)
Al were he short, or long, or blak, or whit;
(Whether he was short or long or black or white)
I took no kep, so that he liked me,
(I didn't care, as long as he liked me)
How poore he was, ne eek of what degree.
(Nor how poor he was, nor of what degree.)

What a different sense of Chaucer (and of the Middle Ages as a whole) we would have if we started with this, the Wife of Bath's confession of being doomed to promiscuity by her astrological signs and inbred appetites. And while I realize there are high schools where such subject matter might not go over so well, if the instructor can't explain that this is humor—and particularly medieval humor—then there's not much hope for literary education. If you're going to try to get students to read something as alien and challenging (even in translation) as Chaucer, the first task is to get them to care. And what better way than showing them that medieval stuff can be both funny and a little racy? (And, yes, I know you're shocked to hear this argument coming from me, positively shocked.)

The thing I always tell my students is that medieval England and Europe in general were highly religious places, but the literature of the time—as we've already seen with Boccaccio—was often quite licentious and fun-loving (and this is true of the literature of every age, by the way). Each of the three major literary languages of the Middle Ages—Italian, French, and English—put forth a brainy, bawdy masterpiece that is considered a classic to this day. *The Decameron* was Italy's, Rabelais' *Gargantua and Pantagruel* France's, and *The Canterbury Tales* England's. All three knew well of "that art the olde daunce" and of that "perilous fyr that in the bedstraw breedeth." And it's a good thing that they did, for as tough as it is to read medieval languages (trust me, I had to learn four of them), if all one got as a payoff was a bunch of homilies—sermons barely masquerading as short stories—nobody would bother, and all the literary wit and genius from the first century to the birth of Shakespeare would have been flushed down a Roman cloaca.

Thankfully God, in his infinite wisdom, willed that the wit and genius of the Middle Ages be rendered palatable, reaching its apex in Chaucer's *Canterbury Tales*. Like the stories of *The Decameron*, *The Canterbury Tales* are told by a variety of different speakers, but this time, they're passing the hours on a pilgrimage to the town of Canterbury, not waiting out the plague. Chaucer borrowed a lot from Boccaccio, and you should read the *Tales* with the same mischievous eye as *The Decameron,* appreciating the trickery, the sex, and the playful parables. But Chaucer reached further in his book than Boccaccio did in his, adding the chivalry of the Knight's Tale, some genuinely pious tales (not all of which are anti-Semitic), and, of course, quite a few more fart jokes (see "What People Don't Know" on page 90). And don't worry, I give you a complete tale-by-tale breakdown in "What to Skip" on page 93.

But first I need to acknowledge the difficulty that Chaucer's 500-year-old English poses to the contemporary reader. The biggest problem for today's would-be Chaucer lover is whether to read him in the Middle English original version (with annotations) or in a modernized rendering. You can see in the quote above that the actual lexical difference isn't vast, but the two sides do provide pretty different reading experiences. To my eye at least, the modernization has that flat, detached feeling you get from most translations, while the original, to most of your eyes I suspect, looks a little like an ESL dropout dictated it to a four-year-old doing the typing. There are a few tricks, though, that will ease the pain of trying to muddle through Chaucer in Chaucerian.

1. Go slowly. It probably goes without saying, but to catch his humor and verbal alacrity, you've got to go word by word.

2. Don't worry about spelling. Standardization of spelling didn't take place till centuries after Chaucer's death, so he's likely to spell words quite differently than we spell them. He sometimes even spells the same word differently in the same sentence (why he would, I really have no idea).

3. Since the spelling can look odd, sound out the word in your mind to help identify it. If you go back and look at the Wife

of Bath quote above, you'll see that once you start pronouncing the words, it's pretty easy to see what they mean.

4. Use the notes. When you come across a word or a passage that doesn't make sense, a good edition of Chaucer (like the Riverside) will have a same-page note that explains it. If your copy doesn't have these kinds of notes at the bottom of each page, get another edition.

5. Enjoy the new vocabulary. What could be more fun than learning some oddball medieval words? I tell you, I've really been the life of the party throwing around gems like *saucefleem* (pimply), *dronkelewe* (being an alcoholic), *unwemmed* (undefiled), *swynke* (work), *yex* (snore), *swyve* (better look that one up), *dighte* (that one too), *tuvel* (uh . . .), or *towte* (never mind). Okay, maybe life of the party is a bit of an exaggeration; as often as not someone tells me to *stynt* my *clappe*. Still. Follow these helpful tips and ye carls will be glosing Chaucer forthwithal, or I don't *yclepe* Jack Murnighan.

The Buzz: Chaucer in America tends to get the same treatment as Dante in Italy, so most people, if they know anything of the *Tales,* only know the opening lines (the tragedy of this I discussed above). The most famous character is the Wife of Bath—and with good reason. She's one of the greatest literary voices ever created, a perfect embodiment of the garrulous alewife we might not expect when thinking of the Middle Ages and their Christian piety.

What People Don't Know (But Should): Chaucer could easily be dubbed Poet of the Fart. Flatulence plays an important role in the Miller's Tale ("a fart / as great as if it had been a thunderclap," 3806–7) and a pivotal role in the Summoner's Tale, beginning with "grope well behind / beneath my buttock there shalt thou find / a thing I've hid in privety" (2140–3). The trick of this whole tale rests on whether a fart can be divided equally into twelve parts. If you want to know how the dilemma's resolved, the fart is finally blown through a wagon wheel, with each spoke delivering an equal portion to the awaiting friars (2243–86).

Best Line: There are many zingers in the Wife of Bath's prologue (which you've gathered by now I'm a big fan of), but my favorite single line comes from the Knight's Tale: "Who may be a fool but if he love?" i.e., who can be a fool if he's never been in love. And just so you don't think Chaucer's against the blazing of the ventricles and atria, here are my favorite of all his lines, from one of his short poems, "The Parliament of Fowls" (note, "th'assay" means the work, "dredful" means awe-inspiring, and "slit so yerne" means slip away so quickly):

> The lyf so short, the craft so long to lerne,
> Th'assay so hard, so sharp the conquering,
> The dredful Joy, that alwey slit so yerne,
> Al this mene I by love.

What's Sexy: Lots. I'll do it tale by tale (but don't miss the more general discussions of each tale in "What to Skip":

Miller's Tale: Nicholas and Alison doing "the revel and the melody" (3652) and Absolon kissing Alison's "nether eye"—"At the window out she put her hole / and Absolon . . . with his mouth he kissed her naked arse / full savourly, before he was aware of it / Aback he started, and thought it was amiss / for well he knew a woman has no beard / and the thing he felt so rough and long-haired"

(3732–3738). The adolescent male's pantheon: Beavis, Butthead, and Chaucer.

Reeve's Tale: The daughter who gets her "jolly whistle well a-wet" (4155), the wife who snored like a horse snorting and took no heed "of her tail behind" (4163), and the clerks who "swonken all the long night" (4235).

Wife of Bath's Prologue: All of it—seriously. She's swyved five husbands to the grave (one who was half her age) and is looking for a sixth (or eighth): "Of bigamy or octogamy / why should men speak of it as villainy?" (33–34). Dozens of lines could be quoted here, though if you read the Wife of Bath in a modernized version, 99 percent of her charm is lost. At least here, fight your way through the original. It's worth it.

Wife of Bath's Tale: Tells of a knight who can't perform on his wedding night because his wife is too ugly (1081–95), ends with the prayer (in part): "Jesus Christ us send / husbands meek, young, and fresh abed" (1259–60).

Merchant's Tale: Amid general discussions—and tests—of old men's abilities to please young wives (no Viagra in the 1390s), this delightful maxim: "There is no workman whosoever he may be / that may both work well and hastily" (1832–33).

Shipman's Tale: Rewrite of *Decameron* VIII, 1 (the one about not paying to sleep with another man's wife) and similarly riggish.

Quirky Fact: In the otherwise forgettable Franklin's Tale, Chaucer refers to "the wide world, which that men say is round" (1228). I bet you didn't know that since the 8th century, all the major cosmographers in Europe agreed that the earth was a globe. Any other myths about the Middle Ages that you want me to dispel?

What to Skip: A few of the tales are unfinished and thus skippable, and unless you're interested in immersing yourself in medieval theological debates and critiques, you won't mind skipping quite a few more. In order, then, take a pass on these:

Cook's Prologue and Tale

Man of Law's Tale

Squire's Tale

Franklin's Tale (okay, but like any old *Decameron* tale)

Physician's Tale

Prioress's Tale

Sir Thopas (read the prologue and then the end, when the Host interrupts Chaucer)

The Tale of Melibee

Monk's Tale (though the interstitial "Here stynteth the Knight the Monk of his tale" is priceless)

Nun's Priest's Tale

Second Nun's Tale

Canon Yeoman's Tale

Parson's Tale

That still leaves quite a few good ones. Here's a brief what-and-why for the rest of *The Canterbury Tales*:

General Prologue: Introduces the plot and the various characters on the pilgrimage. Some descriptions are pretty funny, like the Friar who "lisped for wantonness," the hollow-looking Clerk (student), the Miller and his hairy-moled nose, the beardless "gelding" (the Pardoner), and the "seemly" Host, the organizer of the pilgrimage and subtle hero of the book.

Knight's Tale: Adapted from Boccaccio's *Teseida*, a chivalric story of virtue and love. Entertaining, if a bit long.

Miller's Prologue: Very funny, as the Miller confesses he's drunk and might not make any sense and offers an epigram Boccaccio would have endorsed: "Who has no wife, is no cuckold" (3152). The narrator then apologizes that the tale will be scurrilous and warns gentlefolk to turn past it.

Miller's Tale: Racy fabliau of a student, Nicholas, getting the best of a carpenter (and his wife), and her other suitor Absolon getting a "kiss" of her arse (see "What's Sexy" above) before Nicholas gets a hot poker in his.

Reeve's Prologue: He's a carpenter, so he's offended by the Miller's tale and intends to retaliate. Laments in passing on age's impact on one's sex life, borrowing the leek metaphor from Boccaccio: to have a white head but a green tail (3878–79).

Reeve's Tale: A bed-mixup tale similar to *The Decameron*'s IX, 6 but with a lot more to it and with this all-too-true line about scholars: "The greatest clerks weren't always the wisest men" (4054).

Introduction to the Man of Law's Tale: The Man of Law makes fun of Chaucer (he's a character on the pilgrimage too) for not doing rhyme or meter well (47–48) but praises him for telling "of lovers up and down / more than Ovid made mention of" (53–54). The tale that follows is long and eminently skippable, as is the epilogue.

Wife of Bath's Prologue: The crown jewel of the Tales, as I mention above (see "The Buzz"). If you read nothing else in *The Canterbury Tales,* at least read these thirteen or so pages. Dame Alisoun's prologue, in which she describes how she manages her husbands and gets the "nicety" (see "What's Sexy") is one of the great comic monologues in the history of literature. She also laments how authors portray women, accounting for the misogyny by saying that the writers can't get it up anymore! (705–11). It's a tour de force of wit, insight, voice, salaciousness, and brio.

Wife of Bath's Tale: A knight rapes a maid and gets the death sentence, but the queen says she'll commute it if he can tell "what thing it is that women most desire" (905). An old hag promises that she'll tell him, on the condition that he'll marry her. The answer is not necessarily what you'd think.

Friar's Prologue: Says he's going to tell a tale about a summoner because they run around taking money to pardon people for the sin of fornication (1284).

Friar's Tale: Humorous critique of summoners' corruption in which the devil comes and makes it clear that they're in the same business.

Summoner's Prologue: He gets his licks back, saying that Satan's ass is full of friars (1690–1)—a scene visually rendered to, let us say, powerful effect in Pasolini's film version of *The Canterbury Tales.*

Summoner's Tale: Skip to 2124. A friar tries to swindle a householder who says he'll give the convent something as long as all the brothers share it equally. He then farts on the friar's hand (see "What People Don't Know" above), but the friar can find no "arse-metric" (2222) to divide it with. By the end, the riddle is solved—frat house humor at its finest.

Clerk's Prologue: Gets berated by the Host for being studious instead of merry, then says he'll tell a story he learned from the great Italian poet Petrarch (who actually learned if from Boccaccio, though Chaucer doesn't say so).

Clerk's Tale: An adaptation of the Griselda tale told in *The Decameron* X, 10.

Merchant's Prologue: Laments that his wife is Griselda's opposite: "We wedded men live in sorrow and care" (1228).

Merchant's Tale and Epilogue: Highly lascivious story of January (old man) and May (young wife)—perhaps the errant source of the phrase "December/May romance." Debate over whether to marry, and if so, whether to pick a young or old spouse (if you're old).

Pardoner's Prologue: Skip the intro for the fabulous prologue, where the Pardoner confesses his various tricks—and that he's a drunk, womanizing hoax. Clearly Chaucer and Boccaccio weren't big on pardoners, friars, or summoners.

Pardoner's Tale: Skip the sermon that begins it (to line 660). Read the tale of the three young men who ask an old man, "Why livest thou so long in so great age?" and he responds, "For I could not find a man . . . that would change his youth for my age" (719–24)—beautiful. Then they ask where they can find Death, for they want to get him to stop the plague. The old man says he left him buried with some gold beneath a tree. And, yes, he's still there . . .

Shipman's Tale: Rewrite of *Decameron* VIII, 1 (the freebie-sex one). If you already read that, you can skip this one, or vice versa.

Manciple's Prologue: Makes fun of the cook's breath (37–41) and his drunken state.

Manciple's Tale: Parable of a tattletale crow. Poor bird didn't know the Glengarry rules.

EDMUND SPENSER
(1552–99)

The Faerie Queene
(1596)

Think of it like a tasty dish that's reputed to be good for you, intricately spiced and deeply layered in flavor, but served steaming hot in a sink-sized cauldron filled to the brim. It's good, you might even love it, you know it's healthy, but dear Lord are you supposed to eat the whole thing? Spenser's *The Faerie Queene* has the impressive if somewhat dubious distinction of being the longest epic poem in the English language. Spanning well over 30,000 lines (over 1,000 pages in most annotated editions!) and composed of more than six books, it is still but a quarter of the work Spenser originally set out to write. Much as I love *The Faerie Queene,* I number my voice among those scholars who are quite thankful that the great Elizabethan's pen faltered prior to completion. One bucketful is more than enough—even for Monty Python's *The Meaning of Life* guy, right?

With that lead-in, you might be surprised to hear that until fifty years or so ago, the brightest planets in the sky of English poetry were Shakespeare, Milton, Chaucer, and Spenser, in that order. Today, Shakespeare still wears the garlands (though in many cases more for reputation than familiarity), Milton and his megalith are barely read, Chaucer the comic genius is presumed to be a bore, and Spenser is all but forgotten. It's a shame, but in

Spenser's case, it wouldn't have been hard to predict. *The Faerie Queene* takes as its subject the Christian moral virtues of holiness, temperance, chastity, friendship, justice, courtesy, and constancy, and adopts what was already, by the end of the 16th century when it was written, a throwback faux-medieval style and intricate allegorical apparatus. None of this bodes well for the modern reader.

Yet *The Faerie Queene* is not without charms, and, *vox clamantis in deserto*, I will still insist (you knew this was coming) that there are good reasons to read *The Faerie Queene*—at least in part—and ways of actually enjoying it. For one, the poetry can be truly outstanding, as in world-class, and the fact that all one thousand pages are written in nine-line, iambic pentameter ababbcbcc-rhyming stanzas is stunning if you think about it. I'm not saying that too too many of the stanzas will jump out at you, but probably at least one per canto (and there are twelve cantos per book) is utterly amazing, and quite a few more really impressive—not too bad if you're a poetry fan. There's a reason Spenser was thought of as the fourth best English poet of all time.

Then there's the fact that Spenser had as sophisticated a sense of epistemology and poetic representation as anyone ever. His negotiation of truth vs. falsehood, art vs. nature, surface vs. depth, appearance vs. reality, and all such similar dichotomies can be amazing to follow along with, if you can keep one philosophical eye open as you read.

Finally, you don't have to ingest very much not only to get it, but to claim you've read the whole thing. Like a massive poetic fractal (or a tub of saag paneer), each tiny unit reflects the totality of the rest. *The Faerie Queene* can thus be read from almost anywhere and at any length, and you'll get a pretty good sense of what the remainder of the poem is like. Even reading only a scene or two—and there are a few I'll recommend (see pages

100–3)—you'll taste Spenser's unique flavor and get a sense of his prodigious poetic acumen. Combine that with the fact that, as my old professor Stanley Fish used to say, nobody can remember the whole plot of *The Faerie Queene* (and if they say they can they're lying), and you're covered for cocktail parties. If someone refers to a section you happen to have skipped, no worries—it just slipped your memory; happens to us all.

Now if you do find yourself reading *The Faerie Queene* conventionally, as in from the first page and without jumping ahead, and detect yourself being irresistably captivated by the adventures of its first hero, the Redcross Knight, against the evil triplets Sansloi (lawless), Sansfoi (faithless), and Sansjoi (joyless)—I kept waiting for the appearance of a fourth sibling Sansroi (kingless), but then I remembered Spenser wrote during spinster Elizabeth's reign and that wouldn't have gone over so well—good for you. You can watch him and subsequent Spenserian good guys tackle a host of equally imposing allegorical villains on their way to helping Spenser in his expressed intent of "fashioning" a gentleman. The good money says you won't.

But if you do, you will find yourself, amid the creeping hypnosis of Spenser's interminable rhymes, shocked awake here and there by a profound conceptual insight, a majestic turn of phrase, or by the robotic sidekick of the hero of the Justice book chopping the limbs off a little girl (oops). And then you will know, by the end, that you've triumphed at a great endurance event and will faintly feel the gaze of literary marathoners everywhere as they look up at you from their pools of vomit, impressed. And you might even find yourself saying, in the very words Spenser loaned you:

> But whether dreams delude or true it were,
> Was never heart so ravished with delight,
> Ne living man like words did ever hear,

As to me she delivered that night;
And at her parting said, she Queen of Faeries hight [is
    named]. [I, ix, 14]

The Buzz: Okay, maybe saying that there's a buzz about Spenser is a bit of a stretch at this point; I'd be surprised if his name comes up at any cocktail party on any given New York night— unless I'm pedantically buttonholing some ovine listeners. But the base facts to know are that Spenser sought to portray the moral virtues allegorically—one characteristic at a time—and that the title refers to Queen Elizabeth, with whom Spenser had an intermittently problematic relationship (she didn't always like his poetry). Spenser reaches new depths of bum-kissing in the introductory stanzas of Book III, saying that Elizabeth will find herself represented in the poem by two of the poem's heroines: "In mirrors more than one her self to see, / But either *Gloriana* let her choose, / Or in *Belphoebe* fashioned to be: / In th'one her rule, in th'other her rare chastity."

What People Don't Know (But Should): In the last canto of Book V, a new monster appears, the oddly—yes, horribly— named Blatant Beast, whose tongue "pours his poisonous gall" to defame the good. There was already a villain named Sclaunder (slander), but the Blatant Beast poses more of a threat to poets and books, including Spenser's. At the conclusion of Book VI, the hero, Calidore, captures the beast temporarily, but it breaks the iron chain and escapes.

"So now he rangeth through the world again,

. . . .

Ne spareth he most learned wits to rate,
Ne spareth he the gentle Poet's rime,
But rends without regard of person or of time.

> Ne may this homely verse, of many meanest,
> Hope to escape his venemous despite" [VI, xii, 40–41]

It was a poetic convention in the Renaissance to end your works indicating your unhappy awareness that they might get panned. Rarely, though, do such fears entail creating a monster who spareth not most learned wits and poets; Spenser's really covering his derriere.

Best Line: Apart from the good knight Pyrocles' shield's device "Burnt, I do burn" (kind of sums things up, doesn't it?), my favorite short bit of *The Faerie Queene* is probably this stanza in which the warrior-woman Britomart is asked "why make ye such monster of your mind" (III, ii, 40). She confesses to feeling worse than Narcissus at the unreachability of her beloved who, being far away, is even less than a reflection in a pool—merely an image in her head.

> "But wicked fortune mine, though mind be good,
> Can have no end, nor hope of my desire,
> But feed on shadows, whiles I die for food,
> And like a shadow wex, whiles with entire
> Affection I do languish and expire.
> I, fonder than Cephisus' foolish child,
> Who, having viewed in a fountain sheer
> His face, was with the love thereof beguiled;
> I, fonder, love a shade, the body far exiled." [III, ii, 44]

What's Sexy: I bet you thought I'd have to leave this one blank, didn't you? But actually there's a decent amount of naughtiness in what is supposed to be such a pious poem (now fancy that!). In addition to the lusty ladies described in the Bower of Bliss (see

references below) and to the maiden Serena being tied up and
stripped bare by cannibals in Book VI (viii, 34–end), there is a
scene that stands out in classic literature as being one of the few
depicting, if metaphorically, the female orgasm. I'm not positive
that Renaissance England was aware that the big O for women involved a significant rushing of blood to the pelvic region, but
clearly Spenser, as you'll see, had a sense of what was going on—
and found the perfect poetic image.

> And ever and anon, when no one was aware,
> With speaking looks that secret message bore
> He gazed at her, and told his hidden care
> With all the art that he had learned of yore.
> Nor was she ignorant of that seductive lore,
> But in his eye his meaning wisely read,
> And with the like answered him evermore:
> She sent at him one fiery dart, whose head
> Empoisoned was with secret lust and jealous dread.
>
> .   .   .   .
>
> Thenceforth to her he sought to intimate
> His inward grief, by means to him well known:
> Now Bacchus' fruit out of the silver plate
> He on the table dashed, and overthrowed
> The cup of fruited liquor overflowed
> And by the dancing bubbles did divine
> And therein write to let his love be showed;
> Which well she read out of the learned line:
> A sacrament profane in mystery of wine.
>
> And when so of his hand the pledge had passed
> The guilty cup she fained to mistake,
> And in her lap did spill her brimming glass

Showing desire her inward flames to slake.

By such close signs they a secret way did make

Unto their wills, and watched for due escape . . . [II, ix, 28–30]

Quirky Fact: You'd think Spenser was a pretty good guy, what, with writing a thousand-page poem on the moral virtues and all, but he sure had a dark side. Having lived for a while among my potato-eating forebears, he wrote a tract called *A View of the Present State of Ireland* that suggested various ways of "passifying" the headstrong locals: principally by invading, bringing the sword, and letting famine do the rest. Nice.

What to Skip: As I indicate above, I would encourage you to start *The Faerie Queene,* read a little from the beginning, then when you start to fade, jump ahead to the best parts. From my vantage—and remember, I have your reading pleasure at heart— I'd suggest these scenes (cited by book, canto, stanza): the knight Cymocles waylaid by ladies in the Bower of Bliss (II, v, 27–end); Pyrocles and his "flames" at the Idle Lake (II, vi, all); the Bower of Bliss again, this time with another knight named Guyon (II, xii, 42–end); Malbecco and Hellenore's parable of jealousy, from which the "What's Sexy" quote is taken (III, ix and III, x in their entirety); and the very end with the Blatant Beast (VI, xii, 40–41).

WILLIAM SHAKESPEARE
(1564–1616)

❦

General Introduction—
and free reader's guide!

Let's hope Shakespeare is looking down on us from some-where, because at the time he died, the Bard didn't have the slightest sense that he would come to be considered the greatest writer ever to dip a quill. Unlike Dante or Milton, he never an-nounced that he was turning literature on its head; he simply did, perhaps not even knowing he was. And though he was success-ful in his lifetime, he was not unrivaled (competing with Mar-lowe first, then Jonson). He was buried in his birthplace, Stratford-upon-Avon, not in "Poets' Corner" of Westminster Abbey with Chaucer, Spenser, and that same theatrical compeer, Ben Jonson (whose name is misspelled on his slab—oops). Even-tually Shakespeare received a monument in Poets' Corner, but not until over a century after his death. Nor does Shakespeare's headstone (apparently written by himself) attest to any great-ness—quite the opposite: "Good friend for Jesus sake forbeare, / To dig the dust enclosed here. / Blessed be the man that spares these stones, / And cursed be he that moves my bones." Did Shakespeare think he might be dug up and moved, or tossed aside by a sexton like Yorick's skull in *Hamlet*? How tragic that our language's most incandescent author could die untrumpeted, worrying for the safety of his grave, rather than exulting in the assurance of his legacy.

Thankfully, time, the patient tutor, has helped us understand the enormity of Shakespeare's achievement. The most inventive, dexterous, diverse, and brilliant voice in the history of upright man, he was a very thaumaturge of language, wielding his pen like a wand. And like his great character Prospero in *The Tempest,* he called sprites to do his bidding, neologizing and conscripting roughly twice as many words as any other writer ever has. And not only did he use more words, but his combinations, his artistry, the conjurer's handkerchiefs he was forever pulling from his sleeve, are so varied, so exquisite, so original and ornate, that no other writer's can compare.

But to see the consummate magician perform the utterly miraculous, you have to be up close. The joys of Shakespeare don't become apparent with a passing acquaintanceship; until you feel at home in Shakespeare's language, only the rudiments of his artistry will register. And I'm not talking about the vocabulary, mind you; that's what the notes are for. But you have to get used to his tricks, how he uses metaphors, the indirection of his diction, the way he constructs sentences, when he's joking, when he's exaggerating, when he or the character is being ironic, when he's likely to be punning, when the verbal stakes are high or low. Each scene is almost like a poker game, with some characters bluffing, some concealing, some entrapping, and some simply being guiled down the primrose path. But if you pay close enough attention, each will tip his hand.

It's certainly not impossible to get comfortable with Shakespeare, but it does take endeavor, and the obstacle is larger than college or high school teachers seem to realize. I taught Shakespeare once (at Duke, not a bad school, even off the basketball court), and at first my students could barely comprehend the basic meaning of Shakespeare's lines, much less appreciate the jukes and jabs. And as to the sublimity? Not a chance.

But it wasn't their fault; no one had ever sat them down and showed them how to read Shakespeare point by point. So guess what; that's what I'm going to do for you. In brief, a few techniques to help you be able to feel for yourself what the Shakespearean hubbub is all about.

1. As with Chaucer, go slowly, as slow as you can. Shakespeare takes more opportunities to insert little witticisms and verbal play than anyone this side of Georges Perec. If you let your attention drift, you'll miss everything. Plus you'll need to take your time just to figure out what in the Sam Hill he's saying.

2. With that said, keep your eye especially peeled for puns. As I'll show you with an example below, punning spins the Shakespearean wheel, and catching them can make his plays a lot more interesting, humorous, and downright naughty.

3. Get used to his indirection. Rarely does Shakespeare "just say something"; he puts a twist in almost every line, making you make the connections. So you have to learn to read what's behind his ever-present metaphor and metonymy (having something stand in for another thing that it's connected to, as when Polonius says of his son, "Let him ply his music," the word "music" refers not only to playing and dancing, but to all the pleasures—and vices—that Laertes might be engaging in. Once we see it as kind of racy, it's a great euphemism).

4. Use the notes at the bottom of each page (and make sure you have an edition with notes at the bottom), but keep a dictionary—especially an *OED*—at hand anyway. As with Chaucer, one can learn a lot of funny stuff looking up the words you don't know in Shakespeare ("wassail"—riotous

drinking, "eliad"—an amorous look). Plus the notes will sometimes admit that nobody knows what a line means; it makes you feel a little better when even the pros have no idea.

5. Don't give up on a line till you've given it a few tries. If there's no note to explain it, take a few more perusals before you trundle past. There will be plenty that doesn't unravel, but Shakespeare is actually nowhere near as alien as he seems to be at first glance.

6. Know whose words to pay special attention to and whose not to. Every play has the smart guys (normally clowns, fools, workmen, faeries, the hero or heroine and the bad guy or daughters) and dullards (those getting in the hero's way, flunkies, straight guys). The introduction to each play should give you a quick heads-up, and the rest you can figure out in context. In *Hamlet*, for example, don't bother with Claudius or Gertrude; whereas Hamlet and Polonius, they're worth parsing out.

7. Pay attention to when Shakespeare switches from prose to poetry (instead of block paragraphs, the lines will be divided and each new one will begin with a capital letter), and note how he often rhymes the last couplet of speeches for effect. Shakespeare uses verse and rhyme like salt to add a little extra flavor when he feels like it. You'll get more out of the lines if you notice.

8. Finally, and most importantly, know as you go that you're reading the greatest stylist the world has ever known. The more you look, the more you'll find, emotionally, intellectually, and poetically. Every play is a trove, and if you're not unearthing Shakespeare's genius, you've got to keep trying. As with almost all the writers in this book, once you start writ-

ing "wow" and "!!!" in the margin, you'll know you're actually reading Shakespeare, not just looking at him.

Let's do a quick practice run, taking Hamlet's first speech as our example. His mother Gertrude has just been explaining how all fathers die, arguing that Hamlet shouldn't be so upset about losing his. She then asks him, "Why seems it so particular with thee?" Here's Hamlet's response:

> "Seems, madam! nay it is; I know not 'seems.'
> 'Tis not alone my inky cloak, good mother,
> Nor customary suits of solemn black,
> Nor windy suspiration of forced breath,
> No, nor the fruitful river in the eye,
> Nor the dejected 'havior of the visage,
> Together with all forms, moods, shapes of grief,
> That can denote me truly: these indeed seem,
> For they are actions that a man might play:
> But I have that within which passeth show;
> These but the trappings and the suits of woe." [I, ii]

The first line, with multiple puns on Gertrude's "seem," already gives us a lot to chew on. First, Hamlet is saying that "it" (things with him) doesn't just seem particular, it *is* particular (i.e., you are now married to my father's brother while he's still warm in the grave—that's pretty particular). Then he's saying that that isn't at all "seemly" (meaning "appropriate, proper, in good taste"). Finally, and here's the pun that will condition the rest of his speech: he knows not "seams" as in clothing—neither, as he will explain, in the sense of being able to show in his garb (i.e., in any part of his outside dress or behavior) what he's feeling on the inside (a metaphor Shakespeare uses repeatedly in almost all the plays), nor that he recognizes the royal robes that his uncle Claudius is now wearing but doesn't deserve, either on the outside or the inside.

There's no question that Shakespeare intended all these meanings simultaneously, but don't be alarmed. Many of Shakespeare's puns will announce themselves (and some are truly awful—I don't think he could help himself), and you'll get better and better both at spotting them and at anticipating where he's likely to have one. Plus, not many lines will be as intricate as the ones above, not even in Hamlet's speeches. So it's up to you how much of a scavenger hunt you want to go on. The puns aren't actually necessary to loving the language, but if you miss them, you get less of a three-dimensional effect—each sentence will point only one way, not scaffold up an edifice.

Even if you choose simply to read straight ahead—and I do that too—I hope you can see the regal beauty in "the fruitful river in the eye" (marking how much one can cry) and why he's arguing "all forms, moods, shapes of grief" can't "denote" him (i.e., show what he's really feeling). It's because they can all be faked ("actions that a man might play"—another theme that runs through all the tragedies), whereas what Hamlet's feeling, he wants to insist, can't be acted. Of course, all the while this is being said by an actor, in the midst of a "show," so you see the irony behind what the player as the character Hamlet finds himself saying. Shakespeare probably felt pretty often that he had "that within which passeth show," but shows were what he wrote (and produced and acted in), and that's about all we ever found out about him. Pretty sad.

I'll stop, but you can see why the plays must be read and not just seen on the stage. The very fact that they weren't as successful in Shakespeare's day when audiences could actually follow the language as the actors were speaking as they were later when the texts become available says all you need to know. For us, there's zero chance of getting the literary richness when it goes by at the speed of dialogue. And do today's actors even understand the lines they're reciting? I have my doubts.

I'll admit that the kind of reading I'm talking about takes work—maybe more work than you want to put into something that's supposed to be giving you pleasure. It's a fair point, but think what's at stake: it's the difference between always wondering why this guy is singled out as the best of all time and being able to tango step-for-step with the most gifted man ever to take up a pen.

WILLIAM SHAKESPEARE
(1564–1616)

ᗊᗨᗟ

Hamlet
(c. 1600)

Hamlet is often called Shakespeare's supreme work, and the reason is clear: its protagonist is simply the best talker in the history of literature. Young Hamlet's speeches are supreme not only in their overall grandeur, but in their intelligence, wit, speed, and perpetual gyration of phrase. Line by line, there's more going on, more to wow you, and more to reward close scrutiny than any gab by anyone anywhere. In *Paradise Lost,* Satan and the host of rebel angels do some good jawing; Ishmael's got a few stellar soliloquies while scanning the seas for Moby Dick; *Ulysses'* Stephen Dedalus and Buck Mulligan do their fair share of intricate verbal fox-trotting, and the Judge in *Blood Meridian* can muster some rather impressive biblical orotundity; but still they lose out. None of them is Hamlet.

But the prince of parlance doesn't just walk around monologuing; there's actually a pretty good story too. To recap, Hamlet is told that the ghost of his dead father, former king of Denmark, is strolling about the castle walls at night, creeping everybody out. Hamlet goes to see, and the ghost tells him he was murdered by his brother, Claudius, who usurped his crown and wife to boot. Hamlet decides to play insane till he figures out what to do, and starts speaking innuendo-laden incomprehensibilities to his friends, family, and fair Ophelia, his sugar. Then a troupe of actors comes by whom Hamlet instructs to put on a play simulating the murder; they do so and Claudius storms out. Hamlet goes to speak to his mother, Gertrude, sees Claudius praying and considers killing him but decides to wait (killing the king mid-prayer might send his soul to heaven). Hamlet proceeds to browbeat his mother and accidentally kills the spying Polonius (Ophelia's father) thinking him Claudius (even though the king was just on his knees in the other room). Claudius finds out and decides to send Hamlet to England, but Hamlet averts the trap. Polonius' son, Laertes, hears of his father's death and wants revenge. Claudius plots with him to kill Hamlet by envenomed foil (in fencing) and also poisons some wine as a backup plan. Ophelia loses her marbles and drowns—perhaps self-dunked. Hamlet and Laertes fight, Gertrude unknowingly drinks the poisoned wine, Laertes stabs Hamlet with the poisoned foil, they scuffle, switch foils, and Hamlet wounds him back. Laertes knows they're both done for and confesses the treachery. Hamlet stabs and kills Claudius, and they all die. That's why it's called a tragedy.

Critics tend to say that *Hamlet* is the greatest of the Shakespeare plays because its protagonist is deeper than any other character in Shakespeare (though Falstaff, Prospero, Timon, and Troilus maybe give him a run for his money). But how much does that really mean? And if you're looking for psychology, why aren't you reading a Russian novel? Sure, our troubled hero oscillates between resolve and delay—to off my stepfather or not to off my stepfather, that is the question—but Shakespeare's investigation of the flipflopping only skims his cerebellum. No, Hamlet is not like his counterpart, the action-man Fortinbras (meaning "strong in arm"—a bit obvious, no? Why not add Lance for good measure?) who's off to conquer a worthless piece of Poland (a very forced bit of plot, by the way), but so what?

Commentators always talk about Hamlet's "procrastinating," but he has to murder his uncle, after all. Wouldn't it take any non-hothead a few tries to muster up the cojones? So, yes, there's psychology in Hamlet (both character and play), but it's not especially deep or surprising.

It isn't Shakespeare's fault. These are plays, after all; they're not going to be able to compete with a well-made novel in terms of character development, motivations, or internal richness. Even if Shakespeare went as far as five acts will take you, Tolstoy could continue for fourteen hundred pages if he wanted—and did. Psychology is not the route for really appreciating *Hamlet* or Shakespeare as a whole (nor is the "invention" of "personality" or inwardness either, as has been asserted. One can easily find those in literature of all ages).

No, the way to find yourself loving Shakespeare, as I argued in the general introduction, is to meticulously unfold his origami sentences until their full wonder becomes visible. And nowhere is this more true than in *Hamlet*. There is enormous genius in the Bard's formulations, and in *Hamlet* even more than any of the other plays, it comes packaged in some of the world's finest poetry. I tried to show you the glory of Hamlet's first speech in my general intro, but even simple lines like when he calls actors "the abstract and brief chronicles of the time" (II, ii) imbricate exquisite, nuanced shades of meaning. What, you want another walk-through? Well, since you asked so nicely . . .

The first meaning is twofold: As "chronicles of the time," actors can portray periods in history (like Shakespeare's plays about various kings of England), but they also incidentally represent their own era, all theater being a mirror of its own moment (we learn about Elizabethan England by studying Shakespeare's works). But calling actors "abstract and brief" also suggests that they provide especially focused embodiments, and therefore perhaps the best access you can get either to their subject or their age. That in itself is pretty tidy, but this is Shakespeare, so there's one more meaning as well: The actors' *lives* are both abstract and brief, played out in roles, not truth, and then not for long. There is a quiet sadness here, similar to what we saw in the "passing show" lines I talked about above: a sense of both the glory and tragedy of being an actor but perhaps never being able to be yourself.

If you read *Hamlet*—and especially the prince's lines—for this level of verbal subtlety, it's both inexhaustibly rich and consistently dazzling. Shakespeare is doing his magic routine again, and never does he pull more out of his hat and faster. In the final act, Hamlet says, "There's a divinity that shapes our ends" (V, ii)—perhaps even Shakespeare suspected, coming to the close of his finest play, that a higher hand was helping guide his. It certainly seems that way.

The Buzz: Apart from all the famous lines (a few of which I'll quote shortly), the element of the play that tends to get most of the spilled conversational ink, as I mention above, is Hamlet's internal conflict between thinking and doing. *Hamlet* is also rightfully famous for its extended meditations on death—the most in any Shakespeare play, and certainly a contributing element to its greatness.

First I'll give you a few of the shorter oft-quoted lines, then the two most famous soliloquies (try, though, to read them in context sometime; they're all a lot better set within the play as a whole):

"How weary stale, flat and unprofitable / Seem to me all the uses of the world" (I, ii).

Polonius' fatherly advice: "Neither a borrower nor a lender be . . . to thine own self be true," etc. (I, iii). Rather ironic since Polonius turns out to be true to nothing but his own machinations.

"Brevity is the soul of wit" (II, ii).

"There is nothing either good or bad, but thinking makes it so" (II, ii).

"What a piece of work is a man! how noble in reason! how infinite in faculty! in form and moving how express and admirable! in action how like an angel! in apprehension how like a god! the beauty of the world! the paragon of animals! And yet, to me, what is this quintessence of dust?" (II, ii).

"To be, or not to be: that is the question:
Whether 'tis nobler in the mind to suffer
The slings and arrows of outrageous fortune,
Or to take arms against a sea of troubles,
And by opposing end them? To die: to sleep;
No more; and by a sleep to say we end
The heartache and the thousand natural shocks
That flesh is heir to, 'tis a consummation
Devoutly to be wish'd. To die, to sleep;
To sleep: perchance to dream: ay, there's the rub;
For in that sleep of death what dreams may come
When we have shuffled off this mortal coil,
Must give us pause" [III, i]

What People Don't Know (But Should): *Hamlet* is the most celebrated work of Western civilization (apart from the Bible), but, like *King Lear* and many of Shakespeare's other plays, there's no definitive text. *Hamlet* has come down to us from three different documents (one probably an actor's notes), but none of them is authoritative, and only two hundred lines are identical in all three. It doesn't seem that Shakespeare authorized any of the printings, so editors are forced to hypothesize on what he wanted many of the lines and scenes to be and then cobble from the three options a "proper" *Hamlet*. But how the author actually wanted it or how it was performed on-stage, we'll probably never know.

Best Line: Apart from the famous ones listed above, I love this reference to the speed with which Gertrude married her brother-in-law after her husband's death: "to post with such dexterity to incestuous sheets . . . the funeral bak'd meats / did coldly furnish forth the marriage tables"—ouch. Also implies that Gertrude herself was leftovers; damn!

Some of my other favorites are from Laertes. First, when Claudius asks him, "What would you undertake, / To show your-self your father's son in deed / More than in words?" to revenge himself on Hamlet (who killed his father), Laertes responds: "To cut his throat i' the church" (IV, vii). Studly! Then when the priest refuses to give Ophelia all the rites at her funeral since she's a sus-pected suicide, Laertes says, "I tell thee, churlish priest, / A min-istering angel shall my sister be, / When thou liest howling" (V, i). Sorry, Hamlet, "to be or not to be" is nice, but telling off priests, that I love.

What's Sexy: At Ophelia's funeral, the priest suggests that she was a virgin, but can we be sure? While watching "The Mouse-trap" (the play within the play), she and Hamlet have this saucy dialogue:

> Hamlet: Lady, shall I lie in your lap?
> *Lying down at Ophelia's feet*
> Ophelia: No, my lord.
> Hamlet: I mean, my head upon your lap?

Ophelia: Ay, my lord.

Hamlet: Do you think I meant country matters?

Ophelia: I think nothing, my lord.

Hamlet: That's a fair thought to lie between maids' legs. [III, ii]

Psychoanalytic critics have gone bananas over the idea that Shakespeare was afraid of the "nothing" between women's legs—i.e., the Freudian lack (which I never understood. Call me crazy, but as far as I can tell, there's actually always something there). I'm not saying that Shakespeare had an unproblematic relationship to sex; Hamlet does describe Gertrude and Claudius's as "the rank sweat of an enseamed bed, / Stew'd in corruption, honeying and making love / Over the nasty sty" (III, iv)—eeks. Pretty grim, but it is his mom and uncle sleeping together, after all.

Anyway, even if the Bard is often misogynistic and perhaps terrified of women or sex or their genitals, he's nonetheless a naughty boy. Still at the play (who knew theater then was like the back row of movies now?), Hamlet prompts Ophelia, "Any show that you'll show him: be not you ashamed to show." Then when she chides him, he retorts, "It would cost you a groaning to take off my edge." Pretty saucy, but the "would" suggests he hasn't yet made it to the "forfended place" (cf. *Lear*).

After Ophelia goes insane, however, there might be a little evidence in one of her crazed ditties:

"By Gis and by Saint Charity,
Alack, and fie for shame!
Young men will do 't, if they come to 't;
By cock, they are to blame.
Quoth she, before you tumbled me,
You promised me to wed.
So would I ha' done, by yonder sun,
An thou hadst not come to my bed." [IV, v]

Couldn't this (and her later comment that "it is the false steward, that stole his master's daughter") be referring to a secret liaison between herself and Hamlet (or someone?). I'm not sure when Hamlet could have fit it in (bad puns are contagious)—he had a pretty tight schedule between saying it would cost her a groaning and her going batty—but you never know.

Finally, just so you know I was paying attention, there's this flower mystery: we are told that there's a bloom, the "long purples," that maids call "dead men's fingers" but that "liberal shepherds give a grosser name" (IV, vii). And what, pray tell, might that be?

Quirky Fact: I always found it odd that Claudius kills King Hamlet by pouring poison in the ear. His *ear*? Wouldn't that have woken him up and given him time to swimmer-tap it out?

Then, when young Hamlet is trying to get his friends Marcellus and Horatio to take a pact of secrecy, there's a very kooky slapstick moment. As they're speaking, the ghost of the king calls up from under the stage, "Swear!" and the prince says, "Come on, you hear this fellow in the cellarage, consent to swear" (I, v). Not only would the king's phantom, chthonic voice sound ludicrous coming from underneath, but referring to the ghost of your murdered father the king as "this fellow in the cellarage"—that's pretty flip.

I also have to point out the oddity in IV, vii: an unnamed messenger arrives with letters from Hamlet. Claudio asks, "Who brought them?" and the messenger responds, "Sailors, my lord, they say, I saw them not. They were given me by Claudio. He receiv'd them of him that brought them." But who's Claudio? We never heard of him before, he's not in the dramatis personae, nor does he reappear. Why is the speaking messenger unnamed but this guy is? Why mention this gratuitous middleman at all? And why does he have the same name (in the vernacular version) as the king? My theory is that Shakespeare's having fun, putting extra levels of mediation and twists in just to let you know that there will be such twists elsewhere. Or maybe he just screwed up.

What to Skip: One can easily skip Hamlet's early interaction with the actors (II, ii, 325–521). You can also skim much of his crazy talk in Act II, as well as Ophelia's in Act IV. The end is also skippable (V, ii), unless you want the details of the slaughter.

WILLIAM SHAKESPEARE
(1564–1616)

❧

King Lear
(c. 1605)

King Lear, Shakespeare's second most reputed play, begins absurdly but soon displays the Bard at his most emotionally moving. The motivating conceit is laughable: Lear asking his three daughters—Regan, Goneril, and Cordelia—who loves him the most. The two bitchy ones (R and G) say they love him above all things, whereas the devoted Cordelia says, "I love your Majesty according to my bond." We're reading Shakespeare, so of course "bond" could mean three things: the loving bond I have with you (probably what she meant), the familial bond of daughter to father (less good), or the bond of duty I owe you since you sired me (how Lear took it—not good). But Cordelia, darling, why use language so ambiguous? You are speaking to the father you adore. I appreciate your honesty and all, but couldn't you have just said, "My actions have always spoken for me and always will, my beloved progenitor"? Wouldn't that have made it a lot easier on everybody?

Anyway, despite a lifetime of mutual love, Lear disowns her immediately and gives his kingdom to the evil not-stepsisters. Bad move. First the one tells him he can't keep all one hundred of his manservants with him at her place, causing Lear to pout like Achilles and wish her womb forever barren (clearly the appropriate response), then the other joins league and they lock him out of doors in a terrible storm. Of course he realizes his mistake immediately but is too proud to go to Cordelia and apologize. And there you go: such is the psychology of *King Lear*.

Yet while the character Lear is disappointing and barely likeable or even pitiable until the end, there is still much in his play to make the ducts draw forth their droplets. It's easy to see why many people like this Shakespearean play best of all, for what *Lear* loses in language compared with *Hamlet*, it makes up for in strumming of the soul-strings.

My favorite scene—the one that most twists my guts around—is in the parallel plot, where the good brother, Edgar, is betrayed by the bad bastard brother, Edmund, to their father, the earl of Gloucester. Then Edgar (in disguise) leads his blind father to the "cliff" of Dover, from where he "shall no leading need." Edgar knows his father wants to commit suicide, knows the guilt his dad feels for falsely accusing him of betrayal, so he "leads" the sightless man without them going anywhere, telling him all the while how the way is getting steeper. They're walking in a field instead of to the cliff, so when Gloucester goes to jump, to "shake patiently [the] great affliction off," he simply falls on his knees to the ground. To imagine a son watching his parent try to kill himself and seeing how helpless he is—that is purest pathos. (And if you're wondering, as I was, why Edgar doesn't reveal himself here—as Hamlet didn't to Gertrude about the murder—I think it's because he wanted to retain his secret identity until he could revenge himself on Edmund. Perhaps he feared that Gloucester would out him—though I would have thought letting his father feel his forgiveness would have been worth it.)

That scene alone vaults *King Lear* toward the top of Shakespeare's plays, but there are other exquisitely plangent moments as well. Lear's servant Kent's goodness and devotion throughout warms the cockles, and his speeches are top-notch. Lear's fool, though he jibes Lear incessantly about having cast away his pearl of price, (Cordelia's love), nonetheless stays with the deranged king into the storm and is the play's great source of verbal wit.

The reunion of Cordelia and Lear, however, is where Shakespeare will really get you, mostly because Lear's broken-man humility upon seeing her makes you finally care for him. Then his speech to her (see "Best Line" on page 124), as they are about to be locked in prison by the bad daughters, is as sublime an indictment of the world and glorification of the sweet escape into love and finding "the mystery of things" as you will ever read. Lear says it to his daughter, but you will want to take your loved-one's hand and whisper, "Come, let's away . . ."

On the other end of the pleasure spectrum, you can lick your Schadenfreude chops at a variety of excoriating—and odd—taunts. Kent, among a litany of invectives, manages this shockingly orthographical dig at one of the sisters' henchmen, "I'll . . . carbonado your shanks . . . thou whoreson zed, thou unnecessary letter!" (II, ii). What's he going to call him next, a gerund? But Lear's daughter Goneril has a tongue truly made of hydrochloric. Having just had Gloucester blinded, she says, "Let him smell his way to Dover" (III, vii). Ouch! Then, in reference to her mild husband, Albany, first she sells him down the river— "It is the cowish terror of his spirit / That dares not undertake"— and then disses him to his face, "You are not worth the dust which the rude wind / Blows in your face. . . . Milk-liver'd man, that bear'st a cheek for blows" (IV, ii). Egads. Let's hope his other cheek is not formed for similar enterprise.

Finally, for maximum enjoyment of *King Lear*, pay special attention to the two-line rhymes at the end of a lot of the speeches. They are magnificent, perhaps the most beautiful in all of Shakespeare.

The Buzz: The standard interpretation says that Lear was a tragic figure who made the mistake of asking his daughters to say how much they loved him and then trusted the wrong ones. I actually think he was a little more daft than anyone (except Regan and Goneril) seems to acknowledge—look at his reactions, aren't those the stuff of a doddering old man?—but that probably puts me in the bad person camp. Alas.

What People Don't Know (But Should): Though *Hamlet* is much more famous for the paternal advice it contains (from the smarmy Polonius), I actually prefer both the message and the speaker of this marvelous jingle from Lear's fool:

> "Have more than thou showest,
> Speak less than thou knowest,
> Lend less than thou owest,
> Ride more than thou goest,
> Learn more than thou trowest,
> Set less than thou throwest;
> Leave thy drink and thy whore,
> And keep in-a-door,
> And thou shalt have more
> Than two tens to a score" [I, iv]

Best Line: I love Lear's plaintive (if histrionic) "Be my grave my peace" at the beginning (I, i) as well as this terse maxim: "To wilful men, / The injuries that they themselves procure/ Must be their schoolmasters" (II, iv). Later, when the daughters are having Gloucester's eyes boot-heeled from his head, there's the grim "Out vild jelly! Where is your lustre now?" (III, vii)—eeks. One of the sadder moments comes after an old man tells Gloucester, "You cannot see your way" and he responds, "I have no way, and therefore want no eyes; I stumbled when I saw"—the last bit a five-word damning of the entirety of his life. But, as mentioned above, my favorite by far is this, Lear's final speech to a living Cordelia, the best of all:

> "Come, let's away to prison:
> We two alone will sing like birds i' the cage:
> When thou dost ask me blessing, I'll kneel down,
> And ask of thee forgiveness: so we'll live,
> And pray, and sing, and tell old tales, and laugh
> At gilded butterflies, and hear poor rogues
> Talk of court news; and we'll talk with them too,
> Who loses and who wins; who's in, who's out;
> And take upon's the mystery of things,
> As if we were God's spies: and we'll wear out,
> In a wall'd prison, packs and sects of great ones,
> That ebb and flow by the moon." [V, iii]

What's Sexy: To support his disguise, Edgar invents a past in which he says he "served the lust of my mistress' heart, and did the act of darkness with her . . . slept in the contriving of lust, and waked to do it . . . and in woman out-paramoured the Turk" (III, iv). "Did the act of darkness"—there's one euphemism; here's another: "Have you never found my brother's way / To the forfended place?" (V, i), and a third: "Take thou my soldiers, prisoners, patrimony; / Dispose of them, of me; the walls are thine" (V, iii). He really knows how to not say it, Shakespeare.

Unfortunately, he doesn't circumlocute some egregious misogyny, having Lear deride his ungrateful daughters with this speech:

> "Adultery?
> Thou shalt not die: die for adultery! No:
> The wren goes to 't, and the small gilded fly

Does lecher in my sight.
Let copulation thrive; for Gloucester's bastard son
Was kinder to his father than my daughters
Got 'tween the lawful sheets.

.   .   .   .

The fitchew, nor the soiled horse, goes to 't
With a more riotous appetite.
Down from the waist they are Centaurs,
Though women all above:
But to the girdle do the gods inherit,
Beneath is all the fiends'." [IV, vi]

Leaving the woman-bashing aside, we can at least endorse the line "Let copulation thrive," right?

What to Skip: You can skip III, vi, with no loss; the disguised Edgar and banished Lear simply swap madman-speak. I know it's not much, but the rest of the play is pretty damn incredible.

WILLIAM SHAKESPEARE
(1564–1616)

༄

Macbeth
(c. 1605)

Of Shakespeare's best-known plays, *Macbeth* is the most plot-driven but has the least development of character or dialogue. It's an action and scenery play, very moody, and the only one of his tragedies that's almost better viewed than read (and I highly recommend Akira Kurosawa's feudal Japanese film adaptation *Throne of Blood,* if for the moving-forest scene alone). The plotline is familiar and intriguing: Macbeth and his buddy Banquo see some mysterious witches who prophesy that Macbeth will wear Scotland's crown but Banquo's sons will keep it. Of course, that plants the seed of aspiration, and Macbeth, with the rather forceful encouragement of his icicle-hearted wife, begins to eliminate the obstacles to his taking charge.

To be completely honest, it's hard for me to see why *Macbeth* tends to be considered Shakespeare's third must-read play, while other, to my eye more nuanced ones like *Troilus and Cressida* or *Timon of Athens* remain unheralded. It contains a fair number of oft-parroted lines—"Say it is not so" (II, iii); "What's done is done" (III, ii); "Out, damn'd spot" (V, i) as well as the all-time-great "Out, out brief candle" speech (see "Best Line" on page 130)—but the language overall is far less rich than in *Lear* or *Hamlet.* The Bard still does his fair share of punning and

double-entendre-ing, especially in Lady Macbeth's speeches, but
few characters have the trademarked rakish Shakespearean word-
play (the exceptions are the thane Macduff's little son and the
saucy-tongued porter). Nor can the action be said to be especially gripping; the murders are banal in the extreme, and even
the mystery of how the witches' various prophecies (they come
back a few times) are going to play out has less payoff than a Boccaccio gimmick. To get the most out of reading *Macbeth*, I think
you need to do three things: enjoy what great lines there are (and
this is Shakespeare, after all, so there are still plenty); appreciate
the cold-as-a-razor-blade severity of Lady Macbeth (sort of a
cousin to Regan and Goneril); and pay special attention to a few
key concepts: manliness, sleep, and ambition.

The main thing to follow is manliness and the word "man."
Upon receiving Macbeth's letter detailing the witches' prophecy
and then a message that King Duncan is coming that very
evening, Lady Macbeth—her name almost a joke, no lady
there!—asks to have her woman's nature eliminated so she can
steel herself to help murder the king:

> "Come, you spirits
> That tend on mortal thoughts, unsex me here,
> And fill me from the crown to the toe top-full
> Of direst cruelty! make thick my blood;
> Stop up the access and passage to remorse,
> That no compunctious visitings of nature
> Shake my fell purpose, nor keep peace between
> The effect and it! Come to my woman's breasts,
> And take my milk for gall." [I, iv]

From here on, there will be no question who's wearing the
pants in the Macbeth household. A scene later, Macbeth will try

to back out of their plan, saying, "We will proceed no further in this business," but it takes his "lady" less than fifty lines to bring him back. The pivotal line is when Macbeth says, "I dare do all that may become a man"; he means, I'll do anything that speaks honorably of me. She of course reverses the significance, saying, "Be so much more the man," i.e., be more than you are now, be what man you can become. Then, to seal her argument, she reminds him that he promised (yeah, so . . .), and to show him how far *she*'d go to not break her word (and that she's not restrained by unmanly sentiments), says that she'd take her own newborn "while it was smiling in my face, / Have pluck'd my nipple from his boneless gums, / And dash'd the brains out, had I so sworn as you / Have done to this." Well, that certainly ups the ante.

A second concept to follow is sleep, "that knits up the ravell'd sleeve of care" (II, ii). Shakespeare quietly stakes a claim as the greatest poet of Hypnos' dominion, especially of troubled sleep and bad dreams (remember Hamlet's "rub"?). Here both Mr. and Mrs. Macbeth are undone by guilty dreams, but if you read all his plays, you'll be surprised just how many times the bad-night's comes up. Somehow I don't think the Bard did very well in bed. I mean . . .

And finally, Shakespeare really wants you to notice what he's saying about ambition. Lady Macbeth uses the word in her first lines, fearing that her husband has too much of "the milk of human kindness" to be properly ambitious. From there, Shakespeare repeats it a bunch more times, and the whole play is clearly supposed to be a cautionary tale, summarized in the clause: "ambition, which o'erleaps itself" (I, vii). To my mind, Milton will do this much more impressively with his punning on "aspire" in *Paradise Lost*, but still, if the two greatest writers in English history send the same message, maybe we should take note.

The Buzz: Bloody hands don't come clean. Even Lady Macbeth, feral and ruthless though she seems, can't help but do a little somnambular OCD postmurder paw-washing—to no avail.

What People Don't Know (But Should): Another cheery tale of a devil woman (cue the Cliff Richard) bringing down a virtuous man—or that's how *Macbeth* is normally seen. And, yes, she does reconvince him to go through with the murders when he momentarily gets cold (or moral) feet, but even before he spoke to her, he was plotting his way to the crown: "The Prince of Cumberland! that is a step / On which I must fall down, or else o'erleap, / For in my way it lies. Stars, hide your fires; / Let not light see my black and deep desires" (I, iv). She goaded him on, but he was no innocent schoolboy.

Best Line: Macbeth's response to the report of his wife's death is a threnody for the ages. And though "Out, out brief candle" is the line people remember, I love the preceding "All our yesterdays have lighted fools / The way to dusty death." Wow.

> "To-morrow, and to-morrow, and to-morrow,
> Creeps in this petty pace from day to day
> To the last syllable of recorded time,
> And all our yesterdays have lighted fools
> The way to dusty death. Out, out, brief candle!
> Life's but a walking shadow, a poor player
> That struts and frets his hour upon the stage
> And then is heard no more: it is a tale
> Told by an idiot, full of sound and fury,
> Signifying nothing." [V, v]

Faulkner obviously gets his novel title (and premise) from the penultimate line, but did he not catch the bit that follows?

What's Sexy: Though it sounds (and is meant to sound) promising, the line "Screw your courage to the sticking place" (I, vii) is just Lady Macbeth telling her momentarily wusso husband—in a pretty manhood-on-the-line manner—to be brave and have the king whacked.

However, you might not remember a brief treatise on what's sometimes referred to as "Intoxicated Richard," told from my favorite bit character, the Porter: "Drink, sir, is a great provoker of three things . . . nose-painting [think W. C. Fields], sleep, and urine. Lechery, sir, it provokes, and unprovokes; it provokes the desire, but it takes away the performance: therefore, much drink may be said to be an equivocator with lechery: it makes him, and it mars him; it sets him on, and it takes him off; it persuades him, and disheartens him; makes him stand to, and not stand to; in conclusion, equivocates him in a sleep, and, giving him the lie, leaves him" (III, i).

Finally, near the end of the play, Malcolm, the rightful heir to Duncan's throne, will say, "There's no bottom, no bottom, none, / In my voluptuousness: your wives, your daughters, / Your matrons and your maids, could not fill up / The cistern of my lust, and my desire / All continent impediments would o'erbear / That did oppose my will" (IV, iii), but it turns out he's faking and is still a virgin. Oh well.

Quirky Fact: One of Macbeth's lieutenants is named "Seyton." I understand that the play takes place in Scotland (and thus the name was going to be pronounced with a Scottish accent), but still, doesn't that cause problems?

I also want to point out, being the PC guy you all know me to be, some of the less-savory elements in the witches' brew. To go with the familiar "eye of newt, toe of frog" did you recall them going to the larder for "Liver of blaspheming Jew . . . Nose of Turk and Tartar's lips, / Finger of birth-strangled babe /

Ditch-deliver'd by a drab [a prostitute]" (IV, i). Now that's not very nice.

What to Skip: Act I, scene ii only recounts Macbeth's achievements in war, all rehashed in the subsequent scene. The short scene III, vi, which paraphrases the happenings, adds literally nothing. We've already seen everything that's retold.

MIGUEL DE CERVANTES
(1547–1616)

~~~

Don Quixote
(1615)

"There's no greater foolishness in the world than for a man to despair. . . . Great hearts, my dear master, should be as patient in adversity as they are joyful in prosperity."

Oftentimes, great literature can be that much greater if, while reading, you think about—and feel—the writer behind the book. I don't mean in a biographical way, though that can help too; I simply mean by imagining the kind of person that comes seeping through the lines, the "pale usher . . . ever dusting his lexicons" as Melville calls himself in the prologue to *Moby Dick*. When we read Dickens, for example, we can't help but feel the Dickensian vivacity, again and again, and I for one delight in knowing that such a human being existed, someone that exuberant, that wise, witty, and life-affirming. Reading Virginia Woolf or Proust or Gabriel García Márquez, you marvel that human beings can be that sensate, can register such delicate amplitudes and wavelengths—much less express them. What a gift that we can read their books, imagine their selves and their lives, and then strive to make ours more like them.

With *Don Quixote* you'll want to separate the dancer from the dance, for, separately or together, both the life and the fiction of Miguel de Cervantes are incredibly inspiring. The fictional part you'll probably remember: Don Quixote is an aging gentleman who reads a bit too much chivalric literature, fancies himself a knight, mounts a nag that he thinks is a warhorse and trundles into the countryside pursuing an especially errant version of knight-errantry. It's literature's foremost tale of inspired madness—and what a great life lesson: that to see beauty and romance and adventure in error is better than to see the truth as it actually is.

In reality, however, Spain's greatest writer lived heroically (if tragically) even before penning his country's most beloved novel. A soldier and war hero, he had a hand mutilated in a battle with the Turks, was taken political prisoner, organized and led his fellow inmates on repeated but failed escape attempts, was somehow allowed to live and be ransomed back, returned home, wrote the most popular work of his century, but (because Binky Urban wasn't alive at the time) still lived out his days penniless, finally succumbing to dropsy. What every biographer says about Cervantes is that he was a great man, indomitable of spirit, a combination of the great optimism of the Don and the stalwart strength of his servant, Sancho. Because he had it all inside him, he was able to give us two of the more compelling characters in all literature (Sancho's good-humored willingness to believe the Don's delusions ultimately helps him steal the show). But it's precisely that they coexisted in the same real human being that compounds their greatness, triangulates them into three dimensions, and, against Cervantes' backdrop of tragedy and privation, makes them that much more powerful.

Sadly no English translation has been able to capture the wryness and fluidity of Cervantes' masterpiece. That makes the author's bio that much more important to remember, for if you don't commune a little with Cervantes and can't access the liveliness of the original, you might well find *Don Quixote* a little monotonous. It's not easy being a comic novel, as the author tells us over and over (and over). It's not easy playing the fool but showing wisdom, which is clearly the entire trick of both Quixote and Sancho—and their loving author. Being a one-trick pony is no crime if the trick is really good, but when it goes on for 1,050 pages, we have to be a little concerned. Any time a book tips the scales at over a grand, I ask, Is it *Rememberance of Things Past*? Is it *War and Peace*? And no, *Don Quixote* can't compare with the wide-gauge masterpieces of Proust and Tolstoy. In defense, critics will tell you that Quixote's "errors" and wisdom are part of a satiric critique of this and that in the Spanish culture of the time. That may well be, but to me, the pleasure of satire has a rather short-burning wick, and no matter how bright it is, it doesn't sustain. Plus, an effective satire of one thing can be read as a satire of almost anything. Cervantes' pillorying of the conventions of chivalric literature could be said to be mocking his contemporary politics, religion, or epistemology, among any number of other things. As with any good allegory (like the white whale in *Moby Dick*), a lot of interpretations can be made to fit. But in *Quixote*'s case, I'm not sure any of them will enhance the pleasure of the novel all that much.

So, as I indicate in what to skip below, the solution is simply to read *Don Quixote* until it stops making you laugh. Enjoy Sancho's endless epigrams and homespun—if often accidental—wisdom, enjoy the Don's slapstick shenanigans and euphuistic oratory, enjoy Cervantes' authorial play and intrusions, but only enjoy them as long as you want to. If you stop reading, you won't miss much except more of more or less the same. And if you do make it to the end, don't take seriously the final chapter, where Quixote renounces chivalry on his deathbed and embraces Christianity; it was simply Cervantes' way of staving off the religious persecutors of his day. And take the rest simply for what it is: a great embrace of life by a man whom life had wronged. Yes,

Don Quixote is a one-trick pony, but there's no question it's one of the best tricks going.

The Buzz: In one sense at least, *Don Quixote* is not unlike *Remembrance of Things Past*: people always refer to a single scene in the book, and that scene occurs rather early on. And since you almost never hear references to any other parts, my suspicion is that people either read to these passages and stop or else pick them up from hearsay never having read the books at all. In Proust, it's the madeleine scene, of course, and in *Don Quixote* it's the Don "tilting at windmills" (in Chapter VIII—he takes them to be giants and charges on his mighty steed, trying to lance them). These days it's as if you couldn't mention the novel without repeating that goofy translation (*tilting*?), but what about his other hallucinations—like the bladders of wine he stabs or the country girl he takes as his damzell Dulcinea—or even Sancho finally getting an island to govern well into Part II? Oh well . . .

What People Don't Know (But Should): Apart from not knowing the biographical elements that I mentioned above, a lot of people seem to think that *Don Quixote* was the world's—or at least's Europe's—first novel. The former title tends to be given to Lady Murasaki's *The Tale of Genji*, an honest-to-goodness novel written in Japan more than 600 years before *Don Quixote* (I'm sure earlier books than *Genji* will emerge—the first novel ever probably doesn't jump on the scene at over one thousand pages as *Genji* did—but it's a decent placeholder for now). *Don Quixote* isn't really Europe's first novel either; there were many chivalric romances or quasi-romances or even hodgepodges like *The Decameron* or *The Canterbury Tales* that could conceivably hold the title. At the end of the day, however, it's fair to say that *Don Quixote* reads like it could have been written today. For a book published in its two parts in 1605 and 1615, that's a pretty incredible achievement.

Best Line: As the narrator of *Don Quixote* says: "To be witty and write humorously requires great genius. The most cunning part in a comedy is the clown's."

What's Sexy: Although the sex in *Don Quixote* consists primarily of innuendo and playful punning, there is a film adaptation that turns the novel into a bawdy soft-core musical: *The Amorous Adventures of Don Quixote and Sancho Panza*. Not recommended.

Quirky Fact: Cervantes and Shakespeare died on the same day: April 23, 1616.

What to Skip: For a Eurail trip through the best and most famous parts of *Quixote*, read Part I, Chapters I–VIII (getting to the windmills) and LII (the last chapter); then read Part II, I–V and the scenes of Sancho governing the "island," Chapters XLV, XLVII, XLIX, LI, and LIII. All told, that's less than two hundred pages.

Alternately, as I say above, *Don Quixote* can be an opt-in read. It doesn't change a whole hell of a lot (nowhere near enough, in my mind, to go on as long as it does), so if you decide you're sick of it, well, that's when to put it down. Wherever that is, don't feel bad; you will have gotten a representative taste of Cervantes' masterpiece.

JOHN MILTON
(1608–74)

∽∾∽

Paradise Lost
(1667)

"To stand approved in sight of God, though worlds / Judge thee perverse . . ."

I can barely contain myself. I love Milton to the point of giddiness. I want to write in all-caps and with five exclamation points after every word or just fill the page with puffy balloon hearts written over and over until this chapter looks like the diary of a ten-year-old girl. But none of that would help you that much, would it? So maybe I'd better channel some of the emotion. First I've got to calm down.

For starters, let me say this: *Paradise Lost*—Milton's epic tale of Satan's rebellion, the creation of the world, the fall of man, and his deliverance by Christ—is the greatest single prodigy of a human pen. One work, one mind, the best. Nor is the competition close; Dante in his *Commedia* rivals it in scope but not in consistency; the Shakespearean oeuvre as a whole eclipses *Paradise Lost,* but the Bard conceived no single work on anywhere near the same scale; the Bible, Koran, and Upanishads are all the work of multiple hands; even Homer and Virgil, majestic though their great works are, grand though their themes may be, simply didn't try to bite off as big of a chunk as Milton did.

But that's really not helping either, is it? I need to prove it to you, to show you, to help you see the lines through my eyes a little bit because Lord knows this is probably the first time anyone ever told you that *Paradise Lost* is a literary orgasmatron, right?

Okay, the first thing you need to know is that John Milton, in the history of man, might well have been the biggest jerk. He was a complete asshole, went blind in his twenties and never stopped being pissed off, dictated poems to his daughters in languages they didn't understand and caned them if they made mistakes, so hated both sides of the English Restoration religious controversy that he called himself "a church of one" (I love that), and had a permanent chip the size and temperature of Greenland on his shoulder. No Mahatma Gandhi, Mr. Milton.

Keeping in the back of your mind that he was the sternest, meanest, least yielding person imaginable pays dividends when it comes to hearing what Milton's poetry is supposed to sound like, because it's supposed to sound like a wrecking ball. Milton, against the fashion of the day (of course), chose to write *Paradise Lost* without rhyme, not simply because he thought rhyme was "the invention of a barbarous age to set off wretched matter and lame metre" (see what I mean about being a dick?), but because he purposely wanted to slow down his verse, to keep it from being smooth, to gum up the wheels so that you wouldn't slide along or have any sense of lightness. To this he added new techniques of syllabilization that further tar-pitted the language, pulling it at times to near a dead halt for one purpose and one alone: he was setting up his thunder.

But his most important poetic device to bring down the heavy gavel was enjambment, which is just a fancy poetic term for breaking off a poetic line halfway so you don't get its full meaning till the next line. And Milton didn't just enjamb; he set up his lines like necks under a guillotine blade with the basket beneath to catch the heads. You read a line, then down your eye drops to the next line and Whoosh! Thud. Clarity.

That's how his poetry works.

Let me give you an example. In Book III of *Paradise Lost*, Milton, speaking of his blindness, says:

> With the year
> Seasons return; but not to me returns
> Day, or the sweet approach of even or morn,
> Or sight of vernal bloom, or summer's rose,
> Or flocks, or herds, or human face divine;
> But cloud instead, and ever-during dark
> Surrounds me, from the cheerful ways of men
> Cut off, and for the book of knowledge fair
> Presented with a universal blank
> Of nature's works to me expung'd and ras'd,
> And wisdom at one entrance quite shut out. [40–50]

At the beginning of the third line, wham! If you didn't get it, read it out loud; you should hear a funeral drum dong at the word "Day" and then again at "Cut off." Once you train yourself to see and hear this stuff while reading and feel the incredible power that Milton harnesses as a poet, you're one step closer to loving *Paradise Lost* (and his shorter poems too, especially "Samson Agonistes," where there are similar lines and Milton empathizes, not surprisingly, with the blinded Samson surrounded by Philistines).

A last and vital reading technique—and, yes, we still be enjambin'. What I'm about to tell you is a mode of reading Milton pioneered by the great Stanley Fish. I took his *Paradise Lost* class as a neophyte grad student, and Fish not only taught me how to appreciate Milton, but in some ways how to read, period. His insight is that Milton is perpetually trying to scold you (no surprise there either, right?) for not being pious enough, and the way he does it is by creating linguistic ambiguity, traps for misreading, so if you're not entirely on your guard, you'll conclude (or suspect) one thing, then the enjambment will come (whoosh!) and you'll be *corrected* (pronounced like the phantom bartender in *The Shining*). So, for one example among thousands, the beginning of the poem:

Of Man's first disobedience, and the fruit

Stop there. Anyone thinking that fruit—i.e., reward, product—is a good thing? Bzz. Busted. Here's how it continues:

Of that forbidden tree whose mortal taste
Brought death into the World, and all our woe,

Stop again. Here I want you to feel the apposition (meaning the restating for effect of something just said) of "Brought death into the world" and "all our woe." That's the "fruit" of man's disobedience—ouch. And notice too how you can't help but slow down when reading "and all our woe"; he's put peanut butter on your palate, right? It's on purpose; you're supposed to think not only that now we die, having lost Eden, but every single bit of misery we have comes from Adam's mistake. Milton wants you to crawl along, unable to avoid feeling the full implications of that catastrophic oops.

Now rewind, redo it, and watch where the rest of the line goes (I took out the obscure references to muses):

Of Man's first disobedience, and the fruit
Of that forbidden tree whose mortal taste
Brought death into the World, and all our woe,
With loss of Eden, till one greater Man

Restore us, and regain the blissful seat,
Sing, Heavenly Muse . . .
  . . . I thence
Invoke thy aid to my adventurous song,
That with no middle flight intends to soar
Above th' Aonian mount, while it pursues
Things unattempted yet in prose or rhyme.

Note the enjambment (happy this time) with "restore," then the buildup of "no middle flight" as if to say, "Don't even think for a minute we're taking it down a notch." And then he gives us the incredible "things unattempted yet in prose or rhyme," the most audacious claim in English poetry, ten syllables dragging their poetic feet through cement to tell you that John Milton is an utter stud and that *Paradise Lost* is going to be like nothing written before, since, or *ever*.

That's just the first sentence, if you're scoring at home. From there we have a little bit of action, say, Satan and a horde of rebel angels waging war against God in heaven.

Against the throne and monarchy of God
Raised impious war in heaven and battle proud
With vain attempt. [I, 42–44]

So much for "proud." Thump—another pumpkin into the basket (and still on page two!). And in case you thought maybe "battle proud" was a good thing, think back on the seven deadly sins. Proud wasn't the result—they literally got their asses handed to them—pride was the *cause*. Satan rebelled out of pride; that was his downfall. But that's not what you were thinking, was it? The blunt severity of "with vain attempt" corrects you in your mistake. (Of course, Milton, like almost all religious poets, doesn't make a point of addressing his own pride.)

The point here is that you can't trust the first, literal meaning of *Paradise Lost*'s lines; Milton employs them again and again as conceptual snares to trip you up. In the next few pages, Satan will talk about "outshining" (sounds good but implies hierarchy), "merit" (thus evaluation), "mind" (identity), "will," "glory," "freedom"—all these things that might look positive at first blush but all point to difference and thus are radically antithetical to the unified celestial consort of heaven, the oneness of God and all his angels singing an eternal hallelujah. Satan fell because he wanted to be distinguished, to step out of the group, to be himself, to exist. *Bad.* Both here and later in Eden, Milton will make it clear that if you're not down with being part of the harmonious total, if you need an identity, then you would have fallen like Satan or eaten the apple like Eve. It's okay to be a church of one on earth, but you have to be a team player upstairs.

Once you're aware of Milton's trick, it's easy to understand why all those generations of readers thought that Satan was the most appealing character—even the hero—of *Paradise Lost*: Milton made him that way as a warning (clearly unheeded), seducing you just as the asp seduced Eve. And who's not going to fall? Of course Satan's appealing; evil sounds great, piety is hard, and virtually nothing any of us stand for would have served us well in heaven or in Eden—or in our hopes of being saved (Milton's point). But that's what *Paradise Lost* is all about: letting you know that your fallen way of understanding things is flawed, and if you want a chance for a room on the top floor, you'd better start paying attention.

That probably doesn't sound like the most fun reading experience, and in itself it wouldn't be, but *Paradise Lost* becomes really amazing at the moment you enter into awe. You should feel struck, feel wonderous, be utterly blown away by what Milton's pulling off. I don't care if you don't agree with a single tenet of his philosophy—I barely do—you still have to delight in the fervor, the mind, and the utter mastery of technique behind *Paradise Lost*. Not only does it have the most ambitious story of any narrative in English, it's the most methodical line by line. It's breathtaking.

So, yes, this is what Milton's like: word-turner, verse-torturer, master inflictor of hurt. No poet constricts the reader like Milton does, *not* leaving it open to interpretation, *not* letting you choose your own adventure. *Paradise Lost* works the reader like a heavy bag, in sound, rhythm, and effect. But this is a good thing. There is simply no book that reads like *Paradise Lost* (Hegel's *Phenomenology of Spirit* probably comes the closest). Once you get used to what he's doing, you won't be able to keep from saying, "Oh my God, what a prick. Oh my God, what an ass. Holy shit, that's amazing. How'd he do *that*?" over and over and over. It is the single greatest poetic achievement in what we know of as history.

A few more notes in passing:

- Don't miss the puns. Take "aspire": the act that got Satan into trouble, aspiring, desiring to be more than just an angel but leading to *asp ire*: Satan the serpent's anger at Adam and Eve. There are lots of puns like this—and they're intentional.

- Note the incredible majesty and variety of the devil's speeches in Pandemonium, from the start of Book II to line 466—absolutely stunning. If you want to test *Paradise Lost* out for a bit, definitely read this first, followed by Satan's realization: "Only supreme / In misery; such joy ambition finds" (IV, 91–92)—wow.

- Pay attention to the rhetorical guile and gifts of the devils when speaking together, of Satan when convincing Eve, of Eve when convincing Adam, etc. etc. The quality and beauty of argumentation is simply stunning, as are the debates later between Satan and Gabriel.

• Compare the devils' speeches with how flat and goody-goody Milton makes God's and Jesus' speeches at the beginning, but how their language changes in Book VI once they're pissed ("So spake the Son, and into terror changed"—look out!) and in Book X after man has fallen (616–40).

• For one battle scene among many, enjoy the angels picking up and throwing mountains on the devils ("which in the air / Came shadowing") (VI, 636–56) just before God says to Jesus, "Bring forth all my war / My bow and thunder . . . Then let them learn, as likes them, to despise / God and Messiah his anointed king" (712–8)—incredible.

• Note the tender moment in the dedication at the beginning of Book VII where Milton says to God that he's "fallen on evil days . . . In darkness and with dangers compassed round, And solitude; yet not alone, while thou / Visit'st my slumbers nightly" (25–28) and in Book IX where he fears lest "years damp [his] intended wing" (45)—i.e., that he might die before he finishes. Of course, he didn't stay humble for long; in the first case, he switches back to astronomically arrogant claims almost immediately; in the second, he had just made them: "more heroic than the wrath / Of stern Achilles" (14–15).

• Milton makes God's bad-boy self-declarations even more bad-ass than the ones in the Bible: "I am who fill / Infinitude . . . My goodness, which is free / To act or not, necessity and chance / Approach not me, and what I will is fate" (VII, 168–74). That's killer.

• Note how differently Eden is described pre-Fall to post-. The sound of the poetry literally goes from a reed symphony to a simpleton banging on pots. That's intended too; with the Fall, came the jarring. Adam: "All that I shall eat or drink or shall beget is propagated curse" (X, 728–29).

- Note the great repetitions: The "dark unbottomed infinite abyss" that the devils are thrown in (II, 405)—somehow I don't think they get let out "for a season" like Satan does in Revelation; God as "omnipotent, / Immutable, immortal, infinite / Eternal king" (III, 373)—so he's The Man?; Satan as the "false dissembler unperceived" (III, 681) and then eleven lines later the "fraudulent imposter foul" —are you saying he's not trustworthy?—and finally, this grenade regarding the angel Abdiel (who apparently a certain "Church of one" is identifying with), the densest description of alienation and defiance in all literature:

. . . faithful found
Among the faithless, faithful only he;
Among innumerable false, unmoved,
Unshaken, unseduced, unterrified,
His loyalty he kept, his love, his zeal;
Nor number, nor example, with him wrought
To swerve from truth, or change his constant mind,
Though single. From amidst them forth he passed,
Long way through hostile scorn, which he sustained
Superiour, nor of violence feared aught;
And, with retorted scorn, his back he turned
On those proud towers to swift destruction doomed. [V,
    896–903]

God, I love Milton.

The Buzz: As I mention above, almost everybody concludes that Satan is more appealing than Jesus and wonders if Milton endorsed the devil (a common theory), screwed up (also common), or was in his cups (least likely). Of course, none of these are true, as I hope I made clear.

What People Don't Know (But Should): Satan is bad. You're not supposed to side with him. See above.

Best Line: This is from Adam's description of first seeing Eve, and demonstrates a different tack for Milton's poetry: the purely elegant:

> ". . . so lovely fair,
> That what seemed fair in all the world, seemed now
> Mean, or in her summed up, in her contained
> And in her looks; which from that time infused
> Sweetness into my heart, unfelt before,
> And into all things from her air inspired
> The spirit of love and amorous delight." [VIII, 471–77]

What's Sexy: Well, apart from Sin being born out of Satan's head, having sex with him, and giving birth to Death who then rapes her (II, 758–96)—which, admittedly, isn't so sexy—there are Eve's "mysterious parts" (IV, 312) which didn't need to be covered (pre-Fall), and her and Adam's "youthful dalliance" (348). Milton says that Eve never "the rites / Mysterious of connubial love refused" (742–43) leading directly into this shockingly pro-(married)-sex Miltonian interjection:

> Whatever hypocrites austerely talk
> Of purity and place and innocence,
> Defaming as impure what God declares
> Pure, and commands to some, leaves free to all.
> Our maker bids increase, who bids abstain

But our destroyer, foe to God and man?
Hail wedded love. [744–50]

Tell 'em, brother. (Of course then he goes on to talk about all
the vileness of "casual fruition" and "mixed dance," 777–78. It
was good while it lasted.) Later Eve will want to "solve high dispute / With conjugal caresses" (VIII, 56–57). And then . . . a sex
scene! Adam says:

"To the nuptial bower
I led her blushing like the morn: All Heaven,
And happy constellations, on that hour
Shed their selectest influence; the Earth
Gave sign of gratulation, and each hill;
Joyous the birds; fresh gales and gentle airs
Whispered it to the woods, and from their wings
Flung rose, flung odours from the spicy shrub,
Disporting, till the amorous bird of night
Sung spousal," (VIII, 510–19)

"Disporting till the amorous bird of night / Sung spousal"—
that's actually kind of hot, no?

And later, another sex scene! This one happens just after eating the apple—which apparently works a little like green M&Ms.

"Now let us play,
As meet is, after such delicious fare;
For never did thy beauty, since the day
I saw thee first and wedded thee, adorned
With all perfections, so inflame my sense
With ardour to enjoy thee, fairer now
Than ever; bounty of this virtuous tree!"
So said he, and forbore not glance or toy

Of amorous intent; well understood
Of Eve, whose eye darted contagious fire.
Her hand he seized; and to a shady bank,
Thick over-head with verdant roof imbowered,
He led her nothing loth; flowers were the couch,
Pansies, and violets, and asphodel,
And hyacinth; Earth's freshest softest lap.
There they their fill of love and love's disport
Took largely, of their mutual guilt the seal,
The solace of their sin; till dewy sleep
Oppressed them, wearied with their amorous play. (IX,
124–45)

Perhaps even more surprising than there being two bona fide sex scenes in *Paradise Lost* is a little conversation Adam has with Raphael immediately following his kissing-and-telling routine (see "Quirky Fact" below). Finally, how can I not mention the seriously bad sexual punning at IX, 581–85, including "teats of ewe"?

Quirky Fact: Adam asks Raphael the following question about how they, um, knock boots in the higher spheres—and Raphael answers:

"Love not the heavenly Spirits, and how their love
Express they? by looks only? or do they mix
Irradiance, virtual or immediate touch?
To whom the Angel, with a smile that glowed
Celestial rosy red, Love's proper hue,
Answered. Let it suffice thee that thou knowest
Us happy, and without love no happiness.
Whatever pure thou in the body enjoyest,
(And pure thou wert created) we enjoy

In eminence; and obstacle find none
Of membrane, joint, or limb, exclusive bars;
Easier than air with air, if Spirits embrace,
Total they mix, union of pure with pure
Desiring, nor restrained conveyance need,
As flesh to mix with flesh, or soul with soul."
[VIII, 615–29]

That sounds awesome!

What to Skip: You can skip the background of the demons (I, 397–521) and what the devils did in Hell while Satan was gone (II, 514, 618). Then begin but skim through God and Jesus' conversation after the famous "Sufficient to have stood, but free to fall" (III, 99) up to 344. Finally, one can stop for good at XI, 354, as the rest is just stories from the Bible prophesied to Adam. Those we know.

HENRY FIELDING
(1707–54)

❧

The History of Tom Jones,
a Foundling
(1749)

Every human sentiment should have a book that fully embodies it, so the feelings irreverence and mirth are happy to
have *Tom Jones*. In the early decades of the English novel, having
already cut his teeth with satires both dramatic and narrative,
Henry Fielding, incapable of containing the superabundance of
bonhomie coursing through his mortal frame (so I'd like to
imagine), took quill to inkstand and let it all out in the nearly
one-thousand-page *The History of Tom Jones, a Foundling*. And
Mister Tom Jones, foundling, whose childhood, young manhood,
and oft-challenged quest for the heart and hand of fair Sophia
Western make up the plot of the novel, is the kind of character
you're likely to like: seducer of women, imbiber of rum punch,
gallavanter, cutup, and bosom mate. A thousand pages might
seem like a lot, but it's hard to get too much of *Tom Jones*. Fielding gave us the best English novel of the eighteenth century, and
the world has been laughing ever since.

The experience of reading Fielding's *Tom Jones* is akin to that
of Cervantes' *Don Quixote*: it's hard not to have a persistent sense
of its bighearted author breathing behind the scenes. History has
given us a short list of people simply too charming not to write
a beloved classic, and Fielding can walk across that proscenium

with, to name a few, Chaucer, Byron, Goethe, Pushkin, and Dickens. He is clearly the least gifted writer of the bunch, but, like a prankster at a wedding, you're still always glad you invited him. In his constant amiable interjecting to the reader, Fielding seems to be having quite a grand time, and his vivacious protagonist is clearly doing likewise. It is the writer and the novel's sybaritic commitment to life as joy that makes *Tom Jones* a book to relish, despite the seeming challenge of its formidable girth. It's a light-footed elephant, and it keeps dancing.

One doesn't have to wait long to be entertained, for even the table of contents of *Tom Jones* is hilarious (Chapter VI—*An apology for the insensibility of Mr. Jones to all the charms of the lovely Sophia; in which possibly we may, in a considerable degree, lower his character in the estimation of those men of wit and gallantry who approve the heroes in most of our modern comedies*) and utterly endearing (Chapter VII—*Containing such grave matter, that the reader cannot laugh once through the whole chapter, unless peradventure he should laugh at the author*). I'm not sure exactly how many books you can judge by their tables of contents, but here is one that, in good 18th-century tradition, gives you both a précis of the contents and a foretaste of the manner. And both, needless to say, are likable in the extreme.

Now, following the 18th-century style myself, I will provide you a few topics for consideration:

A note on history, perhaps a bit academic and thus ripe for skipping, but which pedantry compels me to disclose: Despite a popular misconception owing, one assumes, to some spotty history, *Tom Jones* was not the first English novel, not only because, as I've said regarding *Don Quixote,* what constitutes a "novel" is a matter up for some debate, but, more significantly, because others came before. Nor is it even the first 18th-century English

novel. That title belongs—as far as scholars currently tell us—
either to one of Daniel Defoe's works, *Robinson Crusoe* or *Moll
Flanders,* depending on which the critic prefers (both of which
seem like novels to me), or to Samuel Richardson's interminable
Pamela, of which Fielding later wrote a satire, called *Shamela,*
which I prefer.

But while it might not be its century's first novel, *Tom Jones*
is clearly its most popular, and that's why I'm including it here.
Some of the fruits of that fertile period were more literary—
Jonathan Swift's outrageous satire, *The Tale of the Tub;* Richardson's *Pamela* and *Clarissa* both; Lawrence Sterne's *Tristram
Shandy* (which also takes the garlands for the weirdest book
of the century, at times almost postmodern in both good and
bad ways, at times utterly brilliant but at others supremely
annoying)—but *Tom Jones* appears to be the one history is going
to remember, probably because it is the most human. The 18th-
century novel as a whole is going the way of the mastodon, similarly undone by its own bulk, but *Tom Jones'* legs aren't buckling
anytime soon, and its inner vitality should keep it going even into
the digital age.

*A note on acquistion, rather less academic and having the advan-
tage of being potentially salubrious equally to the reader's wallet
and well-being:* my scholar's edition of *Tom Jones* with its half-
page running footnotes is positively gargantuan, but honestly
there's no point to committing the extra money and weight to
such a beast; any one of the myriad cheap pocket paperbacks is
all you need. There's no real demand for extensive notes or schol-
arly apparatus; apart from some historical and literary references
(which, if you don't catch, only means you miss a few jokes) and
a slight foreignness to the language, nothing about *Tom Jones* is
especially challenging (unless you purposefully buy an edition

that retains the 18th-century spellings). Don't get an expurgated edition, however, because they are sure to leave out the prevailing sauciness that makes up much of the pleasure of *Tom Jones*—both character and book.

A note on celluloid, for here, unlike the majority of instances, your congenitally surly author has a nice thing or two to say about a film rendering: *Tom Jones* adapts well to film, or, rather, Albert Finney as a young man adapted well to *Tom Jones*. The early '60s hit was somewhat scandalous, like its literary papa, but only a few hours long, unlike dear old dad. Of course, literate jokes are always more funny on the page—if you try to pack too much into film dialogue, no one understands anything (cf. Shakespeare adaptations)—but for the base exuberance and story line of *Tom Jones,* the film will do.

The Buzz: In truth, there's probably more buzz these days about the film version of *Tom Jones* and its for-the-time raciness than there is about the novel. But regarding the paginated version, one is likely to hear either that it's a jolly good time or that it is really quite confoundingly long or, yet more accurately, that it manages to be the former despite the latter.

What People Don't Know (But Should): It might sound contrary to our sense of history or to typical preconceptions about old books, but 18th-century novels tend to be more fun than 19th-century ones. Something about the age of satire (as the 18th century is often called) seems to have made novelists feel especially free in the way they expressed themselves. This opened the door to a lot of playfulness, and *Tom Jones* is clearly one of the high points. By the 19th century, the corset strings were pulled a little tighter all around.

Best Line: Responding to Sophia's protestations regarding one of her suitors, a more experienced woman delivers her theory of marriage: "What objection can you have to the young gentleman?" "A very solid objection, in my opinion," says Sophia. "I hate him." . . . "Child, you should consult Bailey's Dictionary. It is impossible you should hate a man from whom you have received no injury. By hatred, therefore, you mean no more than dislike, which is no sufficient objection against your marrying of him. I have known many couples, who have entirely disliked each other, lead very comfortable genteel lives . . . I have not an acquaintance who would not rather be thought to dislike her husband than to like him. The contrary is such out-of-fashion romantic nonsense, that the very imagination of it is shocking" (VII, iii).

What's Sexy: Since I didn't tax you overly with my introduction, and since it happens to be a Mrs. Robinson tale told over two centuries earlier (and includes a Milton reference as well), I'm going to give you this scene with only minimal pruning:

> Mr. Jones was in reality one of the handsomest young fellows in the world. His face, besides being the picture of health, had in it the most apparent marks of sweetness and good-nature. . . . It was perhaps as much owing to this, as to a very fine complexion that his face had a delicacy in it almost inexpressible, and which might have given him an air rather too effeminate, had it not been joined to a most masculine person and mien; which latter had as much in him of the Hercules as the former had of the Adonis. . . .
>
> Now Mrs. Waters and our hero had no sooner sat down together, than the former began to play the Artillery of Love upon the latter. But here, as we are about to attempt a description hitherto unessayed either in prose or verse, we think

proper to invoke the assistance of certain aerial beings, who will, we doubt not, come kindly to our aid on this occasion.

"Say then, ye graces, for you are truly divine and well know all the arts of charming, say, what were the weapons now used to captivate the heart of Mr. Jones."

First, from two lovely blue eyes, whose bright orbs flashed lightning at their discharge, flew forth two pointed ogles . . . and immediately from her fair bosom drew forth a deadly sigh. A sigh, which one could not have heard unmoved, so soft, so sweet, so tender. . . . Then the fair one hastily withdrew her eyes and leveled them downwards as if she was concerned for what she had done: though by this means she designed only to draw him from his guard, and indeed to open his eyes, through which she intended to surprise his heart. And now, gently lifting up those two bright orbs which had already begun to make an impression on poor Jones, she discharged a volley of small charms at once from her whole countenance in a smile. Not a smile of mirth or joy, but a smile of affection, which most ladies have always ready at their command, and which serves them to show at once their good-humor, their pretty dimples, and their white teeth. This smile our hero received full in his eyes, and was immediately staggered with its force. He then began to see the designs of the enemy, and indeed to feel their success. To confess the truth, Mr. Jones delivered up the garrison without duly weighing his allegiance to fair Sophia. In short, no sooner had the amorous parley ended, and the lady had unmasked the royal battery, by carelessly letting her handkerchief drip from her neck, than the heart of Mr. Jones was entirely taken, and the fair conqueror enjoyed the usual fruits of her victory. [IX, v]

Quirky Fact: Despite all *Tom Jones'* freewheeling frolicry, Fielding himself actually worked for a while as a magistrate—

and even helped found an early British police force. That's a switch.

What to Skip: *Tom Jones* is another long comic novel where you won't want to skip anything as long as the humor keeps you amused. But if the page count ultimately outlives the laugh count, don't feel guilty. As long as you've luxuriated a bit in *Tom Jones'* warmth, the novel did its work.

JANE AUSTEN
(1775–1817)

~~~

Pride and Prejudice
(1813)

Dashing Mr. Darcy, the "proudest, most disagreeable man in the world," seeks to ensnare the smart and independent Lizzy, precisely the kind of girl who would never fall for such a thing . . .

Such is the setup of *Pride and Prejudice,* and the standard logic suggests that if you want to ascertain if you will like a Jane Austen novel, you must simply think of your trips to the bathroom; if you typically find yourself sitting down, you will almost certainly like it; if you remain standing, perhaps the news is not so good. The truth of the matter, however, is that even those of us with prominent Adam's apples and that pesky Y-chromosome can enjoy Jane Austen, especially this her wittiest and probably finest book (at least the first two-thirds).

If you are a woman, you're probably only reading this chapter to find out how it is that I like Jane Austen or to discover how to impart that appreciation onto your meaty beaux or brethren. Fear not; I'll confess shortly. If you're a man, I already applaud you for taking an interest in an activity, like midwifery or attentive listening, with which our gender has had little historical affiliation. In either case, a few words will suffice to acquaint the uninitiated with Ms. Austen's oeuvre as a whole, and then I can move on to explain what makes *Pride and Prejudice* a great read to both genders.

Jane Austen was obsessed with marriage, though she herself never took the vows—apparently she was close, but changed her mind at the last moment. But her obsession has a twist that creates an essential tension at the heart of Austen and her works, providing their crux and (to my eye at least) the source of much of their sustained interest and gratification: she sometimes believes in marriage but doesn't seem to believe in people. Though she attributes the following position to Charlotte, a friend of the novel's protagonist, Lizzy, it clearly sums up a part of Austen's own feelings on the subject: "Without thinking highly either of men or matrimony, marriage had always been her object; it was the only honorable provision for well-educated young women of small fortune, and however uncertain of giving happiness, must be their pleasantest preservation from want." It's easy to detect the irony and misdirection in this, as in the famous first line of the novel: "It is a truth universally acknowledged that a single man in possession of a good fortune must be in want of a wife." My guess is that it represents only half of Austen's feelings, a response to the practical position she was in and the pragmatic voice in her head that probably argued that she herself ought to wed. On the other hand, it's not hard to hear a dolorous resignation and implicit wish that there was another choice, to live in a world more like today's with many more opportunities available to women.

But even this isn't the whole story. Though she clearly distrusts the bulk of humans, suspecting that they are rarely worthy or capable of deep and true love, generosity, or self-awareness, she does seem to hold out the hope that the proper union would redeem them. She chose not to marry, but almost all her characters do in the end. My guess is that Austen was waiting and dreaming of a kind of coupling that would fulfill all her (and her readers') romantic fantasies. At one point Lizzy says to her sister Jane: "There are few people whom I really love, and still fewer of whom I think well. The more I see the world, the more am I dissatisfied with it; and every day confirms my belief of the inconsistency of all human characters, and of the little dependence that can be placed on the appearance of either merit or sense." But we know she will change her tune by the end. Circumspect, perspicacious, and incisive as Jane Austen was, she was still a dreamer, sitting beneath candlelight with her quill, vivifying romantic heroes.

This seeming contradiction in her work allows her the latitude on one hand to criticize and parody her characters to no end (and to great humorous and philosophical effect) and on the other to encourage and satisfy the heartstring longings of her lovelorn female readers (more on them in "What People Don't Know" on page 162). She simultaneously allows readers the option of focusing either on the critical side of things or on the happy endings, depending on what they prefer. Similar in this regard to Dickens' better novels, Austen at her best, especially in *Pride and Prejudice,* can appeal both to the most pessimistic and optimistic of outlooks—and even more so to temperaments that span both sides of the spectrum.

For the pessimistic, there is the steady overt mockery of the various buffoon characters: Mrs. Bennet, Mary, Lydia, Mr. Collins, and Lady de Bourgh. But there's also a more subtle, incisive critique of Mr. Darcy and Lizzy herself: both come close to being undone by their own vanities and shortsightedness, thus the message behind the book's title.

But foremost of *Pride and Prejudice*'s pleasures, to the less romantic gaze at least, is Austen's great comic achievement: Mr. Bennet. One of my favorite minor characters in English literature, his lines alone make *Pride and Prejudice* worth reading— and place it above her other novels. He is an archcynic ("very laconic in his expressions of pleasure") and assumes the worst in all human couplings (as he shackled himself to an intellectually insipid woman for reasons that are only glancingly explained). To three of his daughters, Mr. Bennet is an irresponsible father to say the least, but his deeper nature we see in his love for Lizzy (his favorite), his desire to have her be truly happy (and have her not repeat his mistakes), and his singling her apart from the other three and their mother. For her he has a palpable paternal love, for everyone else some of the better barbs you'll ever read. Don't let any of his lines get past you; almost all of them contain a bit of acid or a velveted jab (and a microlesson in comedic dialogue for all you aspiring writers).

The optimists among you will have no trouble relishing *Pride and Prejudice* as a whole, but to my admittedly rather cynical eye, the first two-thirds of the novel are far superior to the final. Appealingly romantic as it may be, I'm not convinced that the Mr. Darcy of the book's end can reconcile with his character of the beginning (nor, in fact, did I ever really understand why Lizzy would have fallen for him in the first place). So perhaps in lieu of simply taking the story on face value, one should surmise that Austen worked into the end the precise tension I describe above, desiring something she didn't necessarily believe in, calling it to being in her novel as an alternative to not finding it in reality.

The Buzz: It would be rather remiss of me not to mention the enormously popular (again, especially among women) film versions of *Pride and Prejudice,* the 2005 big-budget remake with Keira Knightley as Lizzy, or the much-lauded 1995 BBC production, where Colin Firth steals the show (and female viewers' hearts) as Mr. Darcy. Many people say that the BBC version is the best adaptation of a book to the screen; I think too much of Mr. Bennet's wit gets lost, but it is certainly good entertainment. The 2005 film's tagline calls it "the greatest love story of all time."

Despite my adoration for gushing, ignorant-of-history hyper-
bole on the back of DVD boxes, I can't exactly second that claim,
though the worthy Lizzy's ability to "somehow" win over the
dreamy and rich Mr. Darcy strikes many readers (and viewers) as
swoony. As noted above, I have a rather different take on it all.

What People Don't Know (But Should): Okay, here cynicism
might be getting the best of me, I'd like to believe that the whole
last third of the book—where Darcy turns out to be not such a
bad guy and maybe, just maybe, will finally get to marry Lizzy—
is Austen giving in to the expectations of the conventional early-
19th-century reader. Not unlike today's films, the novel of that
time was a popular and generally lowbrow medium, and just as
Hollywood today wouldn't be able to keep Lizzy and Darcy apart,
maybe Austen couldn't either.

Best Line: Here are Lizzy's wise words—still often true—
regarding the so-called battle of the sexes: "It is very often
nothing but our own vanity that deceives us. Women fancy ad-
miration means more than it does. And men take care that they
should."

What's Sexy: The implications of the rakish soldier Wickham
running off with the trampy youngest daughter, Lydia, are pretty
clear ("their passions were stronger than their virtue"), but other
than that, it's pretty G-rated.

Quirky Fact: Mr. Bennet has an interesting way of evaluating his
sons-in-law: giving them preference by the measure of their
hypocrisy and folly, the more the better. Yes, it's a joke, but it's
nonetheless pretty telling of his worldview (and probably
Austen's).

What to Skip: All of Part III can be skimmed to no ill effect (Darcy is great and generous in every way—ugh—and Wickham elopes with Lydia). For the more assiduous, one not only can but I think should still skip Part III, Chapters 4, 5, and 7 (with their not particularly convincing deferral of the inevitable and quite a bit of overplaying of the Lydia subplot).

JOHANN WOLFGANG VON GOETHE
(1749–1832)

乄乄乄

Faust I+II
(1832)

If literature ever had a mind to rival Shakespeare's, it was Goethe's. A complete polymath in every respect, Goethe was a lawyer, a finance and agriculture minister, a botanist, a scientific researcher, and he even wrote a treatise on color. As a literary figure, he was equally wide-ranging, creating masterworks in every form (poetry, prose, drama, etc.) and generating fifty-five volumes of collected works. It's not hard to see why the old folk-tale of Faust—the preeminent scientist and sorcerer who trades his soul to the devil—appealed so much to Goethe; he too had pushed human capacity as far as it could go, yet knew how much was still being missed.

There is no question that Goethe is Germany's best writer ever, and he is still considered to have more or less established German as a serious literary language—putting him in a pantheon with Dante in Italy and Pushkin in Russia. Goethe is the kind of writer who comes along once per people. As Shakespeare's talent and reputation virtually assure that he will never be displaced in English, so Goethe will never be in German. They wrote as men, but history has made them immortal.

Goethe has something on Shakespeare, however, and even on Dante: his countrymen still like reading him. It helps that

Goethe's language is multiple centuries newer (and therefore that much easier to understand), but the real reason is that he wrote with uninhibited gusto, a kind of good-natured mischief of the highest intellectual order. Goethe was a fast-moving amoeba, assimilating everything, as curious as he was gifted, and his works demonstrate a combined vivacity and alacrity perhaps unmatched by any other writer.

The reader of Goethe in English, however, finds himself feeling a bit like Tantalus, forever inches away from a frosty cold one. Goethe in the Engles' tongue is a bit like a Persian rug turned upside down: you can tell there's art and intricacy, but it's hard to make out the finer points. His novel *The Sorrows of Young Werther* suffers the least from translation—and spells out the *Weltschmerz* (disappointment that reality never lives up to your imagination) that so afflicted Byron, Pushkin, and the author you're reading now—but serious problems arise with translations of Goethe's masterpiece, *Faust*.

Technically, *Faust* is a play—though Goethe knew it was too complex ever to be staged in full—and is written in verse, or rather in a jillion different kinds of verse, forever punning, alluding, game-playing, experimenting, jigging, sacheting, and generally goofing off, all the while being pretty damn brilliant. Imagine Shakespeare writing a play with an experimental agenda like Joyce's in *Ulysses*; that's how you get *Faust*. And trust me, translators do their best to follow along, trying to show you just how playful and fun and multifaceted Goethe is. And he is. But they, well, like farmhands on the dance floor, they just can't keep up.

But, my darlings, crescent downward not your mouths; there are tricks to reading *Faust* in English, and they actually almost work. The first requires a bit of doublethink: as you're going along, you have to *imagine* how great it is in German, taking what you get, and amplifying it in your minds till it has the kind of grandeur you know it's supposed to. In the same way that women, when they receive crappy gifts from their husbands or boyfriends, think, "Oh, in his own little way, that was really sweet, and if he had any idea how to give gifts, he would have done so much better—isn't he wonderful?" you have to think: "This is a translation; it can only go so far. I'm pretty sure that there's a ton more behind this, and I'm just going to assume there is and love him like I'm experiencing it."

I'll admit, it's a little pathetic. If you do know some German, definitely use a facing-page edition, like Walter Kaufmann's (which I'm citing in all the quotations but one); that way when you read a line you like or that seems awkward, you can look at the original and see how Goethe put it together before Kaufmann had to abracadabra it into something that rhymes in the Queen's. Limited as my German is, this made the experience considerably richer. (I should note in passing, however, that there is no readily available facing-page edition of Part II. Kaufmann only translates the last act and gives a synopsis of the rest. For most people's purposes, that's probably enough, but I'm never a fan of expurgated books unless I'm doing the purging. For what *I* think you should take a pass on in Part II, see "What to Skip" on page 171).

Then there are other things you can do, and these might prove more useful: don't let the rhythm and rhyme carry you away (why there isn't a quality un-rhyming translation is beyond me); just look for jokes in the short lines and deeper stuff in the longer speeches. Make sure to read the Dedication and the Prologues in the Theater and in Heaven carefully, really paying attention to the poetry, because they're phenomenal. Then treat the rest like a plate of nachos: best at the beginning, less and less good as they cool. It's early in *Faust* where you get most of his finest speeches; once the devil takes him for a ride and starts to show him the world, he almost disappears as an interesting character. Mephistopheles, our infernal little friend, is cheeky and hysterical throughout—be sure to appreciate all his charm and irreverence. Margaret (more often called Gretchen for "short") and her story take up most of the second half of Part I; she's pretty two-dimensional, but don't miss the fact that Faust impregnates her with the child she will then not-so-explicably murder between the scenes "Martha's Garden" and "At the Well"— whoa. Finally the Walpurgisnight (witches' carnival) scenes, bizarre and funky as they are, lose even more than the rest crossing the border, so don't worry if you're not that into them.

Two things to monitor the whole time: one, the idea of striving. In the Prologue in Heaven, Mephistopheles will echo a sentiment we saw in Shakespeare and in Milton—"Man errs as long as he will strive" (line 317)—but Faust himself pretty much stands for striving, using the word again and again (as in the beginning of the quote in "What People Don't Know" below). And then near the very end of Part II, Faust's striving is going to make or break him; the devil will take his soul or he won't (I don't want to spoil it, but here's the citation if you want to teleport right there: II, 11, 936–37).

The other is Faust's somewhat parallel fixation with the idea of his status vis-à-vis the gods. Note how often he says "superman," "god," "godlike," or "image of God" but invariably knows he still has feet of clay.

In Act V of Part II, Faust as emperor will attempt an act of purest aspiration, attempting to reborder the ocean. Hmm . . . subduing nature, eclipsing what humanity has ever done before—it's pretty clear what Faust was after (remember God in Jeremiah: "Will ye not tremble at my presence, which have placed the sand for the bound of the sea?"). And small surprise, considering his gifts, that Goethe could conceive of someone trying to perform the deeds of a deity. Few human pates were ever as close as his to scraping the bottom of heaven—or felt the distance that remained so acutely. Goethe: a one-man Babel.

The Buzz: Even if you don't know *Faust*'s most famous line—
"Art is long, but life is short"—or that it appears in two forms,
you've definitely heard how the character Faust gets approached
by the devil and trades his soul for, for . . . uh, for what, though?
The standard answer is knowledge, but that's not quite right. For
the real story, keep reading.

What People Don't Know (But Should): Knowledge isn't what
Faust sold his soul for; knowledge he had—he was already sum-
moning spirits to do his bidding—and had actually already given
up on the progress man could make ("I loathe the knowledge I
once sought"). That's why he wanted to commit suicide; he felt
he had gone as far as knowledge could take him and still not become godlike (this is one of the strains that makes the early part
fascinating). No, at first the trade is not for some quality (like
being able to convince people that literature is amazing), Faust
simply agrees to be the devil's servant in the afterlife if the devil
will be *his* servant while living. The lines where Faust then says
what he wants to get out of it are magnificent: He asks
Mephistopheles, "What would you, wretched Devil, offer, / Was
ever a man's spirit in its noble striving / grasped by your like?"
(1675–78). He then spurns gold, sex, even honor as unworthy
desiderata. He doesn't want enjoyment, he doesn't want contentment (he actually says that if he becomes content, the devil
can take his soul right then and there). Finally he says what he
really wants:

> Let every wonder be at hand!
> Plunge into time's whirl that dazes my sense,
> Into the torrent of events!
> And let enjoyment, distress,
> Annoyance and success

Succeed each other as best they can;

. . . .

I have no thought of joy!
The reeling whirl is what I seek, the most painful excess,

. . . .

I shall enjoy deep in myself, contain
Within my spirit summit and abyss,
Pile on my breast their agony and bliss,
And thus let my own self grow into theirs, unfettered,
Till as they are, at last, I, too, am shattered. (1754–75)

What's incredible here is not only the desire to experience feeling at every point—good and bad—along the spectrum, but his longing in the end to be actually obliterated by experience. That's what I think is fascinating: that he goes from trying to end his life with a draught of poison to wanting to end it by being utterly decimated by feeling. What a great switch.

Best Line: There are *tons* of great lines in *Faust*. The entirety of the Prologue in the Theater is an incredible display of Goethe's various stylistic and personality types—he's clearly *all* the parts, as he is both Faust and Mephistopheles as well—and believes all their arguments. My favorite line, though, is when the poet says that art has the ability "to carry the world back into his heart" (142). That's amazing. But this passage, where Faust faces his human limits, is forced to acknowledge that he isn't a god, might be the best (my translation this time):

I, the image of godhead, who sought to
See the mirror of eternal truth,
And thought myself amid heaven's light,
As if I had stripped off my mortal man;

Become, more than angel, with unbounded might
Even to flow through nature's veins,
And feel th' joy of creation: God's domain.
Ah, the presumption, source of my pain,
One word of thunder swept me off my height. [614–22]

What's Sexy: The devil, well he's a horny little guy (sorry, I tried not to say it), as was Goethe, who apparently amassed an impressive collection of penis-themed memorabilia and had a variety of AC/DC dalliances. Hardly a shock, then, that *Faust* is piebald with innuendo, scurrilous songs, seduction tips, and a few exceptionally dubious metaphors ("at wisdom's copious breasts / you'll drink" 1892–93). But here's the part that most editions—even the German ones—bowdlerize (from "Walpurgisnight" of course):

Faust (*dancing with the young one*):
    "A pretty dream once came to me
    In which I saw an apple tree;
    Two pretty apples gleamed on it,
    They lured me, and I climbed a bit."
The Fair One:
    "You find the little apples nice
    Since they first grew in Paradise.
    And I am happy telling you
    That they grow in my garden, too."
Mephisto (*with the old one*):
    "A wanton dream once came to me
    In which I saw a cloven tree
    It had the most tremendous hole;
    Though it was big, it pleased my soul."
The Old One:
    "I greet you with profound delight,

My gentle, cloven-footed knight!
Provide the proper grafting-twig,
If you don't mind the hole so big." [4128–143]

Quirky Fact: There is a character called Proktophantasmist, who Kaufmann tells us is based on a half-rate intellectual of Goethe's time who parodied *The Sorrows of Young Werther* (calling his *The Joys . . .* yeah yeah) and admitted to having been plagued by ghosts till he got rid of them *by applying leeches to his ass.* As a result, his character: the Ass-ghoster.

And if you want one more good one, keep reading.

What to Skip: In the scene "Before the City Gate," one can skip up to line 1011 when Faust and his student Wagner start speaking; from there it gets good. You can skip the entire "Auerbach's Cellar" scene; its point is just to show Faust how the vulgar amuse themselves—kind of lame. The "Walpurgisnight's Dream" (which comes right after the plain old "Walpurgisnight") is disjointed and doesn't make much sense. Losing the poetry of the original, there's not much point left.

That's all in Part I. Then there's the issue of Part II, which Goethe didn't finish until decades after the publication of Part I—and only a few months before he died. What could be less promising than this back-cover copy of the Penguin edition: "Rich in allusion and allegory, *Faust/Part II* [*sic*] ranges through a host of philosophical and speculative themes. Goethe even foresees such modern phenomena as inflation and the creation of life by scientific synthesis." Should I start letting my blood now?

Don't worry; that hardly does it justice. What's really going on in *Faust II* (apart from that righteous part on inflation) is something of a redux of the story of *Faust I,* but this time Faust travels through a classical Greek otherworld, seduces Helen of Troy (really of Sparta), and has a baby with her (that's what I'm talking about). The child is immediately an adult and tries Icarus-like to fly and fails, causing Helen to follow him to Hades (easy come . . .). Then Faust leads a big battle (one of the instant narcolepsy sections), becomes emperor, has a serious problem with a pair of linden trees (word to the wise), and tries to bound the sea—a metaphor for vain striving.

I will confess, there is much to skip—though there's also some stuff worth savoring. In Act I, read the "Baronial Hall" scene, beginning at Helen's entrance (the Penguin edition doesn't have line numbers, sadly). In Act II, read the first two sections (they're very weird, but how many world classics have as one of their heroes a hermaphroditic bit of human-shaped flame trapped in a test tube?), then skip the rest except the very lyrical "Lower Peneus" of the Classical Walpurgisnacht. In Act III, read the "Inner Courtyard" but only from Faust's first lines to the appearance of Phorkyas. In Act IV, read from the beginning until the drums announce the war. And in Act V, read the whole thing, at least until the victory over Faust's soul is explained at line 11,937 (I'm still not telling who gets it).

ALEXANDER PUSHKIN
(1799–1837)

~~~

Eugene Onegin
(1832)

The opposite of death—okay, I know what you're thinking, but give me a second—might well be Pushkin. Barely a second he lived or a word he wrote exhibits anything but the utmost vitality, the drive to life in some of its strongest manifestations: sex, wit, art, and ego. Pushkin scorched through his life, womanizing, scandalizing, quipping, and managing along the way to solidify Russian as a literary language and set their poetic bar as high as anyone before or since. Considered the father of Russian poetry, Pushkin is adored by his countrymen, especially Russian writers (Nabokov was *obsessed* with Pushkin), as revered there as Goethe is in Germany or Dante in Italy. Most of us will read Pushkin in translation, but still we can glimpse the grace and ease of his art, his enormous seductive power, and his flat-out zest. Pushkin might teach you (he's excellent on the science and psychology of disaffection), he's likely to arouse you, he will certainly make you smile (with bons mots like "He who has lived and thought is certain / to scorn the men with whom he deals"), and he will absolutely entertain you. How marvelous that we can read the father of a great nation's literature for amusement and have that be exactly how he would want us to read him.

174 BEOWULF on the BEACH

Though he drank deeply from life's chalice, Pushkin's chronological time was brief, nipped at 38 in a duel. Dueling was already illegal in Pushkin's Russia, but there was little doubt that their greatest poet would find his end from a pistol ball, either to defend the honor of his own wife (as it happened) or the comely wife of one of his rivals. (Given his lifestyle and reputation, it seems Pushkin should have spent a little more time with his pistols and a little less with his pen and pe——, ahem.) Of course no element of anything can exist in the same way without its attending components, so perhaps if Pushkin had chased fewer wedded women, he wouldn't have had the same verve to instill in his verse and prose. Many great men live long lives, but there are certainly those destined to extinguish quickly—hot, bright, and brief as balsa in a bonfire.

Eugene Onegin is the great artifact he left behind, his longest, most famous, and most complete work. It's a verse novel, which is an author's way of telling you, Not only can I write a novel, I can do it in rhyming meter 'cause I'm just that good. Its hero's last name, though spelled like my nightly drinking regimen, in Russian is pronounced "owe-NYE-ghin" (hard *g*), but in American you can get away with saying it like advice to a cotton farmer ("own a gin"). Onegin is a rake and a dandy, but grows bored of clothing, bored of society, bored of books, bored even of ladies (oh my)—alas, what's a prettyboy to do?

What's shocking about the novel is how dour the rest of the plot sounds: The disaffected Onegin befriends an idealist: Lensky. But being bored, of course, Onegin decides to mix things up a bit by flirting with Olga, Lensky's love interest, despite the fact that Olga's sister, Tatiana, has already confessed her love to our naughty hero. Lensky is outraged and challenges Onegin; they shoot, Lensky dies, and Onegin is left with neither friend nor woman. Eventually he will try for Tatiana's hand, but by then it's too late.

It sounds like a tragedy, but it reads more like a bath in a rose-scented cistern. Pushkin's personality and the seductive force of his poetry so trump any specifics of the plot, that his protagonist could have done almost anything and it wouldn't really have mattered much. The point of Pushkin is Pushkin, and somehow I think he could have written *Paradise Lost* and made it light-hearted and fun.

Eugene Onegin is a book about pleasure: both to be consumed for pleasure and in defense of pleasure. I feel like all classics should be enjoyed, but if there's one that makes it easy, it's *Eugene Onegin*.

A note on my preferred translation: although Nabokov did a meticulous (how shocking!) translation of *Onegin* that is useful for straight comprehension of the text, I much prefer the reading experience of John Bayley's version (Penguin, 1970). Only a few years before Bayley's came out, Clifton Fadiman had said that "there is simply no use in claiming that . . . Pushkin can be read intensively in English with great pleasure." At the time, Bayley more or less agreed: "There is a whole magic [lost]: the touching lyrical beauty, the cynical wit of the poem; the psychological insight, the devious narrative skill, the thrilling, compulsive grip of the novel; the tremendous gusto and swing and panache of the whole performance." Not being able to read Pushkin in the original, I honestly don't know how far his translation falls short, but he certainly re-creates the panache.

The Buzz: In stanza I, xxxviii, Pushkin says that Onegin suffers from an "illness" called "spleen" in English and "chondria" in Russian. These days the word we use—perhaps my all-time favorite—is "Weltschmerz": the "world sadness" I referred to in the last chapter, caused by reality never living up to one's imagination. Lord Byron is Weltschmerz's finest poet in English (especially in the poem "Childe Harold"—which Pushkin alludes to repeatedly—and in his comic masterpiece *Don Juan*) but Pushkin outdisaffects even him. And Onegin defines the type: no young male literary character is more—or more prematurely—world-weary than he. In a culminative moment, Lensky says to Onegin, "This time I think you've been reduced to new depths of boredom." Onegin's response: "No, same" (III, iv).

What People Don't Know (But Should): The one odd part of *Eugene Onegin* is when the "hero" provokes his friend Lensky the idealist into the duel (you know, it gets so monotonous out there in the country) and kills him. It would be hard for anything to put a damper on the poem's irreverence, but that came close.

Best Line: Both of these stanzas refer to the naïf, Lensky, told, more or less, from the perspective of Onegin, I mean Pushkin, I mean Onegin . . .

> He was too young to have been blighted
> by the cold world's corrupt finesse;
> his soul still blossomed out, and lighted
> at a friend's word, a girl's caress.
> In heart's affairs, a sweet beginner,
> he fed on hope's deceptive dinner;
>
> .   .   .   .
>
> And he was loved . . . at least he never
> doubted of it, so lived in bliss.
> Happy a hundredfold, whoever
> can lean on faith, who can dismiss
> cold reason . . .
> but piteous he, the all-foreseeing,

the sober head, detesting each
human reaction, every speech
in the expression of its being,
whose heart experience has cooled
and saved from being charmed or fooled! [II, vii, liv]

What's Sexy: Though the only thing Onegin studied in college was "the science of that passion / of which Ovid sang" (I, viii), there aren't especially racy passages (apart from the foot fetish lines I discuss in "Quirky Fact" below) until this aside in his stanza on champagne: "with its foaming and its playing / a simile of this and that." Naughty!

Quirky Fact: Dostoevsky referred to his great countryman and predecessor as "the poet of women's feet" —and that's no exaggeration. In stanzas I, xxx–xxxiv of *Eugene Onegin*, Pushkin confesses that he's a full-blown foot fetishist: "It fascinates by its assurance / of recompense beyond endurance, / and fastens, like a term of art, the wilful fancies of the heart." Many quills have celebrated women's tootsies, perhaps none more hallowed than Pushkin's.

What to Skip: Because the plot is next to irrelevant compared with the experience, one doesn't have to worry about not finishing the poem. But since it's only two hundred short poetic pages long, you shouldn't have any trouble.

HONORÉ DE BALZAC
(1799–1850)

❦

Père Goriot
(1835)

You are a social historian; rather, you would like to be a social historian, at least of the armchair variety, and at least of France. You imagine taking a time machine back to 19th-century Paris to check things out, take a stroll about, poke your pince-nez into back alleys, workshops, dingy garrets, and all. You are frustrated that novelists like Stendhal and Hugo make their characters so high-class and heroic—realist, yes, but not so real. You liked Flaubert but didn't feel he went far enough. Zola maybe cut a few slices of life and you're glad he did, but hell, you want the whole pie. If you are nodding your head right now, murmuring yes, yes, then you, my friend, are going to love Balzac; he's the man for you.

No writer in history has attempted—and succeeded—in portraying more of society than Balzac. Author of over three hundred books—yes, three hundred—ninety-five of which he loosely strung together and collectively titled *La Comédie Humaine* (The Human Comedy), Balzac undertook what is without a doubt the most ambitious project any fiction writer has set for himself: to represent *everybody*. The multi-shelf aggregate of his literally tireless endeavor is a magisterial—if, mercifully, unfinished—anthropological study, chocolate-coated in fiction, with reappearing characters of all ages and classes, all moralities and motives (though avarice seems the most common) in myriad trades, towns, and travails, adding up in toto not only to a human comedy, but a tragedy, farce, morality play, romance, and everything in between. He tried to get the whole crêpe suzette, and he did a pretty damn good job, considering. He must have known it was like shooting an arrow at the sun, but he must have been proud that it flew as far as an arrow can fly.

For the reader, this is a mixed blessing, for you will run out of life before you run out of Balzac. I confess that after two months of eating microwave burritos and leaving my phone turned off in an effort to get through them all, I still didn't finish even a quarter of the *Comédie.* Day after day I would roll Sisyphus' boulder up the Balzacian mount, but night after night my eyes would glaze and I'd still be back at base camp. Worse still, I began to question the payoff. Balzac's exploration into life seemed to move more laterally than internally. He's anthropological, yes, perhaps but not sufficiently psychological to sustain such a commitment (in contrast to reading a couple thousand pages of Dostoevsky, Proust, or Faulkner, say). I also found that no title stood out as being dramatically better than the rest, so don't be afraid to start with the most famous ones like *Eugenie Grandet, Lost Illusions,* or, my personal favorite (especially the beginning), *Père Goriot.*

Père Goriot, probably Balzac's best-known novel—at least in the U.S.—begins (okay, mid–second paragraph) with a cannonade of the big man at his best: "Paris," he writes:

> that famous valley where cracking plaster is always about to fall on your head and the gutters run black with mud; that valley full of genuine suffering, and of joys that often turn out to be false, and so incredibly tumultuous that it takes something God only knows how outrageous to cause a lasting stir. But here and there some immense heaping up of vices and

virtues turns mere sorrow grand and solemn, and their very sight makes even selfishness and personal advantage stop and feel pity—though that notion of pity is much like some tasty fruit that gets gobbled right up. Civilization's high-riding chariot, like the believer-crushing car of the idol Juggernaut, barely slows down when it comes to a heart a bit harder to crack, and if such a heart gets in the way it's pretty quickly smashed, and on goes the glorious march. Which is what you'll do, too, you who are right now holding this book in your fair white hand, you who sink down in your soft easy chair saying to yourself: Maybe this book is going to be fun. And then, after you've read all about Père Goriot's miserable secrets, you'll have yourself a good dinner and blame your indifference on the author, scolding him for exaggeration, accusing him of having waxed poetic. Ah, but let me tell you: this drama is not fictional, it's not a novel. *All is true*—so true you'll be able to recognize everything that goes into it in your own life, perhaps even in your own heart. [Emphasis in original]

Let's do a quick inventory. Grimy Paris: check. Harsh, unyielding world: check. Assault on reader: check. Claim to veracity—not simply realism, but actual fact: check. What does it add up to? Yes, you guessed it: Balzac. Flaubert once famously quipped of his predecessor, "What a man he would have been had he known how to write," but it seems to me that already this early in *Père Goriot*, Balzac shows some pretty impressive chops.

France's jowly chronicler (cf. Rodin's famous sculpture) is sometimes referred to as the French Dickens, but, despite the charms of the quote above, in no wise does he approach the steady wit and philosophical depth of his English contemporary and fellow workaholic. What they have in common is that each left behind a few phonebooks worth of pages (and Balzac a few more still) and a staggering number and range of characters. But even here they differ palpably; Balzac's people feel like he grabbed them off the street and put them in his books (which he might have; he had a great ear and memory), while Dickens' read like they were summoned from scratch out of dust and India ink and inexhaustible genius. If you want the real as it really is (or was), take Balzac; if you want art, Dickens.

Reality, though, as broad as it was for Balzac, still boiled down to one thing: dough. Money, the "ultima ratio mundi" (the world's final authority, as he calls it in *Père Goriot*), and the machination to get it drive this novel and most of the others, to the point that, somewhere around the halfway or two-thirds mark of his books, you'll be so sick of seeing the word "francs" you might want to hurl your copy against the wall. Balzac couldn't have been much more money- and social-status-obsessed; as Proust put it, "The vulgarity of his mind was such that a whole lifetime could not leaven it . . . he could not conceive how social success should not be the goal of all goals."

In *Père Goriot* the predominant social strivers are Rastignac, a pretty standard boy-from-the-burbs character—in this case a French "southerner"—trying to make it in Paris society, and the social shark Vautrin (referred to as a "bewigged sphinx"!), who expresses Balzac's Machiavellian ethos (see "What People Don't Know" on page 182).

Meanwhile, the title character, Père Goriot the spaghetti tycoon, represents, as Rastignac thinks of him, "paternity incarnate," sacrificing his fortune to support his daughters and their shady husbands, giving away all and more and still not making them happy.

These are the players, but Balzac's foremost subject is Paris, where you had to "sit up all night if you really wanted to know what's going on around you." It's a rough place, the real-deal city, not elegant like the BCBG 17th but a "mud pit" (repeated three times) where love "is unlike love anywhere else . . . basically boastful, shameless, wasteful, an ostentatious fraud." It's Balzac's perpetual potshots at the place we call "gay Pair-ee" that are the real bonbons of *Père Goriot* and many other of Balzac's books. He prided himself on seeing and saying things as they were, and Paris was his obsessive, lifelong study.

So if you are seeking a trip down some of France's squalid memory lanes, taken by an unblinking, perpetually open, perpetually scouring eye, no tour will be as thorough as Balzac's.

The Buzz: The buzz about Balzac is always the same: that he wrote more than everybody else, that he painted the underclasses as they are—petty, hypocritical, and moneygrubbing—and the rich as they are—petty, hypocritical, and moneygrubbing. And if Balzac heard you use the verb "paint" to describe what he did, he'd be very happy. As part of his relentless effort to represent "a truly precise account" of all and everything, he likes to say "were one to paint . . ." again and again—it's clearly his pet metaphor for the approach he was taking. The other word he favors is "drama," always trying to underscore that the lives he's trying to get down were "living dramas . . . that make the heart beat faster, dramas that go on and on and on."

What People Don't Know (But Should): Vautrin, otherwise so unnecessary to *Père Goriot*, actually tips us off to an element in Balzac that's underacknowledged. In lines that anticipate Puccini, Vautrin summarizes himself: "Who am I? Vautrin. What do I do? Whatever I feel like." He is a self-described man of ambition, a dyed-in-the-wool Machiavel who instructs Rastignac to "take a million of these fancy cattle and you'll find ten wide-awake fellows who climb right to the top, laws or no laws. I'm one of them." And later: "I live on a plane far more exalted than other men are even aware of." Like too many intellectuals before and after him, Balzac's jaded views led him to embrace the idea of a Superman who's above the herd, what Vautrin calls the "limp links in a gangrenous social chain." Mixed metaphor aside, the vehemence of Vautrin's (and Balzac's) us/them thinking should be striking. Here too Balzac differs from Dickens and his magnanimity—tragically.

Best Line: There are some great passing descriptions in *Père Goriot*. Two of my favorites are Mademoiselle Taillefel resembling "in her misery, a shrub with yellowing leaves, just replanted in a soil that disagrees with it" and Madame Vaquer going "to her bed every night fairly burning, like a partridge roasting in bacon." The more domestically pessimistic among us might want to memorize these aphorisms: "Marriage is the worst trick in the world"; "You can sleep, you're not a father yet"; or "We understand so little when we get married!" But there is one passage whose back-and-forth of jadedness and hope I find stunning:

> Be young, rich, have titles, be even loftier still, if you can: the more incense you burn before your idol, the more she will shine favorably on you . . . There may be exceptions to these draconian laws, formulated in Paris' iron code, but they're only to be found in lonely places, among souls who refuse to let themselves be carried away by society's rules and regulations, people who dwell close by some source of pure clear water, evanescent but also forever flowing—people who . . . constantly rejoice at the sound of infinity speaking, a voice which they see written in everything, and which they learn to find in themselves, waiting patiently in their wings, feeling only tender sorrow for those who are more worldly. But . . . without some pure and sacred love that fills all of life, [the] thirst for power can become a good thing.

Balzac was capable of realizing an alternative to his grim mercantile worldview, but you get the sense that he didn't have access to the "endless flowing clear water," that he couldn't *not* be worldly and sought to recuperate what he could, knowing there were people who pitied him. Perhaps we should number ourselves among them.

What's Sexy: There's a lot more explicit stuff—both hetero and homo, of course (can't miss anything!)—in the *Human Comedy*, most notably in *Splendeurs et miseres des courtisanes* (translated as *A Harlot High and Low*). But *Père Goriot* too is not without hints of the decadence of the French capital in the early 19th century. At one point, venereal disease is referred to as "Parisian love." Later Goriot's fellow tenants think he has upward of four young "mistresses" visiting him, prompting Vautrin to tell Rastignac that "here in this town we have what might be called 'men of passion.' " I think most dirty old johns would be pretty happy with that euphemism.

Balzac is also the first author I recall who discusses the psychology of the sure thing, pointing out how men can be divided into those who want to pursue an evasive prey and those who want the prey not to evade (a point I think is well-taken).

And, finally, at one point women's breasts are referred to as "biscuits"; that's one I've never heard—and need never hear again.

Quirky Fact: Russian television recently aired a spin-off of *Sex and the City* entitled *The Balzac Age*, following his quote that women over thirty were "the greatest ladies in Paris." I didn't realize the average Muscovite was so familiar with Balzac's bons mots.

What to Skip: Well, I think I'm going to step on a few toes here, but if you accidentally put aside *Père Goriot* halfway through (at the end of Part II) and forget to pick it back up again, I really don't think you'll miss much. Part III is almost completely gratuitous, giving us the unrelated plot line of Vautrin—a weird add-on, if you ask me—and simply spelling out with a yet-heavier hand the ideas of the preceding sections. Section IV meanwhile, draws the bathos rather deep, and if you remember Lear, you'll have no trouble imagining Goriot on his deathbed, wondering if his daughters will visit him before he goes to the great pasta factory in the sky. It probably sounds bad when I say that *Père Goriot* is my favorite Balzac novel and then tell you to pass on the second half, but in a way that's just testament to how much he packed into the first—and to the fact that you might have children to raise or other life concerns that I don't want you to neglect. And don't worry, if you do want more Balzac, you know the well will never run dry.

CHARLOTTE BRONTË
(1816–55)

❧

Jane Eyre
(1847)

There might not be a stranger tale in literary biography than that of the Brontë sisters. Charlotte, Emily, and Anne lost their mother when they were very young and were raised by a domineering, reclusive father who ignored them, ate alone in his room, and sent them to a Dickensian paupers boarding school where they nearly perished from want. They were sickly and socially awkward in the extreme, but they took refuge in each other and in writing. And I'm not talking about the journal notes of the shy—no, in an act of staggering collective will, they managed to coordinate it so that all three finished highly accomplished novels at the same time (see "Quirky Fact" on page 190). Many young people screen themselves from their agonizing lives by reading books; the Brontë sisters did so by writing them.

Tragically, their history of privation would soon catch up to them, leading to their respective, untimely deaths—Charlotte at thirty-eight, Emily at thirty, Anne at twenty-nine. Yet they still wrote seven novels total, and, of the first three, *Jane Eyre* and *Wuthering Heights* are still universally famous, and Anne's *Agnes Grey* is quite good too. But what's even more remarkable is how different each of the sisters' writing styles and concerns are from one another. Considering how little they had in their lives but each other, it's stupefying that three distinct top-shelf authorial voices could emerge under such hardship and in such short life spans. We can only wonder what literary wonders they might have created if the sisters had ever been nurtured and cared for.

I have to confess to not loving the first hundred or so pages of *Jane Eyre,* much of which recounts events similar to those that made Charlotte Brontë's early years so grievous. Having read Dickens' *Nicholas Nickleby* (which treats of similar schools and Dickens' experience in them), I found myself comparing the two, noting Brontë's lack of humor next to Dickens' superabundance, her simplicity of style next to the fuss and flair of his. In short, I was thinking of the novels and the writing instead of the lives and the people. But then, learning more of the Brontë biographies, I realized there was plenty of place in my heart for all three sisters and Dickens too, and that in the reading of *Jane Eyre* we should periodically step back and appreciate not only that the book exists, against so many odds, but that it's precisely that: an artifact of survival, a testament to the resiliency of the human spirit. Charlotte Brontë had Jane think to herself, "I have a rosy sky and a green flowery Eden in my brain, but without, I am perfectly aware, lies at my feet a rough tract to travel, and around me rather black tempests to encounter," but sadly, for the author of *Jane Eyre,* these rough tracts never eased.

And so the character Jane takes up that much more meaning, and her defiance, independence, goodness, and faith can have the impact on all readers that they've had for generations of adolescent girls. Nor does the book's appeal stop there. Beginning in Chapter 11 (when Jane finally escapes the school and secures a post as a governess at Lord Rochester's), both the plot and the style intensify, giving readers quite a bit more to hang their hats on. Rochester is a complicated, headstrong man with a secret, and he and Jane develop a mutual fascination (surprise!) that pushes the plot along. It's still not Dickens, but by this point it is a compelling page-turner.

Apart from its tenacious optimism (and happy ending), perhaps *Jane Eyre*'s most enduring charm—and the reason it can appeal so effectively to both young and old readers—is the softness of its touch. It's a simple read, at no point taxing, and not requiring (or necessarily rewarding you for) the attentiveness one must give a Dickens or a George Eliot. It's a pleasant promenade of a book, one easily taken to the park, the subway, or the shore, read languidly—even drowsily. But the simplicity of Brontë's style is a testament to the skill of the author, not her lack thereof; it takes a masterful hand to write prose that feels so uncrafted. *Jane Eyre* as a novel is much more delicate than Jane Eyre the character, and it successfully balances its feminist impulses, its romantic story line, and its Christian overtones so that none takes complete precedence, nor is any of the three unbounded by the others. Nothing in the book comes across stridently. Instead one simply appreciates the example of Jane herself and understands what is being said through her actions: that the world is often harsh and punishing, but we can endure and ameliorate if we remain steadfast in our knowledge of what's right and determined in our quest to do good. It's a lovely message, gently delivered.

The Buzz: Jane is an excellent model for an independent young woman. She's backtalking (when appropriate), strong-willed, intolerant of injustice, persevering, and aggressively honest—but she also gets her man in the end. And she's the perfect incarnation of the dreamer who wants more than she has known theretofore (see "Best Line" on the opposite page). What could be a better formula for a novel to appeal to girls of all ages?

What People Don't Know (But Should): Though much of Charlotte's earliest biography, written by her friend and contemporary Elizabeth Gaskell, is exaggerated, it does appear true that the eldest Brontë sister was so shy she would sit with her back to her friends when they would visit her. And, to top off the tragedy that was her life, she died while pregnant, having very recently married her father's rector, a considerably older man.

Best Line: Considering how hamstrung Brontë's life was, one can appreciate all the more the vigorous, aspirational imagining embodied in this quote of Jane's: "I climbed the three staircases, raised the trapdoor of the attic, and having reached the leads, looked out afar over sequestered field and hill, and along dim skyline—that then I longed for a power of vision which might overpass that limit; which might reach the busy world, towns, regions full of life I had heard of but never seen; that then I desired more of practical experience than I possessed; more of intercourse with my kind, of acquaintance, with variety of character, than was here within my reach. I valued what was good in Mrs. Fairfax, and what was good in Adele; but I believed in the existence of other and more vivid kinds of goodness, and what I believed in I wished to behold."

What's Sexy: Brontë mutes all the book's potential sexuality in her infinite decorum; she describes Rochester as "irresistible" but makes no mention of his physical being in the passage. Then there's the culminating question late in the book: "Which is better?—To have surrendered to temptation; listened to passion; made no painful effort—no struggle—but to have sunk down in the silken snare . . . fevered with delusive bliss for one hour . . . or to be a village schoolmistress . . . ?" I can't say that you'll be too titillated by Jane's answer.

Quirky Fact: Despite their limited education and resources, Charlotte and her two sisters somehow synchronized their writing so that they each had a novel finished in 1847: Charlotte, *Jane Eyre;* Emily, *Wuthering Heights;* and Anne, *Agnes Grey.* They bundled them together and had them published as a three-part unit. That's some inspirational teamwork.

What to Skip: As mentioned above, I find the first ten chapters weaker than what follows, and I think they can be skimmed. And, for those in a serious rush (running out of summer, perhaps), the last two hundred pages (from Chapter 24 on) can also be skipped or skimmed, although, unless you can't endure the slightest trace of the maudlin, you should lend an eye to the last two chapters (37 and 38) to find out what happens. I don't want to spoil it for you.

EMILY BRONTË
(1818–48)

✼

Wuthering Heights
(1847)

There is a young woman at home dreaming. She is shy and reclusive like her sisters, who are very nearly her only companions. Outwardly she is the most sickly, but on the inside there is a brushfire ready to *blaze*.

Emily Brontë, at twenty-nine years old, having lived a life as restricted and crippling as her sisters', having next to no life experience or any way of collecting the material for her novel (that anyone seems to know about), managed to create *Wuthering Heights*, a murky, gothic, near-horror story, driven by two principal characters who are the very souls of passion and excess. How she did it remains a complete mystery. A year later, she succumbed to tuberculosis and died after refusing treatment.

We should take note of this last fact, the refusal, and both the death wish and the defiance it represents. Another time, having been bitten by a rabid dog, she told no one; she simply cauterized the wounds herself with a hot iron. In one of her poems, Emily had written, "No coward soul is mine, No trembler in the world's storm-troubled sphere." Frail in body, Freya in spirit.

Perhaps we shouldn't be surprised. Defiance—or at least the impulse to it, the fantasy of it—ran strong in the Brontë sisters. Jane Eyre championed in fiction a brashness that Charlotte couldn't in life, but Emily's characters went further: Heathcliff the "fierce, pitiless, wolfish man," and Catherine, the "rush of a lass," are wild, selfish, reckless, boiling-blooded upright-walkers, utterly cut free of the shackles of the superego. Each is filled with what Brontë three times calls "spirit": it's a lust for life and for love, but, like a brushfire, it doesn't stay in bounds.

Heathcliff and Catherine are contrasted to, and are utterly contemptuous of, the mannered and aristocratic but equally "pitiful, silly" Linton siblings whom they eventually marry (for various contorted reasons): the "mawkish, waxen" Isabella and Edgar, the "sucking leveret," the "milk-blooded coward," the "cipher" who, Heathcliff says, "couldn't love as much in eighty years as I could in a day." Damn!

The irony is that it's not only Heathcliff and Catherine, but the weak characters that represent Emily as well: Edgar and Isabella reflect her demure and proper social behavior, and the weak and sickly Linton Heathcliff (Heathcliff's runt issue)—"the ailing, peevish creature," the "whey-faced whining wretch"—her physical self (as does the closed-off oak case with the bed *inside* it in Catherine's room). With such a spirit so contained, Emily no doubt obsessed about ripping free. Heathcliff and Catherine do it for her. Reading *Wuthering Heights* one can almost see Emily pulling the head off a live chicken, painting a pentagram around herself in its blood, calling forth the beasts that boiled inside her, and making them kneel and bow in the service of the novel.

Heathcliff is in fact a demon of revenge, hell-spurred to avenge himself on his adoptive brother, Hindley, for childhood abuse, on Catherine for leaving him, on Edgar Linton for marrying her, on Isabella as a way to get to Edgar, and on the world for making him swarthy, parentless, and penniless. He is the perfect embodiment of vindication. When the housekeeper Nelly tells him, "It is for God to punish wicked peoples; we should learn to forgive," he replies, "No, God won't have the satisfaction that I shall." It's that, the anger that overcomes even piety, that makes me think again about Emily, seething with a deep, hot, smoldering fury—at her father, her body, the horrid schools where she froze and starved—finding no outlet till she was able to cook up Heathcliff in her beldam's cauldron.

With that in mind, it's not much of a leap to recognize in Heathcliff and Catherine's terrorization of Edgar and Isabella a precise reversal—if only in her mind—of how, in reality, Emily's circumstances and health caged her inner tigress. Flaubert's famous "I am Madame Bovary" rings hollow to my ear, but had Emily Brontë, with a voice like the possessed Sigourney Weaver in *Ghostbusters,* said, as her character Catherine does, "I *AM* Heathcliff"—that I'd buy. She was Heathcliff, she simply never got to be him.

One final note: *Wuthering Heights* has the dubious distinction of having, to my mind, not only the biggest wuss but literally the most annoying character in the entire history of literature. Heathcliff's son, the aforementioned Linton, is not only more sniveling and weaker in body even than the young Marcel in *Remembrance of Things Past,* but he also happens to be a shit on the inside. When the plot of *Wuthering Heights* shifts from Heathcliff and Catherine's story to Linton and young Catherine's, I'm afraid it's time to check out (see "What to Skip" on page 195).

The Buzz: It must have been great to have lived in the 19th century, at least in a novel, at least as a man, preferably orphaned and severely spurned. Like the Count of Monte Cristo or Heathcliff in *Wuthering Heights* (among countless others), you can just disappear for a while, then come back, fortune in hand, dressed to the nines, and take revenge on everybody who pissed you off.

Heathcliff the devil-man was a dark, homeless child, taken in by Catherine and Hindley's father. He and his sort-of sibling Catherine develop a violent animal love, but she marries Edgar, the sweet, conventional, rich neighbor. *Very sneaky, sis!* This initiates Heathcliff's obsessive and lifelong retaliation scheme. He is one of literature's great bad-boys.

What People Don't Know (But Should): It's a subtle element in the novel compared with the bombast everywhere else, but Brontë manages a pretty scathing critique of hypocritical Bible-thumpers, embodied in the servant Joseph, "the wearisomest, self-righteous Pharisee that ever ransacked a Bible to rake the promises to himself and fling the curses on his neighbors." Was she thinking of her father, the negligent and heartless curate?

Best Line: It could be that Nelly Dean (one of the novel's two narrators) embodies yet another side of Emily Brontë, at least in her feelings about death that we speculated on above: "I don't know if it be a peculiarity in me, but I am seldom otherwise than happy while watching in the chamber of death, should no frenzied or despairing mourner share the duty with me. I see a repose that neither earth nor hell can break, and I feel an assurance of the endless and shadowless hereafter—the Eternity they have entered—where life is boundless in its duration, and love in its sympathy, and joy in its fullness. I noticed on that occasion how much selfishness there is even in a love like Mr. Linton's, when he so regretted Catherine's blessed release."

What's Sexy: Though there's nothing explicit, this line of Heathcliff's has some sinister sexual implications regarding his detested wife, Isabella: "I've sometimes relented, from pure lack of invention, in my experiments on what she could endure."

Quirky Fact: If you ever wondered just how filthy the conditions of the working classes in England were, here's a line for you: "His clothes . . . had seen three months' service in mire and dust." Wow, that's skanky.

What to Skip: Sadly, after Catherine's death, the novel takes a severe nosedive. The first three-fifths of *Wuthering Heights* are magnificent, as good a soap opera as you will ever read, but beginning at Chapter 18, the narrator fast-forwards twelve years and the protagonists switch from Healthcliff and Catherine to their respective children, Linton and young Catherine. At this point, male readers, unless your taste for Schadenfreude runs stratospherically high, you will be obliged to close the covers for fear of sustained retching. Female readers, you might just puke too. The problem is a single character: Linton Heathcliff. He's intolerable—literally, as I note above, the most annoying character in the entire history of literature. Young Catherine isn't particularly interesting either, but it's Linton who utterly ruins the last 40 percent of the book.

Two more things deserve mention: first, the novel's narrative setup of having the housekeeper Nelly Dean tell Heathcliff's tale to the visitor Lockwood, who, in turn, tells it to us, is clunky and unnecessary. One can skip right to Chapter 4, when she begins to tell the story without his gratuitous mediation.

Finally, even if you skip the last part of the novel, you still might want to read Chapter 29 and the book's final two pages to get the coda to Heathcliff and Catherine's saga. It's a little disappointing but helps "explain" the stuff from earlier.

HERMAN MELVILLE
(1819–91)

༄

Moby Dick
(1851)

The sea monster to end all sea monsters: a ten-ton, sixty-foot sperm whale, white as a baby's butt and just as explosive. Plus a demented old salt, peg-legging himself out of the Old Testament to chase down the demon of the sea (and the soul), and only one sailor saved to tell the tale. What should be considered the greatest adventure novel ever written is often thought of as one of the most boring, unfinishable books you can imagine. But psst, come over here, I want to tell you a secret. *Moby Dick,* you know, that gigantic novel with all that boring whaling stuff in it, is *funny,* I mean really funny, as in one of the funniest books of all time. You're probably thinking that I've been sniffing Elmer's, but it's actually true: *Moby Dick* is a laugh riot; people just don't seem to be able to get past its whalelike bulk to realize it.

Moby Dick, funny? I know my tenth-grade teacher didn't advertise the big kahuna as such; in fact, I pretty much only remember trying to decide whether the main theme was man vs. nature, man vs. the supernatural, or man vs. himself (it's all three and more, of course, though I didn't know it then). But twenty years later, reading it for the third time, it all clicked. Yes, the humor might be trapped in five hundred pages of what can seem like the *Encyclopaedia Britannica* of whaling, but trust me, it's there, it was *meant* to be there, and once you get Melville's sense of humor, *Moby Dick* becomes the classic it really is, and the best novel ever written by an American.

To save the whale, all it takes is to realize that Ishmael, the narrator, is an irreverent wiseacre, forever cracking jokes at the expense of landlubbers, society, religion, his fellow sailors, and himself. He's a terrible shipmate, falls asleep on watch in the crow's nest, is always about to tumble overboard, generally gets in the way of the killing of the whales, and is invariably more involved in his own ruminations than in the spume and storm around him. But as he himself tells us, echoing Cervantes, "A good laugh is a mighty good thing, and rather too scarce a good thing . . . and the man that has anything bountifully laughable about him, be sure there is more in that man than you perhaps think." So, then, with our Ishmael, the former schoolmaster turned loafer who "abominate[s] all respectable toils," who can't keep silver in his pocket (nor particularly cares to), who "has the problem of the universe" revolving in him but helps us along with ours, and who takes us with him on his little jaunt to "sail about a little and see the watery part of the world." He's like Shakespeare's clowns, equal part comedian and tragedian, philosopher and cutup, always ready with the barbed aside or incisive aphorism. About halfway through the book, he gives us a passing summary of his whole character:

> There are certain queer times and occasions in this strange mixed affair we call life when a man takes this whole universe for a vast practical joke, though the wit thereof he but dimly discerns, and more than suspects that the joke is at nobody's expense but his own. However, nothing dispirits, and nothing seems worth while disputing. . . . And as for small difficulties and worryings, prospects of sudden disaster, peril of life and

limb; all these, and death itself, seem to him only sly, good-natured hits, and jolly punches in the side bestowed by the unseen and unaccountable old joker. That odd sort of way-ward mood I am speaking of, comes over a man only in some time of extreme tribulation; it comes in the very midst of his earnestness, so that what just before might have seemed to him a thing most momentous, now seems but a part of the general joke. There is nothing like the perils of whaling to breed this free and easy sort of genial, desperado philosophy; and with it I now regarded this whole voyage of the Pequod, and the great White Whale its object.

Ishmael, as it should happen, proves to be the genial, desperado philosopher extraordinaire. In fact, you'd be hard-pressed to find his equal anywhere in the history of literature. One tiny example should suffice. On the fourth page of the novel proper, having already told us that he's a little down on his luck and light in the purse, he makes the stoical aside that "in this world, head winds are far more prevalent than winds from astern"—sound philosophy from a hard-luck sailor. But then he qualifies his sobering truism by saying, "That is, if you never violate the Pythagorean maxim." Subtle joke, easy to miss, for you're probably thinking Pythagoras, who's that? Oh, yeah, *a-squared plus b-squared equals c-squared*. But that's not the Pythagorean maxim he's talking about. What you need to know (and sadly this isn't explained in most editions) is that there is a two-word fragment of Pythagoras' writings that simply says: *Avoid beans*. This is the maxim Ishmael's referring to, with all its wind-from-astern implications, thereby creating what might be the highest-brow fart joke ever told.

Now, from the very set-sail of the book, Ishmael wants to be our bosom mate. He begins by telling us that when he's feeling a little testy, or when there's "a damp, drizzly November in [his] soul," instead of "pausing before coffin warehouses," "methodically knocking people's hats off," or pulling a Cato and falling on his own sword, he realizes he's had enough of life on land and decides to go to sea.

And so to sea we go. The sea, the big water, the great escape, the ultimate infinite for speculation, "the image of the ungraspable phantom of life . . . the key to it all." Don't worry; Ishmael will tell you everything you need to know about the significance of the two-H, one-O molecule and everything that sails atop it or swims beneath it. And along the way we'll meet Ahab, the monomaniacal monopod whose crazed lust for revenge on the alabaster fish who made a dish of his leg leads Ishmael and the crew of the *Pequod* around the world and back. We'll meet Queequeg, the African harpooner (and Ishmael's best friend and one-time bedmate); the rest of the United Nations of harpooners; the first mates Stubb, Flask, and Starbuck (long before he became a java magnate); and we will meet Moby himself, holy terror of the seven seas, half-monster, half-myth, a comprehensive allegory for all things desired, feared, pursued, or portentous for we wee little walking things called humans.

Long live the fish.

The Buzz: These days, sadly, the biggest buzz around *Moby Dick,* at least in college classrooms, is whether Ishmael and Queequeg get busy when they share a bed at the Spouter Inn (yes, there's a joke here). Somehow trying to figure out if Melville was homoerotic (and just how much) has become more important than enjoying the best and funniest of all American novels. Lord save us. For more on this, see "What's Sexy" on page 201.

What People Don't Know (But Should): We all know that encyclopedias try to contain as much knowledge of as many things as possible, but there's a special sort of encyclopedia called an anatomy that more or less tries to contain all knowledge of one thing. *Moby Dick,* then, is an anatomy of whaling. The reason Melville fans will often tell you that you can find the whole world in *Moby Dick* is because Melville, by compiling everything there is to know about whales, whaling, and whiteness, gave us a near infinity of analogies with which to understand the bulk of human experience. We arrive at the general by a complete understanding of the particular. Each entity in this world reflects the entirety of the universe of which it is part. And thus Melville helps us see that to know one thing truly is to know all things.

Best Line: Among the many, many that I love, I want to underscore this description, first of the whale's head and probable thoughts, then of the rainbowed vapor surrounding it, which becomes a metaphor for intuitions of the infinite that can only emerge in the midst (and mist) of doubt—incredible!

How nobly it raises our conceit of the mighty, misty monster, to behold him solemnly sailing through a calm tropical sea; his vast, mild head overhung by a canopy of vapor, engendered by his incommunicable contemplations, and that vapor—as you will sometimes see it—glorified by a rainbow, as if Heaven itself had put its seal upon his thoughts. For, d'ye see, rainbows do not visit the clear air; they only irradiate vapor. And so, through all the thick mists of the dim doubts in my mind, divine intuitions now and then shoot, enkindling my fog with a heavenly ray. And for this I thank God; for all have doubts; many deny; but doubts or denials, few along with them, have intuitions. Doubts of all things earthly, and intuitions of some things heavenly; this combination makes neither believer nor infidel, but makes a man who regards them both with equal eye.

What's Sexy: In my erstwhile-erotica-writer's opinion, nothing very exciting takes place between Ishmael and his big harpooning buddy (no pun intended), despite all the to-do (see "The Buzz" on page 199). But in case you want to see for yourself, here's the relevant passage (from Chapter IV, "The Counterpane"):

> Upon waking next morning about daylight, I found Queequeg's arm thrown over me in the most loving and affectionate manner. You had almost thought I had been his wife. . . . I could hardly tell it from the quilt, they so blended their hues together; and it was only by the sense of weight and pressure that I could tell that Queequeg was hugging me. My sensations were strange. Let me try to explain them. When I was a child, I well remember a somewhat similar circumstance that befell me; whether it was a reality or a dream, I never could entirely settle. The circumstance was this. I had been cutting up some caper or other—I think it was trying to crawl up the chimney, as I had seen a little sweep do a few days previous; and my stepmother who, somehow or other, was all the time whipping me, or sending me to bed supperless,—my mother dragged me by the legs out of the chimney and packed me off to bed.

Various camps of scholars are going to tell you that this "recollection" of "crawling up the chimney" and getting whipped by his mother and pulled out by his legs is chock-full of conscious or unconscious psychosexual implications. I will admit it comes at an eyebrow-raising moment, Ishmael having just spent the night with Queequeg. But still, who's the harpooner and who's the deckhand here? It seems to me that there's some confusion about who'd be going up the chimney.

Now, for something not exactly sexy but certainly related—in a very large way—keep reading.

Quirky Fact: In the chapter "The Cassock," not only does Melville describe a whale's penis as an "unaccountable cone, longer than a Kentuckian is tall, nigh a foot in diameter at the base, and jet-black," but he then explains how a man called the "mincer" (whose job is to cut the blubber into chunks to boil down in the giant pots of the tryworks) cuts arm holes in the whale's foreskin, turning it into a smock that he wears to protect himself from the flames!

What to Skip: The whiteness chapter (42) does seem to drag (though when taken, as it should be, with as many grains of salt as are in the Pacific, it's a lot more enjoyable). However, the chapters that are most dispensable are 32 (but don't miss the last paragraph) and 55 through 57, all of which contain the more gratuitous of Melville's exhaustive facts on whaling.

CHARLES DICKENS
(1812–70)

❦

Bleak House
(1853)

Based on my nonofficial polling, Dickens is probably the most hated author in the English language. Lugging around one of his novels in my specially designed miniwheelbarrow, I'm often asked: Are you really reading that *by choice*? You don't really *like* Dickens, do you?

Fact is: I love Dickens, and so will you. Granted, you probably remember him as that dreaded homework double-whammy of boring and interminable, but that was high school, and there was no way you were old enough to get it. Try again now and you'll see that each of the novels is a complete page-turner full of suspense, good nature, and mirth. And they're hysterical—all of them. The most popular writer of 19th-century England had an incredible lust for life that comes through in each of his books in virtually every line. He was smarter than all of us and saw people and society for what they were (with every blemish and hypocrisy skewered again and again), yet he was bigger-hearted than any of us too, and maintained belief in the souls of children and the good. Dickens wrote characters that crystallize his faith in man, that show us the way, that are so full of love that we end up being in love with them ourselves—all this in books teeming with plot twists and intrigue. If you like plot, if you like character, if you like comedy, if you like tragedy, if you like style, if you like insight, if you like social critique or a rollicking good time, you're going to love Dickens—wheelbarrow not included.

So what happened? How did his star fall so low having shined so bright? Well, in the midst of all his other classics, he happened to write two Christmas-themed books, one of which came to be considered good reading for children despite the fact that it's in an English now over a century out-of-date. Later he penned one of the best books with a teen protagonist ever (*Great Expectations*; see next chapter), which also somehow became a staple of young adult reading, despite the same language issue, a serious length problem, and a lot of jokes, themes, and turns of phrase that only an adult could make the most of. Sure it would be nice to expose young people to classics, but these really aren't the right ones (what *would* be good to give to them is a subject for another book). Yet teacher after teacher assigns them anyway, thus ensuring that everyone and their brother utterly detests Dickens and prompting further reading of what could and should be one of the most joy-inducing authors of all time.

It's time to fix all that because, in my opinion, of the best of the classic authors, Dickens might well be the easiest to access—for adults—and the most rewarding. It might be sacrilegious to say, but one summer, when I committed myself to rereading Shakespeare's histories and tragedies and as many of Dickens' novels as I had time for, Shakespeare paled a bit. Next to the deft, effortless-seeming manner with which Dickens populated his novels, Shakespeare's characters came off a bit thin. Even Hamlet and Lear weren't as convincing as they always had been, not as deep. I felt, for the first time, the limitation of Shakespeare's writing in plays. Dickens, meanwhile, has all the resources of the novel at his disposal—and he takes full advantage.

With most of his books weighing in at eight-hundred-plus pages, Dickens can take his time, draw out intrigue and nuance, paint his characters with chiaroscuro, and place them on stage after stage. It might be true that many of his characters are one-trick ponies, but they somehow manage to do their tricks so well, we feel them as complete human beings. And yes, the types repeat book after book—read any three Dickens novels and you'll find at least one dutiful daughter, a dissolute young man, a heartless miser, a shameless blowhard, a daft harridan, a drunken house-keeper, a noble savage, and, always, an angelically innocent child who's almost certainly an orphan or a foundling. But despite the repetitions, you still can't help thinking, as he snaps them out of thin air, that Dickens' characters—emblematic as they may be—are still palpably real and his social tableaux true to life. There might never have been an ear for dialogue and an eye for detail quite like Dickens'; even the most prodigious character-builder ever, Balzac, never made them stick quite like his compeer.

Bleak House is Dickens' most ambitious novel, and it brings together the elements that make his other books so wonderful. It has the social critique of *Hard Times*, this time applied to the Kafkaesque legal labyrinth of England's chancery court, "which gives to monied might the means abundantly of wearying out the right"; the humor and warmth of *Great Expectations;* per-haps his most engaging and surprising plot (it's one of England's earliest detective novels); and a cast of characters supreme in any novel in any language. You'll never forget the protagonist, Esther, a paragon of goodness (at times a little overwhelmingly so); Bucket, the detective, and his exquisite manipulations (he's one of my favorite characters in all literature); the Bagnets' golden-years love for each other; the plaintiff Jarndyce—whose inter-minable case sets the plot in motion—and his fair and foul moods; or the lawyer Tulkinghorn's sphinxy intractability, among many, many others.

So laugh with Dickens. Feel the warmth, exult in the joy, rub your belly, and know that no English author has been able to be both as scathing and generous, antihypocrisy and humanitarian, witty, wise, and playful as the original Chuck D.

The Buzz: Everybody says that Dickens was a great social critic, which he was (see "Best Line" on the opposite page), but that's hardly the main thrust of his novels. Yes, *Hard Times* (and almost all his other books) does a great job of representing Industrial Age London and its crimes against working humanity, and because Dickens' family was forced to live in a debtors prison (his father was a bankrupt), he had the insider knowledge to create some of his novels' best scenes. Furthermore, his mistreatment in early schools allowed him to absolutely excoriate the British school system in *David Copperfield* and *Nicholas Nickleby.* But Dickens doesn't stop there; any attentive reader will see that his real objective is not simply to criticize how badly humanity can behave, but to demonstrate, through one noble character after the next, just how well it can and should. In *Bleak House,* even as Dickens is critiquing the British legal system, he puts forth characters like Esther and Jarndyce to show the other side of things— and the noble possibilities that are available to each of us. At the end of the day, Dickens is a relentless optimist, even while being an absolute critic.

What People Don't Know (But Should): Dickens wrote and published virtually all his novels in monthly installments, delivering about forty-five pages at a time. In itself, this is a stunning amount of productivity (no doubt Dickens' oeuvre benefited from getting into such a frenetic rhythm), but even more impressive is the fact that he was so popular in his day, the illiterate waited with bated breath for each new release. No, they couldn't read them, but they would line up outside booksellers' shops just to see the drawing that would advertise that month's section. Now that's a fan base.

Best Line: Here's a perfect example of the deft balance in Dickens between bonhomie and bombast. Note how gently he pillories the English legal system, but note too just how damning his critique:

> The one great principle of the English law is, to make business for itself. There is no other principle distinctly, certainly, and consistently maintained through all its narrow turnings. Viewed by this light it becomes a coherent scheme, and not the monstrous maze the laity are apt to think it. Let them but once clearly perceive that its grand principle is to make business for itself at their expense, and surely they will cease to grumble. [Chapter 39]

What's Sexy: *Bleak House* doesn't have anything sexy, but it does have one of my favorite (and most romantic) couples in all literature: the Bagnets. Mrs. Bagnet, forever cooking pots of hairy and unidentifiable greens, is so loved by her husband that he can't keep from telling you every chance he gets. And when he is asked to give his opinion on something, he invariably refers to the the missus's superior expressive ability—in other words, he has her say what *she* thinks. Is there a more reliable recipe for a successful marriage?

Quirky Fact: *Bleak House* is the first literary work to mention spontaneous combustion. Dickens even had to explain in one of his prefaces that it was a scientifically proven phenomenon so readers wouldn't think he made it up.

What to Skip: Along with *Great Expectations* and *A Christmas Carol,* Dickens' most famous novels are *David Copperfield, Nicholas Nickleby, A Tale of Two Cities, Oliver Twist,* and *Hard Times.* Sadly, the last three are, in my opinion, among his least compelling. *Two Cities* might be the worst, apart from its rightfully famous, utterly amazing, and completely misunderstood first line (which I have to quote just to underscore the sarcasm that people never seem to acknowledge).

> It was the best of times, it was the worst of times, it was the age of wisdom, it was the age of foolishness, it was the epoch of belief, it was the epoch of incredulity, it was the season of Light, it was the season of Darkness, it was the spring of hope, it was the winter of despair, we had everything before us, we had nothing before us, we were all going direct to Heaven, we were all going direct the other way—in short, the period was so far like the present period, that some of its noisiest authorities insisted on its being received, for good or for evil, in the superlative degree of comparison only.

All three are better skipped in favor of *Bleak House, Great Expectations, Nicholas Nickleby, David Copperfield,* and even his first (and perhaps most irreverent) novel, *The Pickwick Papers.*

From *Bleak House* proper, I'd advise skipping every section in which the annoying character Skimpole appears. Skimpole's shtick is that he's a grown-up who claims to be like a child and thus takes no responsibility for his actions, family, or finances. He wears thin quickly and appears in Chapters 6, 8, 9, 15, 18, 31, 37, 39, 43–44, 57, and 61. Best to avoid.

CHARLES DICKENS
(1812–70)

✎

Great Expectations
(1861)

You might have read it in your youth, but, unless you had a dedicated teacher, were already accustomed to reading 19th-century English, or had an especial soft spot for orphans, it probably didn't go so well. But if there is a single classic that deserves a second chance now that you're an adult, it's *Great Expectations*. *Bleak House* has the widest scope of any of Dickens' novels, but *Great Expectations* is surely his most immediately gratifying and accessible—and one of the shortest.

But let's get this out of the way first: it is not, I repeat, *not*, a children's book. Yes, the protagonist, Pip, is a boy when the novel begins; yes it's G-rated, uplifting, and morally benign; but *Great Expectations* calls out to fully formed hearts and active minds, and even an attentive teenager will access only a tenth of its glory (though that tenth might still be enough for them to like it).

Now, I want to stress one more thing: there might only be a few books that you enjoy more than *Great Expectations*—ever. I'm not exaggerating. It overflows with such warmth, humanity, humor, and, dare I say it, sweetness that you literally won't be able to keep yourself from loving it. The fact that everybody doesn't already realize that *Great Expectations* is one of the most delightful books of all time absolutely befuddles me—and is a testament to how badly we mishandle literary education. What should be a cherished favorite in everyone's library is too often squandered by being assigned to people who can't go alone to R-rated movies.

Part of the problem is that Dickens is deceptively hard, or, to put it better, much of his greatness purls just beneath the obvious, so unless you're doing attentive, line-by-line reading, you'll only be seeing the novel's proverbial tip. I don't want you to have to take my word on this, so to prove my point, I'm going to quote from the second paragraph and show you how it works (Dickens really doesn't wait long to get himself going). Pip is speaking:

> As I never saw my father or my mother, and never saw any likeness of either of them (for their days were long before the days of photographs), my first fancies regarding what they were like, were unreasonably derived from their tombstones. The shape of the letters on my father's gave me an odd idea that he was a square, stout, dark man, with curly black hair. From the character and turn of the inscription, *"Also Georgiana Wife of the Above,"* I drew a childish conclusion that my mother was freckled and sickly. To five little stone lozenges, each about a foot and a half long, which were arranged in a neat row beside their grave, and were sacred to the memory of five little brothers of mine—who gave up trying to get a living exceedingly early in that universal struggle—I am indebted for a belief I religiously entertained that they had all been born on their backs with their hands in their trousers-pockets, and had never taken them out in this state of existence.

We're two paragraphs in, and you already have both the glory and the challenge of Dickens. By my count, there are at least two successful jokes and one confusing sentence (I have no idea what the line about his brothers being born on their backs with hands in the trouser pockets means). And there's the problem: if you stumbled on the confusing bit and didn't catch the two jokes that preceded it, I can see why you would already be working up a yawn.

The key is to get the wit. The line about the headstone letters suggesting to him that his dad was square, stout, dark, and curly is meant to be a joke but isn't that funny—to me at least. But the wife's inscription *"Also Georgiana"*—that's great, if subtle. Think of the Industrial Age British. Think of the back-broken, hard-drinking, closed-lipped working-class men of that era. So, in the spouting effusive adoration of the period, the mother gets *"Also Georgiana."* Claim to fame: *wife of the above.* A life lived, a life gone, seven foaled, five dead: *"Also Georgiana, Wife of the Above."* Sad—but also funny.

Then the quip about the brothers giving up early in "that universal struggle" of "trying to make a living"—again gallows humor (for all five boys died young) but again pretty amusing, and no doubt apt regarding the struggle part.

I'm not saying that these jokes are amazing; they're not, and I'm kind of sad they aren't better so you'd get a sense of how good Dickens often is from the get-go (as in the neglected sarcasm of the first line of *A Tale of Two Cities*, as mentioned in the last chapter). But what they do demonstrate is that there's always a lot going on; virtually every line in the paragraph has a joke in it, and if you miss them and only notice the confusing stuff, the ship's all but sailed.

But let's take a better line—again subtle—so you can really get the swing of the Dickens thing. This is from twenty pages into the novel, early in Chapter 4. So far we've had some excellent plot—Pip being forced by a runaway convict to steal him some food, feeling guilty, etc.—and then this description of his guardian, his sister who takes her name from her husband: "Mrs.

Joe was a very clean housekeeper, but had an exquisite art of making her cleanliness more uncomfortable and unacceptable than dirt itself. Cleanliness is next to Godliness, and some people do the same by their religion." The literal level is pretty clear: Mrs. Joe (an unyielding battle-axe whose real name we don't learn till much later) is clean to the point where you'd rather be in filth—it would feel better. We all know people like that, and the phrase nails them remarkably efficiently. But it's the addendum that I really like: "Cleanliness is next to Godliness, and some people do the same by their religion," i.e., they make their religion so constrictive and uncomfortable that you'd rather live among pagans. This is Dickens in a nutshell: quietly, gently sliding his épée deep into the self-righteous. It's brilliant, but it's also really quick and easy to miss.

From there the novel simply blossoms. The plot might be familiar: Pip is sent to play at the rich lady Miss Havisham's, where he meets her pretty and condescending "niece," Estella (who says, "He is a common labouring-boy!" and Miss Havisham responds glacially, "You can break his heart."). The older lady turns out to be a little gaga, having shut herself indoors since being spurned at her wedding decades before, still wearing her dress, stopping all the clocks, and keeping the cake, now spider-covered, at hand. Estella makes Pip wish he wasn't working-class (leading to his famous "It is a most miserable thing to feel ashamed of home" line) and lose track of what he is and has, especially his simple but supremely loving brother-in-law, Joe—heartbreaking. Eventually Jaggers, the shark-to-end-all-sharks lawyer, shows up and declares that Pip has "great expectations" (a sizable trust fund coming his way), and from that point the mystery is on: who is the money from, and how will it turn out? It's a near-perfect class-mobility parable where Pip makes most of the mistakes you can make, but life, as it often does, teaches him—and us—all the right lessons.

Instead of wasting any more of your time or mine trying to convince you to read *Great Expectations,* here's a simple gambit: Go online (google "*Great Expectations* text") and just read Chapter 7 on Joe's illiteracy, what the "drawback" on his learning was, how his wife is "given to government" and "comes the Mogul" over him and Pip. It'll take you twenty minutes, and you'll be sold. I have no doubts.

And once you're fully a-swim, do what one should always do reading Dickens: give yourself over to the story and the characters (you'll love, to name but a few, Pip, Joe, Jaggers, the good-hearted Biddy, Magwich the callused criminal, and Jagger's assistant Wemmick with his "aging parent"—perhaps my favorites), but don't forget about the language either. For once you've trained yourself to read slowly and catch all Dickens' wryness, you'll understand why I've read all fifteen thousand pages of his novels, many multiple times, and can't wait to read them all again.

A final word should be said about sentimentality in Dickens. Yes, he gets a little melodramatic at times (okay, lots of times), and this rubs certain heartless, bad, mean mean people the wrong way. Oscar Wilde, for example, referring to Dickens' novel *The Old Curiosity Shop,* famously said, "One must have a heart of stone to read the death of little Nell without laughing." He's got a point, sort of. Reading Dickens, I occasionally think, "This might turn a few stomachs." Of course everyone will have a different level of tolerance of the Dickensian treacle (and mine, I'll confess, is very high), but you should never lose track of the fact that his sentimentality is never naive and is always balanced elsewhere in the novels by critique. Dickens simply believed in his heart that humanity could, at times, be good, and wanted to put that on display. If we have a hard time believing his noble characters, that's only because of the infrequency with which we see such levels of goodness in everyday life. And that fact alone helps to underscore both Dickens' critiques and his necessity. Now as in his day, Dickens shows how desperately we need models of human goodness.

The Buzz: The three characters people tend to speak of in *Great Expectations* are Pip, Miss Havisham, and Estella. Of course, Miss Havisham's crumbling yellow wedding dress and cobweb-covered cake stick in the memory rather forcibly. As always, though, I think Dickens distinguishes himself through his bit characters as much as through his protagonists, so don't think these three are the only ones that will entertain you.

What People Don't Know (But Should): Apart from *Great Expectations* not being a children's book, people seem to forget the ambiguity of the ending. In the penultimate line, when Estella says to Pip, "Suffering has been stronger than all other teaching, and has taught me to understand what your heart used to be," it seems as if they are going to part forever. But then . . . but then . . . read the last six words and decide for yourself.

Best Line: I'm giving you two. The first shows you again how subtle the Dickensian joke can be (the subject, by the way, is prison): "a certain part of the world where a good many people go, not always in gratification of their own inclinations, and not quite irrespective of the government expense." The second is a summation of the goodness that Dickens not only believes in but puts on such exquisite display: "It is not possible to know how far the influence of any amiable honest-hearted duty-doing man flies out into the world; but it is very possible to know how it has touched one's self in going by." Wow.

What's Sexy: Again, Dickens is not the place to go to for nook-nook. The closest we get is Wemmick's hysterical attempts to put his arm around his girlfriend, Miss Skiffins, at dinner.

Quirky Fact: During the time when Dickens was writing this novel, the weekly magazine he was editing, *All the Year Round,* started to flag in popularity. To fix the problem, he decided to publish *Great Expectations* there, forcing himself to turn it in in weekly chunks (he was used to doing monthly installments), but thus saving his magazine. I'd like to see Tina Brown do that.

What to Skip: Nothing at all. But, as I said in the last chapter, don't fall into the trap of thinking that *Hard Times* or *A Tale of Two Cities* are among Dickens' better novels; they aren't. I actually consider them his two worst—and *Oliver Twist* is near the bottom too.

GUSTAVE FLAUBERT
(1821–80)

⌒⌒⌒

Madame Bovary
(1856)

If you were to read them in quick succession, paying attention mostly to the plot (and nodding off now and then mid-sentence), you might not be able to tell *Madame Bovary* and *Anna Karenina* apart. Two women protagonists—each head-strong, each unfaithful to her low-voltage husband, each ultimately tragic—both fictionalized by 19th-century goody-goody men who may or may not have had any business writing about wayward women who defiantly take the lumps their conservative societies give them. But Flaubert and Tolstoy both did, and the novels they produced remain popular generation after generation. I, for one, am a little surprised.

Flaubert's came first, and I have to admit, the first two times I read *Madame Bovary,* I wanted to put knitting needles into my eyes (and truthfully I couldn't stand what many critics call his chef d'oeuvre, *Sentimental Education,* either). Yes, Flaubert's writing is exquisite—he was as meticulous a stylist as France had ever known—but from my vantage, nothing about the character Emma Bovary was compelling, nothing captivating, nothing even sympathetic (except maybe that she lived in a restrictive era—but big whup). Flaubert once famously said, "I am Madame Bovary," but the internal evidence is a little murkier. At times he is as critical of his protagonist as a church deacon would be. Worse still, to my mind at least, is that Emma's one and only potentially redeeming characteristic is being willing to follow her whims of the moment—a dubious trait at best. Apart from that, she's dumb as a croissant (and just as flaky), picks her men like desserts at a buffet, is mortifyingly plebeian in her tastes but thirsts for what she thinks is culture and sophistication, and doesn't seem guided by ethics or feminism or freedom, just by boredom and mild cupidity. Suffice it to say that I was not moved.

But then I spoke to some female friends, and I finally began to understand the appeal. Women readers—now as in the early 19th century—tend to emphathize with Emma Bovary, ignoring Flaubert's snittiness and romanticizing her "plight," lauding her for her independence, rejoicing in her freedom-taking, and projecting depth onto her seemingly cardboard-deep character. Now the Ph.D.-ed pedant in me wants to argue that this is a misreading, that it's not what Flaubert intended, that the whole novel is supposed to be a critique of Emma and the society she comes from, but maybe I'm wrong, or at least maybe the standard "misreading" is actually a benevolent one, vital to making this book the hit that it's always been. For a few centuries now, Emma Bovary has been understood to be an icon of female daring and expression—a breaking-out of a woman's identity in an age of severe repression—and if you can feel her that way as you read, then you can lend the novel a significance worthy of its place as a classic. If not, you might wonder what the century-and-a-half of ballyhoo has been all about.

None of this is meant to dispute the historical value of *Madame Bovary* as a prose masterpiece or as an important early example of the Realist novel and a boundary-pusher in its frankness about Emma's sexuality (for which it was accused of obscenity—perhaps thereby giving rise to the early fan-base? I'm just saying . . .). There's no question that *Madame Bovary* is and always will be an "important" novel in the sense literary scholars and historians are always talking about—*social critique, symbolic expression, realist technique, metaphoric structure,* yadda yadda—but those kinds of considerations alone rarely result in almost a hundred and fifty years of fans. Instead, I think Emma's reputation has always preceded her, and that that reputation has conditioned how generations of readers have interpreted the book—in a good way.

In other words, unless your French is good enough for you to read *Madame Bovary* comfortably in the original (and thus be able to really feel the precision and elegance of Flaubert's prose), it might be that only by making Emma a heroine can you really enjoy *Madame Bovary.* My hope is that you can read it with one eye open and the other closed (not literally): being able to be critical both of Emma and Flaubert, yet still remaining an advocate of female expression and freedom even if that's not exactly what Emma represents; being able to appreciate the delicacy of the writing even when the author's ninniness starts to shine through. It might be a tough juggle, but if you can manage it, you'll both be able to like *Bovary* and not be deluded in your reasons for doing so.

The Buzz: Yes, on first blush Emma sounds like a protofeminist, but I'm not convinced that Flaubert thought so. When he says, "She no longer concealed her contempt for anything or anybody, and at times expressed singular opinions . . . she longed for lives of adventure, for masked balls, for shameless pleasures," and later quotes her saying, "If only you knew all I dreamed!" we think, oh the poor girl, undone by marriage and society, a swan pinioned. But then we note the word "shameless" and begin to suspect there's something else going on.

What People Don't Know (But Should): In the 19th century, women were thought to be corrupted by novels—and, granted, most of the novels they were reading were as pulpy as the Harlequins of today. Flaubert clearly wants to use book-corruption as part of the explanation of his protagonist's psychology—what there is of it. Emma, he says, "dirtied her hands with the greasy dust of old lending libraries"—and that's not literal grease, mind you—and "tried to find out what one meant exactly in life by the words bliss, passion, ecstasy, that seemed to her so beautiful in books" (I, vi). Later "it was decided to keep Emma from reading novels" (II, vii), but too late. Like Francesca in Dante's *Inferno,* she was already undone. Read the wrong thing, and the damage is irreversible.

Best Line: Well, I know one line that's *not* the best: "The human tongue is like a cracked cauldron on which we beat out tunes to set a bear dancing when we would make the stars weep with our melodies" (II, xii). That could honestly be the worst line in any book discussed in this volume. Gag!

But Flaubert makes up for it. This line, describing Emma receiving her last rites, is phenomenal—and, I can't resist mentioning, makes pretty clear how Flaubert really felt about his "heroine": "The priest . . . began to give extreme unction. First, upon the eyes, that had so coveted all worldly goods; then upon the nostrils, that had been so greedy of the warm breeze and the scents of love; then upon the mouth, that had spoken lies, moaned in pride and cried out in lust; then upon the hands that had taken delight in the texture of sensuality; and finally upon the soles of the feet, so swift when she had hastened to satisfy her desires, and that would now walk no more" (III, viii). Amazing.

What's Sexy: Despite the obscenity charges brought against the novel, most of the sexuality is subtle. Early on, Flaubert somewhat erotically describes the perspiration on Emma's shoulder and then her teasing out the drops of "curacoa" [*sic*] with her tongue from the bottom of a glass (I, iii). Later the worker-boy Leon will be transfixed watching Emma's comb "that bit into her chignon"and her dress moving as she played cards (II, iv). But when Emma eventually gets together with Rodolphe, the highbrow Flaubert descends to hackneyed romance-novel speak: "With one long shudder, she abandoned herself to him" (II, ix)—ugh. However, the primary sexual locus for the author, clearly, is Emma's hair, which makes three more appearances, the best being this scather: "Some artist skilled in corruption seemed to have devised the shape of her hair as it fell on her neck, coiled in a heavy mass, casually reassembled after being loosened daily in adultery" (II, xii). If you want the source of the symbolism, cf. *Paradise Lost* and Eve's "wanton ringlets" (IV, 306).

Quirky Fact: Flaubert was so obsessive a stylist that he was still writing and rewriting *Bovary*—sometimes as many as eleven versions exist of the same paragraph—even though he already had drafts of his novels *A Sentimental Education* and *The Temptation of Saint Anthony* written (as well as a lot of short stories) but *hadn't published anything*. Would that some novelists today could have such restraint.

What to Skip: I can barely stomach Rodolphe's "seduction" of Emma (except as proof that Flaubert willfully makes them both despicable) and have found an expedient means around it: begin the novel at Part II, section XII. What do you miss? That Emma's husband was a dud and she found a lover. From that point, it gets somewhat more palatable.

FYODOR DOSTOEVSKY
(1821–81)

~~~

Crime and Punishment
(1866)

In Dostoevsky we have the great philosopher of abjection. No writer of his stature ever scraped as deep and dirty as Dostoevsky, either socially or psychologically. In work after work, his characters confront the worst of torments that plague both the inner and outer man. Dostoevsky's great novella *Notes from Underground* (an excellent intro to his oeuvre if you're not yet ready for a big book) begins "I am a sick man. I am a spiteful man. I am an unattractive man. I think my liver is diseased," and this is how his protagonists tend to be: depressed, debilitated, dispossessed, and depraved. They are at life's bottom and have often driven themselves there, miserable and dissolute but unable not to heap further degradation and agony on themselves. Nowhere in literature will you find a deeper probing of the psychology of self-punishment and self-flagellation, or the grim ineluctable slipping away into true nihilism.

But nihilistic as his characters often are, Dostoevsky himself was of quite another type. Though he suffered terribly in life (in addition to being an epileptic and compulsive gambler, he was arrested for his early political beliefs, put through a fake execution—psych!—and sentenced to hard labor in Siberia for four years), he should not be confused with being a nihilist or proto-existentialist himself—quite the opposite. His relentless unflinching investigation of misery is actually part of a larger, redemptive project, not dissimilar to Augustine's in the *Confessions* or Milton's in *Paradise Lost*. For Dostoevsky will lead you down the path to faithlessness and desperation, trying to sucker you into believing what his characters believe, but only to show you that there is an alternative, even to the most seemingly lost. In the least preachy, least intrusive way possible (so subtle, readers often miss it), Dostoevsky makes it clear that the alternative to suffering is God, and redemption is always available—even when you don't know it.

As a whole, *Crime and Punishment* enacts this trap perfectly, but also sets it up in miniature early on in one of the most emotionally riveting scenes you'll ever read. Only nine pages into the novel, the protagonist, Raskolnikov, meets Marmaladov, a drunk in a bar who has just guzzled away the money that would have fed his starving children. Marmaladov buttonholes Raskolnikov and asks him if he has known what it is "to plead without hope . . . utterly without hope, sir, knowing beforehand that nothing will come of it?" Marmaladov's point is that you know you have no chance, *yet you do it anyway*. Some part of you wants the rejection, both to punish yourself and to confirm that you've hit rock bottom, that it can't get worse, that life can't give you yet another dose. That's the subtlety both of his question's psychology and Dostoevsky's insight: that the desperate man wants to be broken, *not* to be able to endure, just as the compulsive gambler subconsciously wants to run out of money. For at the end of hope, at least there's cease.

Marmaladov then poses what will eventually become the central question of the book: "Do you understand what it means to have nowhere left to turn?" The distraught man is poised on the very brink Dostoevsky wants to place the reader, the same brink where Raskolnikov will soon find himself, though he doesn't realize it yet. But in Marmaladov's heart there is a flicker of understanding, a flicker of hope, lost on Raskolnikov. He wants forgiveness; he doesn't feel he deserves it but hopes that God might grant it anyway, *precisely because he doesn't feel worthy* (see "Best Line" on page 225). From this point on, the story will become Raskolnikov's descent into abjection and groping for redemption (never quite able to look heavenward) as a counterexample to Marmaladov, the man who understands that he's not as alone as modern life would have him believe.

As a novel, *Crime and Punishment* is a piano wire pulled tighter and tighter, then strummed. At first glance, the plot seems almost a mockery of the title; the murder takes place only a seventh of the way in, and the "punishment" (if considered conventionally—whether Raskolnikov will be arrested and imprisoned) isn't revealed till the very end. But of course the punishment is also his guilt and the exquisite cat-and-mousing of Raskolnikov both by the detective Ilya Petrovich and by his own psyche. This is what most people remember of the novel, the slow teasing out of the evidence—real and imagined—against him, the uncertainty in our minds and his whether the police really have something on him, the psychological thumbscrews that tighten and tighten and tighten. In terms of pacing, it's utterly masterful; in the psychology of guilt, unrivaled; and in the sheer execution of the story, a fully sustained joy to the reader. *Crime and Punishment* is a book to treasure, the perfect combination of the page-turner and the philosophical novel.

Having been utterly rapt—entertained, surprised, impressed, and kept up well past your bedtime, waiting for the next twist—you'll get to the end of *Crime and Punishment* and realize that you just read a supremely religious work. And the basis of this religion, for Dostoevsky as for Marmaladov, is forgiveness. Like a former addict who's become a counselor—but somehow manages to keep from proselytizing—Dostoevsky sees your dark side from within and absolves everything, because he was there. Dostoevsky: a man like any other—maculate, flawed, and all too aware of the fallibility and frailty of us all. But tucked beneath his threadbare coat were the wings of an angel—an angel of understanding, an angel of mercy, an angel who never forgot his humanity.

The Buzz: The desire to confess, how it burns. Ask anybody what *Crime and Punishment* is about and they're likely to remember Raskolnikov's deliberation and tentativity before killing the old woman and the ceaseless guilt that hounds him thereafter. From the moment he commits the crime, Raskolnikov feels the flames licking: "A terrible word trembled on his lips as the bolt had trembled then on the door: now, now, the bolt will give way; now, now, the word will slip out; oh, only to say it!"

Crime and Punishment is literature's greatest inquiry into criminal psychology, both from the perspective of the prosecuted (Raskolnikov) and the prosecutor (Petrovich). The latter offers this gem: "If I don't arrest him or worry him in any way, but if he knows, or at least suspects, every minute of every hour, that I know everything down to the last detail, and am watching him day and night with ceaseless vigilance, if he is always conscious of the weight of suspicion and fear, he is absolutely certain to lose his head." This is effectively the psychology of the panopticon: a prison guard tower invented in the 18th century by Jeremy Bentham that suggests to the inmates that everything they do can be seen. Bentham's breakthrough—understood by Dostoevsky as well—is that once the prisoners believe that the panopticon is staffed at all times, *it doesn't have to be staffed at all.* The very idea of being perpetually watched does the job of watching. Through Dostoevsky's deft narration, Ilya Petrovich allows Raskolnikov to create a panopticon in his own mind.

What People Don't Know (But Should): Late in the novel, we find that Raskolnikov has published an article prepounding a proto-Nietzschean superman theory. (Dostoevsky's source for the idea was possibly Napoleon III's *Life of Julius Caesar,* translated into Russian in 1865. And though Nietzsche called Dostoevsky "the only psychologist who has anything to teach me," it's doubtful that Dostoevsky taught him this. Nietzsche probably first saw a similar theory in Goethe or the Young Hegelians.) It's an awkward addition to the plot, as if Dostoevsky, already halfway through his novel, caught wind of the theory and felt the need to attribute it to his character so he could put it under critique. *Crime and Punishment* does have one other rather bizarre tie to Nietzsche, however: thirty-three years after the novel's publication, Nietzsche went insane upon seeing a horse beaten in a scene similar to the one Dostoevsky describes in Raskolnikov's dream.

Best Line: You'll be hard-pressed to find a level of heartache comparable to this, Marmaladov's prayer, at least since Ugolino's confession in *Inferno:* "This very bottle, sir, bought with her money. . . . She said nothing, she only looked at me in silence. . . . It hurts more when there are no reproaches! . . . Now, who could be sorry for a wretch like me, eh? Are you sorry for me now, sir, or not? Tell me, sir, are you sorry or aren't you? He-he-he-he! . . .

"No, there is no need to be sorry for me! I ought to be crucified, crucified, not pitied! Crucify, oh judge, crucify me, but pity your victim! . . . *He* will pity us, He who pitied all men and understood all men and all things, He alone is the judge. In that day . . . He will say: 'Come unto Me! I have already forgiven thee' . . . And the wise and learned shall say: Lord, why dost Thou receive these?' And He shall say: 'I receive them, oh ye wise men, I receive them, oh ye learned ones, inasmuch as not one of these has deemed himself worthy.'"

Marmaladov will be forgiven. *That* is the religion Dostoevsky champions.

What's Sexy: Zip. Raskolnikov falls for Marmaladov's daughter, the prostitute, but he sees her as an icon of self-sacrifice (which she is) and looks to her for deliverance, not for a roll in the hay.

Quirky Fact: The April 1866 edition of a journal called *The Russian Messenger* contained installments of both *Crime and Punishment* and Tolstoy's *War and Peace*. Two of the greatest novels of all time, both serialized in the same magazine—try topping that, *The New Yorker*!

What to Skip: A number of sections of Book V are quite skimmable; I wouldn't spend too much time on V, i (a scene with Peter Petrovich, the wealthy suitor of Raskolnikov's sister); V, ii (Marmaladov's funeral); and V, v (Raskolnikov with Marmaladov's daughter). Apart from that, you'll be dazzled.

FYODOR DOSTOEVSKY
(1821–81)

❧

The Brothers Karamazov
(1880)

Woe to him who in terrible trouble must thrust his soul into the fire's embrace, hope for no comfort, not expect change. Well is the man who after his death-day may seek the Lord and find peace in the embrace of the Father.

—Beowulf

As great as *Crime and Punishment* is, it is with *The Brothers Karamazov* that Dostoevsky Cousteau-s his way to the darkest depths. In my opinion, no novel delves so insightfully into human psychology—and with as astonishing a range of personality types and behaviors—as *Brothers K.* Like the infamous (and probably apocryphal) Chinese meal where diners slice a tonsure from the skulls of living monkeys to lay bare their brains, Dostoevsky splits his characters open, exposing their inner workings to all. He shows us their deep motivations, digs his nails into their grime, teases out their weaknesses, all in service of making shadow-casting figures that we believe, feel, and recognize in ourselves.

The plot of *The Brothers Karamazov* is intricate in the extreme: Dmitri (a.k.a. Mitya—most everyone has multiple names; it is a Russian novel after all), Ivan, and Alyosha (Alexey) are the title characters. The first has a tempestuous relationship with a woman he blackmailed but owes money, Katarina (Katya), but really loves Grushenka, the mistress of his dissolute father, Fyodor. Ivan meanwhile loves and is loved by Katarina, but she won't leave Dmitri for him. Alyosha is a monk, but he too is loved by a woman: Lise the cripple, one of my favorite characters. Eventually the father is killed, a significant sum of money disappears, and suddenly we have a murder mystery.

Almost all the characters in *The Brothers K* are troubled, but as with *Crime and Punishment*, Dostoevsky is setting us up. For yes, we might see ourselves in Mitya or Ivan's lovelorn anguish, or worse in Lise's self-hatred or Fyodor's dissipation, but it's precisely their hopelessness that we *aren't* supposed to feel. In spreading their psyches for the clear view of the reader, they become cautionary tales, parades put forth for our edification. For despite the on-the-scene despair the characters feel (and that we sympathize with), in every case there is a solution to the problem, and that solution is faith.

The setup is not dissimilar to that of the earlier novel. In *Crime and Punishment,* Raskolnikov embodied the nihilist or the would-be Nietzschean superman desperately groping for redemption, unable from beginning to end to escape Marmaladov's question "Do you understand what it means to have nowhere left to turn?" and, per the quote from *Beowulf* above, thrusting his soul into the fire's, not the Father's, embrace. In *Brothers K,* the types are more complex, the traps more refined, but the early setup not dissimilar. Just over one hundred pages into the novel, Dmitri, of the three brothers the most nihilistic—and likeable—by far, asks his saintly brother, Alyosha:

> "Have you ever felt, have you ever dreamt of falling down a precipice into a pit? . . . I am afraid, but I *enjoy* it. It's not enjoyment though, but ecstasy . . . I'm a Karamazov. For when

I do leap into the pit, I go headlong with my heels up, and am pleased to be falling in that degrading attitude, and pride myself upon it. And in the very depths of that degradation I begin a hymn of praise. Let me be accursed!"

It sounds like a clear case of what psychologists now call reaction formation, but Dostoevsky has Dmitri tell us more: "I can't endure the thought that a man of lofty mind and heart begins with the ideal of the Madonna and ends with the ideal of Sodom. What's still more awful is that a man with the ideal of Sodom in his soul does not renounce the ideal of the Madonna." Everything is rejected, but nothing is renounced—a recipe for obsession, for haunting. And in the culminative moment, Dmitri all but paraphrases Marmaladov, asking Alyosha, "Do you know the meaning of despair?"

Dmitri's virtually limitless self-hatred leads him to a frenzied, ecstatic, almost joyful thumb-nosing of life and success and ultimately the God he desperately wants to believe in. He embodies a type of modern man for whom the author has much pity, not so much the nihilist as the lost, God-less soul, adrift without meaning or faith, even in himself.

All of this is part of what is perhaps the most incisive psychological concept the novel puts forth: that of "laceration" or "self-laceration." The title of one of the novel's sections, it describes how, in a state of horrific abjection, we are compelled to abject ourselves yet further as punishment for our guilt or shame. In *Crime and Punishment,* when Marmaladov knows his family needs the money in his pocket to keep from starving or freezing to death, instead of taking it home, he takes up his glass—almost gleefully—to drink it all away at the bar. His guilt and self-loathing run so deep he has to inflict this last and ultimate indignity on himself, as Raskolnikov will do as well. In *Brothers K,* we see self-laceration again and again: Dmitri taking the money he owes Katarina and blowing it in revels with Grushenka; Katya, Grushenka, and Lise all torturing and humiliating themselves, each other, and the Karamazovs whom they love; Fyodor, in the company of his son's fellow monks, unable not to feel or resist his own degeneracy and buffoonery; and on and on. Dostoevsky takes pains to stress that to be a Karamazov (and who, he might add, is not?) is to bear an internal taint: the impulse to excess and self-destruction, the slide on the slippery slope.

Strangely enough, in a novel so much about character, the most famous brothers trio this side of the Gibbs are somewhat disappointing. Dmitri is easily the most complex, exhibiting self-laceration, guilt, and remorse—though in a rather straightforward way—but Ivan and Alyosha are almost two-dimensional. Ivan encapsulates the modern rationalist—cold and calculating and more soulless than lost-souled. And Alyosha, whom Dostoevsky calls his "hero," the "lover of humanity," is a pious, kindhearted, almost simplistic good guy, the shoulder that everyone cries on and the person from whom everyone wants forgiveness, as if he was the God they otherwise can't seem to find. The strongest characters, in my opinion, are the women: Katarina, Grushenka, and Lise. Each of them attaches to one or more of the Karamazov brothers as a triangulation of their own self-hatred; each is unable to reconcile her internal feelings and acts out in seemingly contradictory ways, ways that demonstrate the layering and internal turmoil of their various psyches. Time and again, when any of these three characters are on the page, I find myself with mouth agape at something they've done or said. If you are going to get the most out of *The Brothers Karamazov,* pay less attention to the brothers themselves and more to the self-lacerating women who love them.

Now the part that people tend to enjoy the most is the famous Grand Inquisitor section, based on a short story that Ivan wrote and recounts to Alyosha, in which Jesus has come back to Earth fifteen hundred years after his death to speak to the leader of the Spanish Inquisition. Their exchange is riveting—as intense as perhaps any scene ever penned, and the Inquisitor could be the most jaded character in all literature. He confesses that he controls the populace out of fear because they need fear, they need to be controlled, and if the Church didn't serve that function, there would be chaos. And he goes on from there in an absolutely damning excoriation of Jesus for giving man freedom, for believing in man's capabilities, letting him fail, and thus forcing the Church to "correct" his work (see "The Buzz" on page 232 for more details).

If you only read the Grand Inquisitor section, you could easily believe that Dostoevsky himself was an atheist or a nihilist with a Realpolitik of the most fatalistic stripe. But there is no question that the Grand Inquisitor is *not* intended to be Dostoevsky's final word. Two chapters later we see the true center of the book: Alyosha's mentor, Father Zossima, delivers a monologue that shows a quintessentially pious alternative to the arch-cynicism of the Grand Inquisitor. In a sense, the entire novel hinges on this revision; again Dostoevsky takes a page from Milton, as if to say, "If you thought you were supposed to believe *that*, let me tell you what you're really supposed to believe."

But what Zossima says might be the single most challenging gauntlet a book has ever thrown at the feet of its readers, the most extreme injunction to morality you will ever read: that we are all responsible for all sin in all men *always*. Yes, you heard that right: everyone, all the time. We are all linked; if one of us sins, we all sin. And so, like Bodhisattvas, we must strive for the forgiveness and deliverance of all humanity. The message is unequivocal and comprehensive. Could any project be more munificent, more humanitarian, but more seemingly unrealizable?

Even if none of us is capable of taking up Zossima's challenge,

Dostoevsky's message and the spirit behind it remain. Like Alyosha, we are not to judge but to accept, all and everything. No wonder people retreat to the Grand Inquisitor's pessimism; it's an infinitely easier mental and philosophical position to take. But to connect one's self with all humanity, to take them all on, and to realize, like Tolstoy does in *Anna Karenina,* that forgiveness and lack of judgment could unite us, that is Father Zossima and Dostoevsky's ambition.

So we think back to Dmitri, to his father Fyodor's antics, to the self-lacerating women, to Ivan in his fatalism, and again we ask Marmaladov's question: Where do you turn? And now we see that *The Brothers Karamazoy* expands on the answer contained in *Crime and Punishment.* For with a person like Father Zossima in the world, there is a second alternative for those who have abandoned hope: It's not only God's mercy there waiting for us, there can be a terrestrial goodness, a grace, a majesty. Dostoevsky wants that to be you.

The Buzz: I've indicated already that the Grand Inquisitor section is the one 99 percent of people mention when they speak of *The Brothers Karamazov*—and no surprise. Its setup is fascinating: Christ meets with the chief figure of the ultrazealous Spanish Inquisition, ostensibly the most pious man on earth. And the Inquisitor says, "Why . . . art Thou come to hinder us? . . . I care not to know whether it is Thou or only a semblance of Him, but tomorrow I shall condemn Thee and burn Thee at the stake." The leader of the Inquisition burning the Savior—you can already see why this section's famous. He goes on to say that "people are more persuaded than ever that they have perfect freedom, yet they have brought their freedom to us [the Church] and laid it humbly at our feet . . . [we] have vanquished freedom and have done so to make men happy." Ouch.

The section is long and intricate, and short citations can't do it justice, but my favorite lines refer to the weakness of human nature and the enormous (and, the Inquisitor says, unfair) expectation of asking men to have faith: "He who created them rebels must have meant to mock at them. . . . How are the weak ones to blame? . . . Canst Thou have simply come to the elect and for the elect?"

Yes, it seems as scathing and damning an indictment as there could be. But don't stop there.

What People Don't Know (But Should): As I say above, people often miss the point of this and Dostoevsky's other books, laboring under the misconception that somehow he was a nihilist. But through Father Zossima, Dostoevsky's message should be loud and clear. And even before his long monologue, Zossima summarizes his message for the monks of the monastery: "Love one another, Fathers . . . love God's people . . . [Each monk] is responsible to all men for all and everything, for all human sins . . . each one personally for all mankind and every individual man. . . . Only through that knowledge, our heart grows soft with infinite, universal, inexhaustible love. Then every one of you will have the power to win over the whole world by love and to wash away the sins of the world with your tears." He's talking to us, all of us. Now do you think Dostoevsky was nihilistic?

Best Line: A few more inspirational words from Father Zossima: "It's the great mystery of human life that old grief passes gradually into quiet tender joy. The mild serenity of age takes the place of the riotous blood of youth. I bless the rising sun each day, and, as before, my heart sings to meet it, but now I love even more its setting, its long slanting rays and the soft tender gentle memories that come with them, the dear images from the whole of my long happy life—and over all the Divine Truth, softening, reconciling, forgiving! My life is ending, I know that well, but every day that is left me I feel how my earthly life is in touch with a new infinite, unknown, but approaching life, the nearness of which sets my soul quivering with rapture, my mind glowing and my heart weeping with joy."

What's Sexy: Though the novel is sex-free, there is a very charged eroticism in Dmitri's blackmailing of Katarina Ivanovna in Book III, chapter 4, for the money to save her father. Then there's Grushenka, the woman of ill repute, described as having "a supple curve all over her body. You can see it in her little foot, even in her little toe." She's a bad girl, and you'll see it in her speech and actions too.

Quirky Fact: Poor Dostoevsky, literally. Despite all his literary success, his was as rough a life as Cervantes'. When you read Father Zossima's valedictory comments in "Best Line" above and remember the severely improverished, epileptic Dostoevsky, broken in body—but not in soul—by a death sentence commuted at the last minute and the subsequent four years in a Siberian prison, you just hope he's right. Zossima's beatific author certainly deserved such a heaven.

What to Skip: Although this is an all-time great novel, it does have one section that's both annoying and doesn't seem to fit: the fifty-odd pages of Book X, "The Boys," a side story of a dying kid and his cronies. I hated it the first time I read it, and then reread it to make sure, and it really does stink. Why it's there, I don't know. Why you should read it, I don't know either. I say don't.

LEO TOLSTOY
(1828–1910)

∽∽∾

War and Peace
(1869)

Sitting on a table, *War and Peace* looks like half a loaf of pumpernickel and weighs about twice as much. Some people call it the world's greatest novel, but almost everyone else imagines it to be among the least readable works in all of fiction. But the only really hard thing about Tolstoy's masterpiece is lugging it around (I cut my edition into three separate chunks for easy transport). As in his other most famous book, *Anna Karenina,* the prose is straightforward—deceptively simple, actually—and the plotlines a compelling mix of Napoleon's march toward Moscow and the lives and loves of various Russian gentry. Intimidating as it might appear at first glance, the truth is that *War and Peace*'s 1,444 pages will rarely bore you, often amaze you, and consistently entertain you.

And even if you don't agree that *War and Peace* is the single greatest novel ever (my vote would probably be for America's homegrown *Moby Dick*), there's no question that Tolstoy, of all history's novelists, is the great poet of understated grandeur, of historiography, of the Russian character, of military tactics, and of spiritual epiphany. In the same novel, we go from hearing Napoleon, Europe's most notorious sixty-two-inch scourge, addressing captured Russian soldiers, to one of Tolstoy's great human heroes, Pierre, beginning to discover the real essence of life, the "significance of everything" in "a happiness beyond the reach of human forces . . . a happiness of the soul alone, the happiness of loving." In a sense the whole book is about struggling, about Napoleon struggling for material victories and failing, about Pierre and Andrei and Natasha struggling for spiritual ones and succeeding. Distances are traveled: Napoleon marches his army from Austria to Moscow, leaves the Russian capital smoldering, and flees back to France. Andrei, the prince turned soldier turned malcontent, goes from saying cheery things like "Life has become a burden to me of late. I see I have come to understand too much" to finding real understanding in piety and love. If the primary historical arc of the novel is the failure of the French campaign in Russia, the primary human arc is the success of the various characters in their soulful, desperate searches for meaning. If the point of the long novel is transformation—and there is no genre that permits the possibility for so much—then *War and Peace* is the utmost realization, the book in which more changes, grows, and transforms than in any other. And we the reader, in Tolstoy's grip for a month or twelve, can transform right along.

Wisdom is never easy to come by, and it's clear that Tolstoy intimately understood the noumenal, metaphysical longing that agonizes many of us. What makes his book's epiphanies especially meaningful—and convincing—is that the characters have to go through significant gyrations and missteps to reach them. They grope pitiably in the darkness before finding something solid to hold on to (there is a verb in French—a language Tolstoy spoke fluently—that describes the fumbling process and pretty much sums up being in the world: *tâtonner*). The something they eventually come to grasp is invariably a sense of larger meaning: Andrei being wounded in the battle of Austerlitz and gazing at the limitless sky, Pierre learning in the abjection of prison what is truly necessary to life. Tolstoy attributes to Pierre—and to Russians—a special capacity for "seeing and believing in the possibility of goodness and truth, but of seeing the evil and falsehood of life too clearly to be able to take any serious part in life," but he, like Dostoevsky or Dickens, could see all the evil and falsehood without having to reject existence. For Dickens, life could be embraced and goodness found amid the dreck; for Tolstoy as with Dostoevsky, life gives us the capacity to love and to anticipate the infinite bounty of Christian salvation.

In that sense, the characters of *War and Peace* make up an impressive, instructional tableau, there both to remind us of ourselves and to help us reach our full potential. In Natasha we recognize our own restlessness and the need to balance free-spiritedness with devotion; in Pierre we see the tribulations and tragicomedy of the search for meaning and the need to attach one's self to the true essence; in Andrei, the rational and world-weary man, we are confronted with the sublimity of acceptance.

We read Tolstoy to learn the history of Napoleonic Europe and we read Tolstoy to learn what calms a troubled soul and enlarges the human spirit. And the answer to that question of questions, Tolstoy's magnum opus both says and shows, is love.

The Buzz: *War and Peace* is *the* historical novel. Napoleon's invasion of Russia not only forms the backdrop of the book, but Napoleon himself has a number of speaking cameos. The battle scenes, especially the famous clash of Austerlitz, are among the most vivid descriptions of war in the history of literature—and the most realistic. Tolstoy goes to great pains to deromanticize and demythologize both military tactics and the real experience of battle. You finish the scene and see that war is just as ugly, hopeless, and indefensible as you thought it was.

What People Don't Know (But Should): *War and Peace* is a far more literary novel than *Anna Karenina*. Among its many breathtaking stylistic moments, and apart from the "Best Line" below, there are two extended metaphors that need to be highlighted: the first, describing the initiation of the battle of Austerlitz like the movement of a large clock (in a metaphor just as intricate), the second the description of the conquered Moscow as a dead beehive, instinctually defended by the last remaining bees, but queenless, lifeless, and ultimately torched and abandoned by the beekeeper. Both metaphors are imagistic and conceptual tours de force and by themselves make the case that this is Tolstoy's masterpiece.

Best Line: Here is one lovely bit of epiphany; again, though, if you read the entire novel and experience it in the context of Pierre's development, it's that much richer: "While imprisoned . . . Pierre had learned, not through his intellect but through his whole being, through life itself, that man is created for happiness, that happiness lies in himself, in the satisfaction of basic human needs, and that all happiness is due not to privation but to superfluity. But now, during these last three weeks of the march, he had learned still another new and comforting truth—that there is nothing in the world to be dreaded. . . . He learned that there is a limit to suffering and a limit to freedom and that these limits are not far away, that the person in a bed of roses with one crumpled petal suffered as keenly as he suffered now, sleeping on the bare damp earth with one side of him freezing."

What's Sexy: The sexiest passage in *War and Peace*—and, granted, there aren't many—concerns Pierre's eventual wife, Hélène, and his original motive for marrying her. "She was, as she always did for parties, wearing a gown cut in the fashion of the day, very low back and front. Her bosom, which always reminded Pierre of marble, was so close to him that his shortsighted eyes could not but perceive the living charm of her neck and shoulders, so near to his lips that he need only stoop a little to have touched them. He was conscious of the warmth of her body, of the smell of perfume, and heard the slight creak of her corset as she breathed. He saw not her marble beauty forming a single whole with her gown, but all the fascination of her body, which was only veiled by her clothes."

Quirky Fact: *War and Peace* has two epilogues: The first tells what happened to the main characters in the decades that follow the end of the narrative proper. The second, though, is an extended (and mostly rather boring) philosophical essay on history, agency, free will, causality, and divinity. It's one thing to sneak a lot of philosophy into your novel proper (Flaubert's *Bouvard and Pécuchet* is the most egregious example of this), but I find it pretty funny to have one narrative epilogue to your novel and then one purely philosophical one. I guess Tolstoy still had a few things to get off his chest.

What to Skip: For a fourteen-hundred-plus-page book, it's all pretty incredible. Apart from the second epilogue, which is expendable, you can also skip or skim the long disquisitions on military tactics (unless you're interested) and, after reading one, skip the remaining and repetitive lectures on the nature of history (and how it's impossible to do properly). He repeats himself repeatedly.

LEO TOLSTOY
(1828–1910)

⌒⌒⌒

Anna Karenina
(1877)

*A*nna Karenina is highly misunderstood by those who haven't cracked its daunting covers; it's assumed to be a rough go because of its length and supremely prestigious author, but it's actually a beach read—if a rather long one—and one of the great page-turners in classic literature. One could go so far as to say that it resembles a very well written and intelligent romance novel, much akin to *Madame Bovary* (as I indicate in that chapter) but far superior in most people's—and my—opinion. Both plotlines center around a headstrong woman risking everything to cheat on her husband, but Anna's motivations are much more interesting and believable than Emma's, and the end result is considerably more satisfying. *Anna Karenina* is like a sundae with a dollop of *Madame Bovary* as its base and a squeeze of melted *Middlemarch* poured over the top.

Like *Middlemarch, Anna Karenina* explores the psychology of a wife unloved by a husband of seemingly pure rectitude. In *Middlemarch,* everyone but Dorothea knew the straitlaced, dried-up academic Mr. Causabon would wilt the poor girl's bloom; in *Anna Karenina,* it's almost the opposite. Her husband is successful and well liked, and Anna's drama occurs privately. About three hundred pages into the novel (from the end of Chapter 15 into the beginning of 16 of Book III), we get a truly incredible scene. Anna has written to her husband telling him she's left him, confessing her affair with Vronsky, asking only that he let their son go with her. She receives back an envelope filled with money and a letter insisting on her return that says, "Our life must go on as before." To this, Anna erupts with this phenomenal soliloquy:

"He's in the right! In the right!" she said. "Of course, he's always in the right! He's a Christian! He's magnanimous! Yes, the mean disgusting man! And no one understands it except me. No one will ever understand it. And I can't explain it. They say, 'Oh, he's such a religious, moral, honest, intelligent man!' But they don't see what I've seen. They don't know how for eight years he has crushed my life, crushed everything that was alive in me, that he has never once thought that I was a live woman who was in need of love. They do not know how at every step he has slighted me and remained self-satisfied. Haven't I tried, tried with all my might, to find some kind of justification for my life? Haven't I tried to love him, to love my son when I could no longer love my husband? But the time came when I realized that I couldn't deceive myself any longer, that I was alive, that I couldn't be blamed that God had made me so, that I have to love and live."

To me, this is truly amazing, and the point where the novel first becomes really great. She's in the wrong—at least in society's eyes—and he's killing her with what looks like forgiveness but is really just more of the same life-sapping neutrality. And, as Fyodor Karamazov demonstrated when speaking to Alyosha's fellow monks, a human being can only tolerate feeling so dirty, so bad, for so long without breaking. Anna knows what awaits her if she returns: the perpetually patronizing gaze of her husband who pats himself on the back for forgiving her, and her own self-hatred for having to endure it. In one of the most damning lines ever, Anna sums up her predicament: "I've heard it said that women love men despite their vices . . . but I hate him for his virtues."

Whereas I never really felt affection for Emma Bovary, it's not hard to feel for Anna, as one does with Dorothea in *Middlemarch*. And beyond mere affection, you can also feel forgiveness, which is (as with his compeer Dostoevsky's foremost books) among Tolstoy's great themes.

In fact, *Anna Karenina* contains a line that, if taken seriously, would revolutionize human relations and perhaps even save us from ourselves. Anna, having already cheated on her husband, says (apropos of her sister-in-law): "If she can not forgive me my position, I don't want her ever to forgive me. To forgive she would have to live through what I have lived through, and may God preserve her from that." It's an incredible moment. Of course we all know that we should try to put ourselves in other people's shoes before we judge and condemn them, but Tolstoy goes further. He's saying that if we actually could truly understand each other, then in every instance we would forgive. In *War and Peace*, Tolstoy cites an old French saying (clearly unheeded): *tout comprendre, tout pardonner* (to understand everything is to forgive everything). It might not seem shocking at first glance, but consider the implications: the criminal becomes an object of pity instead of hatred, the person who wronged you an object of empathy instead of anger. It's what Jesus preached for us to do (at his best moments), and, like his precepts, even if we can't practice them all the time— and lord knows few of us can—we could at least accept the spirit in the idea: that we can never see the whole picture, that every adulteress had reasons, and even her faults and weaknesses might have had causes of their own that were beyond her control. Acknowledging the deep levels of causality behind our actions and the inherent limits of our understanding could give rise to a lot more acceptance, and that by itself would completely change how most human beings treat each other.

Despite Tolstoy's noble insight (which I fear humanity will never learn), I don't think *Anna Karenina* entirely lives up to its august reputation, either in difficulty or in overall quality. It really isn't very hard, and at times one wishes perhaps that it was a little harder. *Anna*'s epic brother *War and Peace* taxes the reader in ways her romance never does, but the bigger book not only contains more, but reaches further, probes deeper, and gratifies longer than *Anna Karenina* at every turn. But if you'd like a shorter and easier introduction to Tolstoy, or if your days at the beach are drawing to a close, try *Anna*. It's Tolstoy lite.

The Buzz: Dickens' *Tale of Two Cities* might still take the cake for most quoted—but least comprehended—first line (and actually it's just the first few words that people cite—"It was the best of times, it was the worst of times"—leaving out the turns that follow), but *Anna Karenina* follows close behind: "All happy families are like one another; each unhappy family is unhappy in its own way." For a century this was the tersest summation of that universal but eminently perplexing formation known as the family. In recent years, however, Tolstoy's great epigram has had a rival in the first line of the poem "This Be the Verse" by the Englishman Philip Larkin: "They fuck you up, your mum and dad."

What People Don't Know (But Should): There is a second main plotline in *Anna Karenina,* but, truthfully, I wouldn't be surprised if you've never heard about it. It's centered around Levin, a Russian aristocrat who plans on writing a book on the farm laborer and manages in his research to put some of Tolstoy's social and religious principles on display. Levin didn't exist in the first draft of the novel, and, much as I hate to say it, it probably should have stayed that way. At the moment Levin has his great revelation

("He felt something new in his soul. . . . 'To live not for oneself but for God' . . . I have never doubted it or could doubt it. And I am not the only one. Everyone, the whole world, understands that perfectly and has never doubted it and everyone is always agreed about this one thing"), I found myself writing "gag" in the margin. Levin is presented as being quite naive (even though he's autobiographical, taking his name from Tolstoy's Russian first name: Lev), and his epiphanies don't carry the same weight as those of Pierre and Andre in *War and Peace*. If you want most of Tolstoy's insights at their finest—and religious revelations that are genuinely compelling—you'll find them there, not here.

Best Line: My favorite lines are quoted in Anna's outburst addressed above, and the most famous line was discussed in "The Buzz," so to avoid repetition I'll cite Tolstoy's summation of the blow that finally jars Karenin (Anna's husband—as male Russian names don't add the "a" at the end) into reality and out of politics, the "reflection" of reality he always lived in—nice idea:

> Karenin was face to face with life; he was confronted with the possibility that she might be in love with some other person besides himself, and that seemed quite absurd and incomprehensible to him because it was life itself. All his life he had lived and worked in official spheres, dealing with the reflection of life. And every time he had come up against life itself, he had kept aloof from it. Now he experienced a sensation such as a man might experience who, having calmly crossed a bridge over a chasm, suddenly discovers that the bridge has been demolished and that there is a yawning abyss in its place. The yawning abyss was life itself, and the bridge that artificial life Karenin had been leading. For the first time the possibility of his wife's falling in love with someone else occurred to him and he was horrified at it. [Book II, Chapter 8]

What's Sexy: The consummation of Anna's affair with Vronsky gets passed over indirectly and somewhat confusingly (it seems that all the good stuff took place between Chapters 10 and 11 of Book II), and immediately after, she feels more shame than joy. As for Tolstoy's take on it all, it's not much more optimistic or approving than Flaubert's: "There was something dreadful and loathsome in the recollection of what had been paid for by this terrible price of shame . . . [as] the murderer throws himself on the body with a feeling of bitter resentment and as though with passion, and drags it off and cuts it to pieces; so he, too, covered her face and shoulders with kisses. She held his hand and did not stir." Eeks. Perhaps they should have just had a smoke.

Quirky Fact: Even if Tolstoy was sympathetic—and made us sympathetic—to Anna's infidelity and the causes behind it, he still leveled a pretty caustic critique at the Russian elite of the time (among whom he's clearly not numbering himself—note the "in the eyes"): "In the eyes of all fashionable people . . . the role of a man pursuing a married woman, who had made it the purpose of his life to draw her into an adulterous association at all costs—that role has something grand and beautiful about it and could never be ridiculous." That's the first I've heard of a whole sector of society that not only condoned but romanticized attempts to get wives to stray. Even in the greatest seduction novel ever, the 18th-century French masterpiece *Dangerous Liaisons (Les liaisons dangereuses),* the philanderers were ostracized at the end.

What to Skip: Though *Anna* crests to over nine hundred pages, there's really no part that you can skip, unless you want to leave out Levin's final revelations at the end. But as you've already made it that far, you might as well finish. And, again, it's a page-turner, so don't be intimidated.

GEORGE ELIOT
(1819–80)

⌐∾∾⌐

Middlemarch
(1872)

There are smart novels, there are smarter novels, and then there's *Middlemarch*. Page by page by page, George Eliot deploys her intellect—for, yes, she's a she—with both the cocksureness of a chess hustler and the soothing wisdom of a tribal chieftain. Eliot's acknowledged masterpiece stages the various props of fiction less for their own sake as for ornamental pedestals to display the crown jewels of her superhuman perspicacity. No one will dispute that her characters are good, that her plot is engaging, and that she kicks some good metaphors, but it's the searchlight pierce of her understanding, punctuating every few paragraphs, that gives *Middlemarch* its hallowed place in literary history. She plumbs psychology, she crafts her epigrams, she shares her prodigious gifts, and I can't help but think that the authors of most so-called novels of ideas are to her as mere prattling freshmen patiently—if barely—tolerated by their Professor Emeritus of Pre-Socratic ontology.

Here's a famous bit of Eliot insight from literally hundreds (trying to pick one is like trying to pick the best line in *Moby Dick;* something calls out on every page):

That element of tragedy which lies in the very fact of frequency has not yet wrought itself into the coarse emotion of mankind, and perhaps our frames could hardly bear much of it. If we had a keen vision and feeling of all ordinary human life, it would be like hearing the grass grow and the squirrel's heart beat, and we should die of that roar which lies on the other side of silence.

Sure, you might be saying, but do I really want to sip from the fount of pure intellect? Aren't I supposed to be reading a novel? I'm on the beach, gosh darn it! I'll confess: the first time I read *Middlemarch*—I was in my early twenties—the literary side of Eliot's charms were all but lost on me. But the last few times through (and, yes, you can go back more than twice), I realized that even aside from all the cerebral fireworks, the novel-y parts of the book are genuinely gratifying as well.

It begins impressively, with a preface meditating on Saint Theresa of Avila (the great sixteenth-century reformer and mystic), lamenting that "many Theresas have been born who found for themselves no epic life." She's setting up one of her principal ideas: that goodness can happen without fanfare, and that greatness can exist without success. It's clearly one of Eliot's fears, that her efforts will be forgotten, but it also makes the reader, especially the intelligent female reader, begin to ask herself if she too could be a Theresa. By the time Eliot says, "With dim lights and tangled circumstances they tried to shape their thought and deed in noble agreement; but after all, to common eyes their struggles seem mere inconsistency and formlessness," no small number of her idealistic readers are saying, That's me! That's me!

Eliot's invocation of Theresa is a clarion blast to action, to ethics, later to be demonstrated throughout the novel by her dearest character, Dorothea. By the end of the preface, it's clear that Eliot both knew her own capabilities and imagined them in other women: "Here and there a cygnet is reared uneasily among the ducklings." She knew she was a swan, and she challenges you to be one too. In a sense, she is the anti-Nietzsche; where he, like Vautrin in *Père Goriot,* imagined a Superman who would be above morality (an idea especially appealing to boys), Eliot puts forth Saint Theresa, herself, and Dorothea—superwomen operating in and through morality. Somehow I think you'll be more compelled by her version.

That said, Eliot herself had no illusions about the difficulty of doing good things in society, and her characters' various attempts and frustrations trying to enact their visions make up the two main plots of *Middlemarch.* The primary story line concerns the intelligent and ambitious Dorothea, who agrees to marry the much older Casaubon, a scholar writing an interminable study of the "Key to All Mythologies." Dorothea wants to commit her life to helping a great individual with a vital project, but it doesn't take long before she's fully disillusioned, both with the work and the man. Paralleling Dorothea's woes are those of a young and idealistic doctor, Lydgate, who comes to Middlemarch, makes his own bad marriage, and soon finds himself pinned between his reformist ideas for the practice of medicine and a certain domestic insistence for pounds and pence. Throughout the book, Dorothea exhibits a serious ethical and social agenda (she goes on to attempt to reform the villages on her estate), but so do all the primary male characters of the book: Lydgate most pointedly, but also Casaubon with his book (however overreaching); Dorothea's father, Mr. Brooke, with his naive political ambitions; and even Ladislaw, Casaubon's dissipated nephew, who adopts a life of good deeds, in part to try to win over his uncle's wife. (Meanwhile the "normal" girls, Lydgate's wife, Rosemond, and Dorothea's sister, Celia, are the ducklings, remaining just silly or self-serving.)

Aspirant as Eliot's characters are, no one in *Middlemarch* goes unfrustrated by reality. It's as if, in her cosmos of characters, Eliot wanted to explore the legion ways that one can try to impact recalcitrant life, and yet her gimlet eye didn't allow her to believe that any attempt would be more successful than any other. One feels Eliot's virtual corset, not only as a woman in the society of the time, but as an active mind desiring social change. She needed a commune to run or an England to minister primely over; hers was not a mind for the 19th century—or for any other where individuals are so highly constrained by their environs.

One last element of *Middlemarch* deserves mentioning, especially to all of you grad students, might-be grad students, or ambitious workaholics biting off more than anyone should chew: Mr. Casaubon, the least appealing character in *Middlemarch,* is a warning to you all. His life's work isn't done, will never be done, and is a telling example of how some projects—especially if they're sizable in the first place—can expand to include far more than you could ever handle. I always tell my students that thought is like an impact on the surface of a still pond: once it pierces, it reverberates and reverberates. Pick your topic prudently; prick the water with a needle; don't throw a cinder block in. And decide when enough's enough. As with this book, which almost got away from me many times, there's always more to read, more to do. You have to keep an end in sight, even if you know it's a provisional end—and it's almost certain to be. But the flip side, caring so much you never complete, is the very definition of self-undoing. As Eliot says, thinking of the dying but far-from-finished Casaubon: "Are there many situations more sublimely tragic than the struggle of the soul with the demand to renounce a work which has been all the significance of its life?" Don't let it be you.

The Buzz: The best-known fact about George Eliot is that, like the French writer George Sand, she was a 19th-century woman writing under a male pen name. Eliot's real name was Mary Ann Evans, and she seems to have picked George as a tribute to her longtime lover. (Curiously Sand also took the given name of her paramour of the time for her first nom de plume: Jules Sand. Subsequently she changed it to George.) Apart from that, you normally only hear people talking about how Dorothea's desire for the life of the mind—as a way out of the constricting gender roles of 19th-century England—led her to the disastrous marriage with the bloodless wanker Casaubon. Eliot's larger point I'll relate in the next section.

What People Don't Know (But Should): Although there is plenty of overt feminism in the contrasting portrayals of the enterprising Dorothea with the shallow and self-serving Celia and Rosemund, the most delicate (and I think strongest) bit of feminism comes near the end of Book IV when Eliot says, "Nature having intended greatness for man . . . has sometimes made sad oversights in carrying out her intention," i.e., she occasionally put that greatness in a woman. Talk about a bait and switch! Remember, her readers of the time thought they were reading a man; Eliot saw the irony of the situation and sharpened her dagger with it.

Best Line: Besides the "grass grow" line I already quoted, I want to sneak in one more for biographical reasons: she describes mornings in Rome where "autumn and winter seemed to go hand in hand like a happy aged couple one of whom would presently survive in chiller loneliness"—a beautiful line in itself, but made more poignant by the aging Eliot's checkered love-life. She had long been part of a happy couple, scandalously living for over twenty years with a married man, the intellectual George Henry Lewes. Following Lewes's death, however, she married a man twenty years her junior, who then either jumped or fell tragically from their hotel balcony during their honeymoon. Eeks.

What's Sexy: The main relationship, Dorothea's with Casaubon (that academic "bladder for dried peas to rattle in") is written to be among the least sexy in history. The only hint of hanky panky is Casaubon's understanding that the marriage entitles him to "receive family pleasures and leave behind him that copy of himself that seemed so urgently required of a man—to sonneteers of the sixteenth century." Is "family pleasures" a euphemism? Since it comes before the offspring, it seems to be.

Quirky Fact: Halfway through the book, a sheepdog belonging to a farmer makes a two-page appearance and happens to bear the unfortunate name Fag. Language drifts unaccountably over time, resulting in some unfortunate anachronistic associations (take the 18th-century novel *Fanny Hill* for another example). Of course, "fag" still means cigarette or cigarette butt in England, but it's still pretty hard on the eye.

What to Skip: It's pretty hard to find anything to skip in *Middlemarch,* but I would advise skipping the rest of her novels, at least until you've reread this one a few times and want to break out. *Silas Marner, Adam Bede,* and even *Mill on the Floss* are all considerably lesser achievements than *Middlemarch,* though *The Mill on the Floss* is the best of the rest.

HENRY JAMES
(1843–1916)

꧁꧂

The Wings of the Dove
(1902)

James's has been called—the concept is itself Jamesian—a
sensibility so fine that no idea could violate it.

—Frank Kermode

There might have been no writer in history more constipated
than Henry James (okay, John Lyly maybe, but who remembers him?). I don't mean literal constipation, though that could
have been the case as well; I mean textual. I mean sentences more
undulant, imbricated and tortuous, in both the conventional
and the etymological sense, coiled and halting, meticulous, at
times redirecting, at others self-referential, self-disclaiming—
disclaimers not appended to every single bit of prose ending in
a period, mind you, only to the notable majority—laden with
commas, alternately gratifying and, by a certain blush, maddening, if but to begin to adumbrate the peculiarity of their
realization.

Yes, that was my attempt at a Jamesian sentence, but honestly,
I can't come close (and, for the record, I'm speaking here about
the later Henry James, of his last three and most distinctive novels: *The Ambassadors, The Wings of the Dove,* and *The Golden
Bowl.* The earlier Henry James reads rather like Edgar Allan

Poe—especially in the short stories and novellas—or like a Flaubert/Tolstoy disciple in *Portrait of a Lady*.) Since I can't give you a decent imitation of his hypotactic habits, I'll quote a representative sample so you know what you're getting into.

> It was doubtless because this queer form of directness had in itself, for the hour, seemed so sufficient that Milly was afterwards aware of having really, all the while—during the strange indescribable session before the return of their companions—done nothing to intensify it. If she was aware only afterwards, under the long and discurtained ordeal of the morrow's dawn, that was because she had really, till their evening's end came, ceased after a little to miss anything from their ostensible comfort.

Perusing dear old Henry James, it often feels like you're wading through cooling magma. So why read an author that makes Faulkner seem breezy? And, more pointedly, how?

The why is perhaps more easily answered than the how. In a clause, James is our Proust. He is as close an approximation as we—meaning America and England, his birthplace and adopted home, respectively—have produced to the fineness of Proust's sensibility, his elegance and convolutedness of expression, the refinement of his critical gaze, his aesthete's arched eyebrow, and his especial and deep appreciation of art, furniture, and women's dress.

Furthermore, there are elements in James that one won't find in Proust. First, a kind of jowliness to his delivery; you sense the speaker's Oxbridge dewlap, it always sounds as if he was perorating from a Louis XV chaise, raising his head from the antimacassar to make sure you're not sleeping, finding you are, but continuing apace, undaunted. One has to roll James' sentences around in the mouth a bit, I would like to say like a Château

d'Yquem Sauternes, for they *are* sweet—and clearly expensive—
but rather more like a fin de siècle port that's taken on a bit of
must *(to the back of the palate, one good swush, there you go . . .)*.
James' sentences don't go down easily, as if they're too chewy and
toothsome to be just words, but read enough of them and you
will sense why: because they're also time. The late Henry James
paced and populated his sentences such that they require a wran-
gle, they can't and won't be transparent or smooth or easy (a trick
Milton strove for as well) and so they're never immediate; they
exist in time—they took time and they take time—and thus they
virtually become things.

The thingyness of the Jamesian sentence, its indebtedness to
the mandible and maxilla, then, is one of the signature reasons
for reading his last three novels, but of course it's also what makes
all three nearly unreadable. How to do it? With the sentences
themselves there's really no mystery—read, parse, mull, reread,
remull—but perhaps one could at least wean oneself into his sensibility by, I don't know, spending extended time with peacocks
or curators or castrati? If none of those are available, you might
simply have to surrender, Nestea plunge into his velvet prison,
perhaps even giving up on the idea of reading any of them *as*
novels, i.e., as in something you begin and later finish. For by the
time you do finish (and trust me, I say this from personal experience), you might well have forgotten what the book was ostensibly about, who the characters were, and why you're reading
something so incalculably snooty in the first place.

But that's it in a nutshell: though he applies the epithet to one
of his characters, the later Henry James was himself the "ele-
phantine snob," and the novels simply allow him to promenade
you around his drawing room, explaining the paintings, the fab-
rics, the gossip on the marquises coming to dinner. Never will
you have read anything where the word "taste" comes up more
often, nor, apart from zoology or Hemingway's Africa novels, the

word "herd." As with his earlier books, each novel is likely to contain a displaced American using wealth as her invitation to the party and her ignorance like the spilling of a drink on someone's gown to prompt a conversation. And yes there will be other Americans, never portrayed uglier, and the expiring echoes of the old European courts. And there will be furniture, "the language of the house itself"—always meticulously described. But none of these will be as relevant as James himself, and his overall effect of—in all senses—class.

But one can also detect, amid the luxury and finery, a hint of tragedy, a hint of anxiety—and perhaps this, too, is one of the subtle pleasures in these last novels. In *The Golden Bowl*, James summarizes an old aristocratic lady, saying, "She looked as if her most active effort might be to take up, as she lay back, her mandolin or to share a sugared fruit with a pet gazelle." My contention: James wanted to be that lady, and the joy and agony of reading his great novels lies in feeling both the success and failure of the realization.

In his lifetime James could already feel that the future was America, and he tried to make himself America's antipode, cleaving to a past so mythic and upwardly immobile it might have existed only in his imagination. But he could never not be American—always the barbarian who learned which fork to use—and he knew it; he had no crest, no device, no heraldry, despite his family's fame (his father was a famous theologian and his brother the philosopher William James). His only defense was to out-elitist the elite, and we would do well to think of his last books as artifacts of overcompensation. Because maybe in the end that's what saves him from being only a peacock, what makes him almost likeable: our pity for the exile, our knowledge of how it must have galled him every night, how having "cleaned" his teeth (as I'm sure he affected saying), he still had to fall asleep remembering where he was born. He was never actually a member of the class he sought so to describe; he could never be "the man in the world least connected with anything unpleasant."

A note on the selection: I picked *The Wings of the Dove* from among the last three novels not because it's the best—I actually think they're all pretty equal—nor because it was James' favorite (*The Ambassadors* was), nor his last (*The Golden Bowl*), but because I think it's the one you're most likely to finish. It's the story of the moribund Milly Theale, an unbelievably wealthy young American, who goes to Europe to get some culture before she bites it. She befriends Kate Croy, who is secretly engaged to Milly's old heartthrob, Merton Densher (and what romantic hero isn't named Merton?). Croy tries to get Milly and Merton to marry, thinking that after the sick girl's death, Merton will come back to her loaded. There are a few plot twists, and I don't want to give away the ending, but, again, my guess is that you'll enjoy the book less for the story and more for James being James.

One final reason that I picked *The Wings of the Dove*: the back cover of the Penguin Classics edition has two elements that would have mortified our petulant perfectionist. First, they cite what could be the worst sentence James ever penned (speaking of Milly's dough: "She couldn't dream it away, nor walk it away, nor read it away, nor think it away. . . . She couldn't have lost it if she had tried—that was what it was to be really rich." *Quel fromage!*) Then they summarize the novel with a blurb that could be grafted onto a Harlequin without changing a word (I'll leave that for you to find). So in a way it's a silver (outer) lining: if you utterly detest the novel, you'll at least be able to get a good laugh at the author's expense.

The Buzz: In James' preface he sums up, as only he could, Milly Theale's plight and the thrust of the novel (if thrust it does): "The idea, reduced to its essence, is that of a young person conscious of a great capacity for life, but early stricken and doomed, condemned to die under short respite, while also enamoured of the world; aware moreover of the condemnation and passionately desiring to 'put in' before extinction as many of the finer vibrations as possible, and so achieve, however briefly and brokenly, the sense of having lived." Otherwise said, she wanted to see some art before sloughing off the mortal.

What People Don't Know (But Should): I've mentioned that the last three novels mark the late Henry James stage—generally considered the apex of his achievement—but there is a novella bridging the earlier and later work that, to my mind at least, possesses the insight and sophistication of the later period but remains considerably more readable—and much shorter: *The Spoils of Poynton*. If you'd like to dip your toe into the Jamesian tarn, this is the point at which to do so.

Best Line: Here's one that summarizes James' feelings on money: "His want of means . . . was really the great ugliness," and one on the origins of sensibility.

> "Men are too stupid—even you. You didn't understand just now why, if I post my letters myself, it won't be for anything so vulgar as to hide them."
>
> "Oh, you named it—for the pleasure."
>
> "Yes; but you didn't, you don't, understand what the pleasure may be. There are refinements—!" she more patiently dropped. "I mean of consciousness, of sensation, of appreciation," she went on. "No," she sadly insisted—"men *don't* know. They know in such matters almost nothing but what women show them."

What's Sexy: The first two paragraphs of "Book Ninth"—two full pages, eighty-odd lines' worth—are where it gets down, I think. My margin note from an earlier go-through reads: "the 'sex scene'—worst ever!" but truthfully, I'm not positive anything actually does or did take place. Kate is said to have "come to him . . . to stay, as people called it" and I'm pretty sure this is an oblique-in-the-extreme euphemism but I can't claim to be certain. In any case, it's somehow perfect for Henry James that you're not sure the sex scene is a sex scene, for we wouldn't want actual blood to ever flow through the veins, now would we?

Quirky Fact: The "was there or wasn't there?" mystery in the last entry played itself out in James' life as well. Until recently he was thought to have been a lifelong celibate (and there are letters that suggest as much), but now there's evidence that he might have done a little vase-polishing with some of his male friends.

What to Skip: The bad news is that no part of the novel stands out as dispensable; the good news is that if you stop along the way, it's no great tragedy.

MARCEL PROUST
(1871–1922)

෨෨෨

Remembrance of Things Past
(1922)

Proust is long—not just long, but the *longest*: over thirty-three hundred pages, one novel. It's so long, deciding to read it is like committing to move into a studio apartment with a lover you've never met. All that time in the same room—you'd better hope you like each other.

Not many people hang around to find out. The normal reader gets through the first fifty-odd pages—which include the most famous scene, where Proust dips a French pastry called a madeleine into a cup of tea—and no more. Some unfortunates quit after *Swann's Way,* the first book of eight (seven in English) but one of the least interesting. Only the truly persevering realize that the longer you read *Remembrance of Things Past,* the more you feel its magic, the more it pulls you into its unique world, the more it does seem like a love affair. We've all had this kind of relationship; it's weird but fascinating—your friends don't really get it, but some of the things he says, his wry wit, his subtle sexiness, you can't shake him, and he has gotten deep, deep under your skin.

The story line, given the girth, isn't as complicated as you might think (though there was a Monty Python skit of a game show in which contestants had to summarize it in thirty seconds or less). Basically it follows the biography of the protagonist, Marcel, an almost-exact stand-in for his author, from his early days as one of literature's foremost wusses, through some romantic difficulties, to his final realizations of the meaning of things and what he's finally going to write a book about (sixteen seconds, yeah!). The first volume, *Swann's Way,* refers to one of the walks he would take along two paths leading from his childhood home (Monsieur Swann being the neighbor whose life will prefigure Marcel's). In the second book, *Within a Budding Grove* (I much prefer the French title, *A l'ombre de jeunes filles en fleurs*—in the shadow of young girls a-blossom), the sickly Marcel is sent to the seaside to convalesce, and there he meets a troupe of girls, including Albertine, whose vexed relations with Marcel will drive the principal arc of the fifth and sixth volumes, *The Captive* and *The Fugitive.* The third volume, *The Guermantes Way,* covers Marcel's young adulthood and infatuation with his noblewoman neighbor. The two-part fourth volume, *Sodom and Gomorrah,* has his most direct treatment of homosexuality. And, finally, in the seventh and last volume, *Time Regained,* Marcel has the realizations that I'll discuss shortly.

That's the plot in bas-relief, but the thing you have to understand about *Remembrance of Things Past* is that it's not really about the events; it's about sensations, about memory, about time, jealousy, habit, lying, relationships, hetero- and homosexuality, and, above all, about the interior life being the only significant one. Proust is the foremost advocate and greatest poet of the déjà vu, the déjà-felt, the déjà-experienced, and only, he argues, when memory involuntarily (or, to a lesser extent, willfully) links disparate moments of our lives together, overlaying two completely different times, can we catapult out of time, holding ourselves and the past fixed and free as if there was no movement of the clock hand, no change, no death. That is the art of living for Proust, and for him it's the only game in town. Sought or unbidden, it's only these mnemonic connections that allow us, as the French title, *À la recherche du temps perdu,* suggests, to succeed in the search for lost time.

In his pursuit of these states, Proust is relentless, dispensing with all the easy joys and distractions that make up the vast majority of what the rest of us call life. He would have us pull away from society as he did—famously shutting himself up in his bedroom and lining it with cork to cancel out noise—and devote ourselves to looking inward instead of being content with meaningless interactions outside of ourselves. To him, the import of everything external is an illusion; we project it there, but only to deceive ourselves. Love, for example, is a thing we want to feel, so we imagine it into being and attribute it to others, believing that our lives depend on our feelings for them and theirs for us (whereas for Proust the value of love is only that it makes the lover suffer, and suffering creates the strongest memories!). Even friendship and socializing in general, he says, are complete wastes of time, simple reprieves from the harder work of seeking the truth within. In other words, better order some cork.

Yes, this sounds extreme, and anyone who hasn't felt the dissatisfaction with reality that Proust expressed will have a hard time empathizing. But at certain times most of us *have* felt that dissatisfaction, even if we train ourselves to move on and look on the brighter side. But for Proust, there is no bright but the inside: the great possibility of the interior man, living and feeling despite whatever vulgarity and chaos prevailed in the outer world. The entirety of Proust's novel asks the question: what matters? And his answer is the self, only the self. And once you commit to memory, further experience becomes irrelevant. Each of us has already lived enough to know all and everything, if only we had been able to get the meaning out of the time we've already been alive. There's no point in gathering more data; instead we should simply go back, searching through all the time that we would otherwise lose, looking to restore its value, attempting to make the things we've lived announce their full significance.

That's the message of *Remembrance of Things Past*, but ultimately I think it's a little gaga. I don't deny that we could reexamine our lives and glean a lot more out of them, but my guess is that most of us would get more out of simply trying to live our presents and futures with our eyes open, instead of sifting through the past to try to get things back. And the ironic thing is that Proust demonstrates just how to do that. Ultimately, he teaches us a lot more by the continual demonstration of his mode of living than he does by the explanation of his mode of recollecting.

That's because no one, in the history of man, felt more than Proust. Like a taut cilium on a microscopic tendril, he could detect the finest, most subtle of all life's vibrations. No person was ever as attuned to the sensory input of smells, sights, sounds, and feelings. It's maddening at times; you imagine him as a youth in his Lord Fauntleroy outfits weeping because Mamma didn't kiss him goodnight or because the hawthorns smell so amazing, and part of you wants to take him out to the ball field and kick his pathetic ass. And yet Alain de Bouton is right (though he got the reasons wrong): Proust *can* change your life. Watching Marcel live, seeing him experience over the course of thirty-three hundred pages, we too get more and more attuned. We can learn from his example, taking his opus grandissimus as a tutorial in feeling, a how-to for being in the world, a user's manual of our empirical and emotive organs. We might not want to follow Proust in much of the crazy stuff that he did, but his book is nevertheless the greatest primer in being sensate to this life we keep on living.

The Buzz: The only thing anybody ever seems to mention from *Remembrance of Things Past* is the scene where Proust dips the madeleine into a cup of herbal tea, tastes the mix of flavors, knows it's evoking something for him (ultimately a morning from his childhood when his aunt offered him a similar morsel), and begins to have the first of his déjà-experienced moments that are the crux of the novel. Conveniently for most readers, the description starts at page 48, where Marcel's other epiphanies don't come until after page 3000. So when people refer to Proust's madeleine, all they mean is a trigger to a memory that bridges two separate moments in time or, in Proust's theory, takes us out of time. That's some pastry.

What People Don't Know (But Should): While Proust's madeleine has become as iconic (and clichéd) a literary reference as Don Quixote's windmills, ultimately for Proust it wasn't the only or even the most important incident leading to the fundamental epiphany in the novel. Late in the last book, Marcel loses his footing on some flagstones and a few pages later presses a stiff dinner napkin to his cheek. Each moment creates the déjà-experienced effect, and only after the napkin does he piece it all together and understand their true meaning and import. His realization comes in a flash: the subject of the book he's been wanting to write (his quest for which is one of the minor plotlines) will be the past, his past, excavated and revivified as only Proust can. The madeleine tipped him off to sense memory, but the napkin and the tripping on the flagstones trigger both the book's conception and culmination. So the next time you hear someone refer to Proust's madeleine, ask them what they thought of his napkin.

Best Line: Proust is one of history's foremost thinkers and stylists, so over the course of thirty-three hundred pages, he notches an enormous number of exceptional lines. He's rightfully famous for being a little long-winded, so I'll pick this one simply because it manages to reach sublimity almost immediately: "I could, if I chose, take Albertine on my knee, hold her head in my hands, caress her, run my hands slowly over her, but, just as if I had been handling a stone which encloses the salt of immemorial oceans or the light of a star, I felt that I was touching no more than the sealed envelope of a person who reached inwardly to infinity."

What's Sexy: Although Proust has myriad great lines on sex, love, desire, and girls in bloom (though he's really talking about young boys), Marcel isn't a participant in either of the two most explicit scenes. In the first, the snooping Marcel hears Charlus, the gay nobleman, getting it on with Jupien the tradesman— don't miss the extra emphasis on the joys of mansex:

> From what I heard at first in Jupien's quarters, which was only a series of inarticulate sounds, I imagine that few words had been exchanged. It is true that these sounds were so violent that, if they had not always been taken up an octave higher by a parallel plaint, I might have thought that one person was slitting another's throat. . . . I concluded from this later on that there is another thing as vociferous as pain, namely pleasure, especially . . . in the absence of fear of parturition.

In the other, Marcel's friend Aimée tells him that Albertine enticed a laundry girl to "caress her with her tongue along the throat and arms, and even on the soles of her feet" before the two girls get naked and start pushing each other in the water. And yes, almost everyone turns out to be gay in *Remembrance of Things Past*. Now why would that be?

Quirky Fact: At the beginning of the fourth book, *Sodom and Gomorrah* (also called *Cities of the Plain*), as Charlus and Jupien recognize the truth about each other, Proust gives us high literature's first demonstration of gaydar, likening (in quite a few extended passages) homosexual men's ability to find each other to a rare tropical flower's ability to attract the particular type of passing bee necessary for its "fertilization."

What to Skip: Okay, this is kind of crazy, but I went through the whole thing a second time and figured out page by page what you can dispense with. The truth is, I think you can skip each of these sections without really missing much but repetitions of plot or observation (all numbers are inclusive and refer to the classic Moncrieff/Kilmartin translation):

Vol 1: 109–14, 133–45, 269–99, 316–74 (read 325, though), 394–445, 496–501, 633–93

Vol II: 11–39, 49–82, 91–132, 136–87 (read 151), 193–293, 381–408, 414–622, 657–795, 799–end

Vol III: 5–57, 61–134, 141–53, 157–79, 191–96, 200–249, 268–484, 488–691, 698–708, 718–36, 744–884, 951–1033, 1044–1083

That cuts the thirty-three hundred pages by 50 percent, which still leaves about a *Harry Potter* and a half.

JAMES JOYCE
(1882–1941)

✎∿∿✎

Ulysses
(1922)

James Joyce's *Ulysses* might well be the biggest pain in the ass literature has ever produced. But if you know what to skip—and don't worry, we'll Swiss the cheese—and get a few pointers as to what to focus on (hint: organ meats), not only will you be able to join the leagues of those who hail *Ulysses* as among the best novels of all time, but no obnoxious snob will be able to lean over his black-and-tan and make you feel bad because he's read it and you haven't.

Now, apart from getting the supercilious to shut their traps—always a worthy motive in my book—there are myriad solid reasons why you'll want to devote a month of bedtimes to the *Citizen Kane* of English-language novels. Here are three: because we can't be as smart as Joyce, we can't notice as much as Joyce, and we can't be as funny as Joyce.

Reading *Ulysses* is like taking a tour of Ireland's most famous brain—a tour agonizingly lacking in a good Baedecker, I'm afraid. But if there's been a more potent combination of intellect and raunch, turn of phrase and eye for detail, sense of the profoundly transcendent and the poignantly ordinary, and both the verve and audacity to push the novel form further than it has ever been pushed before or since, there's no record of it. If you never give *Ulysses* the old post-college try, you'll deprive yourself of the wit, wisdom, sex, boozing, punning, ogling, pontificating, experimenting, and mental masturbating of one of history's great geniuses. There are novels I like more than *Ulysses*—*Moby Dick, One Hundred Years of Solitude, Suttree*—but there might be no novel that has more in it than *Ulysses*. Between its far-spanned covers, you'll be fishing in some deep and turbulent swells, but trust me, your stringer will be full, fuller than you could have imagined, and you'll know you didn't begin to catch a zillionth of the fish that were there. To change metaphors, *Ulysses* has the mother lode, and I entreat you to pick up your pan, prospect, and get whatever nuggets manage to trickle down the river.

The greatest impediment, however, to the appreciation of *Ulysses* is, sadly, Mr. James Joyce. I get the sense that Joyce was one of those guys whose cerebral gifts were indisputable to everyone but himself, and, like a lot of such boys, he felt the need to show them off again and again and again. Much of *Ulysses* is simply an intricate puppet show, with each little doll repeating, "The author's brilliant; the author's brilliant." This is both the tragedy and irony of the novel, for if you take away all Joyce's esoteric and occultating parodies, impersonations, games, and machinations (all, again, in service of showing you how protean his pen was), what's left is the book's spun gold—and one of the sweetest, most human things you could ever read. In trying so damn hard to put his intellect on display, Joyce made his magnum opus almost impossible to read for most people and somewhat mortifying to those who actually do. We pity him for having to try so hard, we feel his adolescence, his insecurity, and our cheeks rouge for the little guy.

But that's when you have to remember Bloom, the counterpoint to all the euphuism and vain virtuosity that mars *Ulysses'* jewel. Some people say that Dublin is *Ulysses'* hero, but to me there's no dispute: it's Bloom, the novel's central character and source of much misreading. Mr. Leopold Bloom, everyman extraordinaire, is much maligned by many readers as a bumbling dolt, but he is really just a sensitive, tentative, intensely thoughtful and woman-appreciating laughingstock, who spends a day walking around the capital trying (but failing) to avoid the man who's shtupping his wife, buying some offal, having a drink here and there (while being mocked by the other patrons), attending the funeral of a man he barely knew, and giving us access, in Joyce's deeply tender portrait, to one of the most finely drawn internal landscapes as has ever appeared in fiction.

To me the entire project of liking *Ulysses* comes down to two things: first, appreciating the rich, sensitive portrayals of Bloom and its other main character, Stephen Dedalus (who's a lot less annoying than he was in *Portait of the Artist as a Simpering Dork,* I mean, *Young Man*); and second, paying attention to the glories of Joyce's dialogue—among the all-time greatest. At its best, *Ulysses* patterns what's human on all vital grounds, none ignored. At his worst, it's simple rodomontade: festooning for Joyce's ego, frustration for us.

A few more general hints for reading *Ulysses*: Don't worry about what you don't understand—and there will be lots. Keep a library copy of *Ulysses Annotated* nearby to help with the obscure bits you want to know, though one of the redeeming things about *Ulysses* is that its most human bits are also its most comprehensible. That said, try to read it in a pleasant environment, so that when Joyce gets annoying, which he will, you don't get too put out (I always read him while sunbathing; almost nothing can put me in a bad mood while sunbathing).

Since there's so much going on in *Ulysses,* I decided to break it down, as I did with many of the old guys, chapter by chapter (note that condescending Joyce-heads call the numbered sections "episodes"—whatever). Here's the main plot of each chapter, some especially great stuff to look for, and a few of my favorite quotes:

Chapter 1: Stephen volleys bons mots with his saucy friend Buck Mulligan. My favorite bits include the meditations on God and faith; the commentary on Irishness and Irish art (a "cracked servant's lookingglass"); the hatred of the body ("Who chose this face for me? This dogsbody to rid of vermin"); Stephen's ripostes, Mulligan's rants, the locker-room-speak and, of course, the drinking ("Today the bards must drink and junket"; "The sacred pint alone can unbind the tongue of Dedalus").

Chapter 2: Stephen teaches a history class, then goes to pick up his wages and delivers a letter. We get more access to his inner workings, especially his embarrassment at getting the money. I love when he calls Kingston pier "a disappointed bridge" and the line "I fear those big words . . . which make men so unhappy." This chapter also has the famous quip: "History is a nightmare from which I am trying to wake."

Chapter 3: This is mostly narrated from inside Stephen's head as he walks around. It's consistently confusing (lots of stuff to look up), but the important thing to understand is that the chaos represents thought and need not be understood line for line. Some reflections contra desire, including references to Aquinas calling sex "morose delectation" (wow), though a girl is said to have "apple dumplings." At the end, he picks his nose and wipes the booger on a rock.

Chapter 4: Bloom is now the principal, and he's introduced with this delightful description: "Mr. Leopold Bloom ate with relish the inner organs of beasts and fowls." Ha! Our organ-eater goes and buys a kidney to eat for breakfast—nice—comes home, cooks and eats it, and then goes and takes a dump, using the prize story in the newspaper to wipe with(!). Though we will know him better further on, let yourself love Bloom. At this stage, his interior processes sound overly similar to Stephen's—a weak spot in the book—but this changes later. Note his devotion to his wife, Molly, despite his playfully wandering eye (and the fact, which we learn in the next chapter, that he's swapping love letters with a woman named Martha).

Chapter 5: Now it's Bloom's turn to walk around, and we see him trying to glimpse a rich woman's stockings (very funny), reading the latest missive from Martha, and thinking generally lascivious thoughts. At the end, he goes to a bathhouse to take a tubbie.

Chapter 6: Bloom gets in a carriage with Stephen's father and they go to a funeral. Some great lines: on sex ("Give us a touch, Poldy. God, I'm dying for it"), on burials ("The clay fell softer. Begin to be forgotten"), and on a drunk's nose ("a lot of money he spent coloring it"). We touchingly find that Bloom's father was a suicide and get some hints about Molly's licentiousness and infidelity.

Note: Joyce's point in these three Bloom chapters is that every bumbly, wrinkled, pudgy everyman on the street might very well be having quiet, poignant thoughts and carrying on epistolary romances and in general living as full an internal and sexual life as you, me, or anyone else. It's not hard to feel the massive humanness of Joyce's document. It has much, perhaps infinite, soul.

Chapter 7: Bloom goes to a newspaper's offices; Stephen arrives as well but they don't interact. Joyce taxes our patience with various writing experiments—easily skipped, though the section on the grandeur of Rome being sewers ("It is meet to be here. Let us construct a watercloset") is pretty funny. And "Dublin. I have much, much to learn" is beautiful—and reminiscent of Balzac's comments on Paris. Only use I've ever seen of the adverb "biscuitfully." He uses it to describe murmuring.

Chapter 8: Bloom walks around some more, thinking about sex and Molly (and her manager, Blazes Boylan—she's a singer—with whom Bloom believes she's having an affair. And she is). Near the end, he accidentally sees Boylan on the street and has to flee. There's a fair amount of Bloom's interior, but sadly most of it is less probing and moving than what we get in later chapters. The whole chapter can be skimmed or skipped outright, though I do love the line "Beauty: it curves: curves are beauty" right after a nice erotic paragraph and the reference to "two fellows who would suck whiskey off a sore leg"—my kind of people.

Chapter 9: Stephen and Mulligan hone their tongues amid some intellectuals at the National Library—way too much wit for wit's sake. Amid the obscurantism, though, there are some great takeaway lines—on Goethe ("the beautiful ineffectual dreamer who comes to grief against hard facts"), art ("the supreme question about a work of art is out of how deep a life does it spring . . . all the rest is speculation of schoolboys for schoolboys"), and, of course, sex (cf. the Shakespeare anecdote and Mulligan's scurrilous "play:" *Everyman His Own Wife or A Honeymoon in the Hand*)—but probably not enough to justify careful poring, unless you're a fan of high-level, superdork pedantry (and, yes, I often am).

Chapter 10: Consists of the meanderings of various Dublin characters—including Stephen—but has little that's moving apart from Bloom being the butt of everyone's jokes. One of Molly's lovers describes them cheating on him virtually under his nose

("She's a gamey mare and no mistake") but then pays the "sheeny" a rare compliment: "He's a cultured allroundman, Bloom is . . . there's a touch of the artist about old Bloom." There's an amusing scene of Bloom buying romance porn for Molly, and this great quote on America: "What is it? The sweepings of every country including our own." Now Stephen's inner thoughts are very heavy-duty and easily distinguished from Bloom's. Still, my attention flagged throughout. Skim this one.

Chapter 11: Bloom has dinner, and, cat away, Molly hooks up with Boylan. Overall it's way too obscure, but, as always, there are a few great lines. My favorite might be: "Woman. As easy stop the sea. All is lost"—was ever the suspicion of being betrayed expressed as laconically and tragically? But I also love the subtle implications of "last look at mirror always before she answers the door"; the language of love (with Martha) paragraph ("tipping her tepping her tapping her topping her"); the glorious lines 1133–38 ("by . . . went Bloom, soft Bloom"); and, of course, the flatulence interlarding the final few pages—classy.

Chapter 12: Just when things were getting unbearable, comes 12 with its winged wit and you're back in the saddle. This is really Joyce at his best: phenomenal dialogue in the bar (look up all the magnificent and often salacious or booze-related slang), but the virulence against Bloom is incredible. Keeps sounding like Dublin will descend on him like a pack of dingoes. Abundant hysterical one-liners—"syphilisation"; "Could you make a hole in another pint?"; England, the great empire "on which the sun never rises"—far too many to transcribe. We also cryptically learn about Bloom and Molly's son who died. Throughout the chapter there are various lists that you can skim or skip if they're not to your taste. Either way, Chapter 12 will leave you laughing till it breaks your heart.

Chapter 13: This chapter is about Gerty MacDowell, a young woman whom Bloom sees in a park, catches him looking, decides "she wanted him because she felt instinctively that he was like no-one else," lets him look up her skirt and masturbates while fireworks go off overhead (in unison with their simultaneous orgasms—egads). If it sounds as awful as improbable, it is. Even if it's a parody of romance novels, it's unbearable. You start to get the impression that Joyce can't write women, including— dare I both denigrate and anticipate—Molly's famous monologue in the last chapter.

The problem with skipping it, though, is you'll miss out on some great Bloom internal thinking—especially about masturbation ("the strength it gives man. That's its secret"), seduction ("First kiss does the trick. The propitious moment. Something inside them goes pop"), orgasm ("kick the beam"—a curious phrase), etc. So focus on Bloom's thoughts and try to skim quickly through the rest.

Chapter 14: Prepare for aggravation. This chapter, where Bloom bumps into Stephen and Mulligan and they have some drinks, is a compendium of parodies of literary styles, but somehow I don't think you'll be any more impressed or amused than I was. If you opt not to skip it (though I think you should), you'll find another reference to Bloom's dead son, one to Stephen being a virgin, some ribald puns on the playwright Beaumont's and his partner Fletcher's names (among others), a witty plan for Mulligan to be the fecondateur in a eugenics farm, and this lovely line to Stephen: "Those leaves . . . will adorn you more fitly when something more, and greatly more, than a capful of light odes can call your genius father." You will also find a reference to the upapa, that anthropophagic avian of medieval bestiaries, and will probably be especially annoyed by this line: "For they were right witty scholars." Yeah, yeah, Jimmie, we get it.

Chapter 15: This chapter is written as a play in which the potted Stephen ultimately gets punched out before Bloom comes to his rescue. It's reminiscent of *Faust* in style but far more randy and much more annoyingly obfuscating. Much of it is hallucinations by Bloom where various women he's tried to seduce make lubricious appearances, and eventually Boylan comes to confess his and Molly's shenanigans. It also contains the first use of the phrase "pisses cowily," a summary quote by Bloom ("I am a man misunderstood"), as well as references to spanking, VD, S/M, condoms, the clitoris, brothels, fetish, scat, enemas, crossdressing, how Bloom sits to pee, and yet more that I can't type from blushing. This chapter isn't good reading, but it is pretty incredible that all this stuff is in a canonized work (Pynchon's *Gravity's Rainbow* is the only other novel generally held to be a classic that goes so far). Oh, and since we're talking smut in high lit, in line 3909 Joyce gives us an anticipation of the famous liver masturbation scene in Philip Roth's *Portnoy's Complaint*. And here I thought Roth came up with that one—not that I keep tabs on this sort of thing.

Chapter 16: Continuing from the end of the last chapter and reintegrating the "play" with reality, the heretofore mostly separate tales of Bloom and Stephen merge fully, as Bloom takes the stumbling Stephen and tries to dry him out by getting him a meal. There's some decent dialogue—"Why did you leave your father's house? To seek misfortune"; "We can't change the country. Let us change the subject"—and this great one-off: "his chamber of horrors, otherwise pocket." Not the most spectacular episode by a long shot—easily skipped.

Chapter 17: Written entirely as answers to scientific-sounding questions (a device that grows wearisome quickly), this chapter, where Bloom offers Stephen a place to stay but is declined and goes to bed, was apparently Joyce's favorite. We learn that Stephen last bathed the previous October (let's hope he showers); details of Bloom's father's suicide but not the precipitating reasons; some nice observations of the galaxy ("the heaventree of stars hung with humid nightblue fruit"; "so-called fixed stars, in reality evermoving wanderers from immeasurably remote eons to infinitely remote futures in comparison with which the years, threescore and ten, of allotted human life formed a parenthesis of infinitesimal brevity") as well as a lovely list of affinities between the moon and woman ("her splendour, when visible; her attraction, when invisible"); the similarities and differences of Stephen's and Bloom's pissing; a plan for a rectal plug; Bloom's inability to resolve if there are bungholes on Greek female deities, but his realization that, yes, that is another man's imprint (and crumbs, and "flakes of potted meat") on his and Molly's bed; the names of all Molly's men, which Bloom responds to with, in order, envy, jealousy, abnegation, and finally equanimity; and SPOILER ALERT the forensic details of their dead son, aged eleven days. This last detail will register here hopefully as it does in the chapter: as a sudden shock after so much science, still expressed clinically but with full emotional resonance. It perhaps makes the chapter worth reading as a buildup to that single moment, though it is a sizable slog.

Chapter 18: Molly's all-but-unpunctuated, 1,600-line, 4,391-word stream-of-consciousness soliloquy is, more than anything, what *Ulysses* is famous for. For the record, let me say that I don't really find it particularly compelling—or even that representative of how thinking works (especially compared to Virginia Woolf's depictions—cf. the chapter on *To the Lighthouse*). Take the highly improbable and laughably lascivious lines 903–4, for example;

what woman calls it her "hole"? But realism aside, Molly's monologue was still a massive breakthrough in the history of literature; no one had ever published anything like it stylistically. Plus,
Molly's as potty-mouthed, jaded, and manipulative as Chaucer's
Wife of Bath, and that's saying something. There are naughty
bits on virtually every page, representing a wide range of sexual
tastes (hers, Boylan's, Bloom's), but sadly there's little else that's
moving—until the end. Then, with less than a full page left,
we get the story of her getting Bloom to propose. Here, finally,
warmth—machination, yes, but warmth. Joyce speeds the rhythm
up, Molly's in the groove, the lack of punctuation becomes more
than a gimmick, and it ends with just the kind of emotion and
feeling that I'm a sucker for. It's a book that frequently forgets its
heart for its head, but it closes, exquisitely, with a touch of love.

The Buzz: While Joyce's competitor for the title of supreme modern novelist, Marcel Proust, is known for the beginning of his
book, Joyce is known for the end of his. The last chapter of
Ulysses, Molly Bloom's internal soliloquy (discussed above), is
often thought to be the first example of modernist, so-called
stream-of-consciousness writing. There had actually been quite
a few narrations of characters' thoughts to themselves throughout the history of literature (and even Joyce had already used
stream of consciousness in *Portrait of the Artist*), but Molly's was
the longest and among the most nonlinear—thus supposedly
more analogous to actual thinking.

   Ulysses is also famous for being the first modern novel that
narrates a character taking a dump. I say "modern" because Sancho also takes one in *Don Quixote.*

   Finally, Joyceans will tell you that each chapter of *Ulysses* cor-
responds to a section in Homer's *Odyssey* (you can see what's
what in any companion volume). The connections are so loose,
though, it really doesn't help your understanding of anything to

know what Homer chapter Joyce had in the back of his mind. It's just a little more of Joyce's game playing.

What People Don't Know (But Should): Though many people think of *Ulysses* as the foremost novel of modernism—which it might be, but who cares?—I'd rather say that it is the foremost novel of three things: drinking, dialogue, and organ meats. And it's not bad on sex, either, if a little teenyboy and pervie.

Best Line: I've already cited a ton of lines—though really only a tenth of what I'd like to have—but I've kept one up my sleeve for good reason. If there's one thing Joyce would want to be associated with, it's Ireland. At one point one of Stephen's cronies says, "Our national epic has yet to be written," and clearly Joyce knew it—and wanted that fixed. But to write the epic of Ireland, you have to mention Guinness. Here is Joyce's ode to the brewers (to whose names he adds "bung") and the brew that has so affected his people:

> Terence O'Ryan heard him and straightway brought him a crystal cup full of the foamy ebon ale which the noble twin brothers Bungiveagh and Bungardilaun brew ever in their divine alevats, cunning as the sons of deathless Leda. For they garner the succulent berries of the hop and mass and sift and bruise and brew them and they mix therewith sour juices and bring the must to the sacred fire and cease not night or day from their toil, those cunning brothers, lords of the vat.

What's Sexy: Sex suffuses *Ulysses,* as it does Joyce's letters, which are riggish in the extreme. The most sustained naughty bits are in Gerty's chapter (13), Bloom's hallucinations—though they're more encyclopedic than technically sexy (15)—and Molly's soliloquy (18). See the chapter breakdowns for more specifics.

Quirky Fact: Among the myriad: do kids of today, when they call shoes "kicks," know that they're citing Joyce? In Chapter 10, a drunk is described as having "a swell pair of kicks on him."

What to Skip: Hopefully the chapter breakdowns I've included allow you to decide for yourself what to plow through and what to take my word for.

THOMAS MANN
(1875–1955)

◡◠◡

The Magic Mountain
(1924)

One should be impressed, intrigued, and not a little horrified when the author of the cinder-block-sized novel you're holding says, in his two-page preface, "Only the exhaustive can be truly interesting." But so it goes with Thomas Mann's hefty, challenging, certainly exhaustive and admittedly sometimes exhausting masterwork, *The Magic Mountain*.

Chronicle of ultraweenie Hans Castorp's visit to an Alpine sanitorium (for tuberculosis, not mental illness), *The Magic Mountain* is an extended, exceptionally probing meditation on human infirmity—psychological *and* spiritual, of course, the kinds we all suffer from. The setup of the novel is brilliant: tuberculosis, a lung disease at one time notoriously difficult to diagnose and cure (though all but stamped out since the 1940s), becomes an analogy for what ails us in general, and the sanitorium a test lab for Mann to show us his experiments and search for a cure. In the beginning, Hans arrives at the Magic Mountain (the nickname for the sanitorium) simply to visit his afflicted cousin, but soon our hero's health comes into question as well. Early on, when the fabulous Dr. Krokowski examines Hans—who has protested that he is perfectly healthy—the doctor's jocular response indicates the stakes and range of the novel's primary metaphor: "Then you are a phenomenon worthy of study. I, for one, have never in my life come across a perfectly healthy human being."

From the get-go, Mann is ready to diagnose modern man as a whole: "In an age that affords no satisfying answer to the eternal question of 'Why?' 'To what end?' " a man lacking "the heroic mold" will find himself subject to "a certain laming of the personality . . . a sort of palsy." Palsied, lamed, paralyzed by a lack of understanding of what's driving it all—sound familiar? *The Magic Mountain* is scalpel-sharp brilliant, and the nuance of its social and metaphysical investigations and critique makes other "philosophical" novels like Sartre's *Nausea* or Camus' *The Stranger* read like child's scribblings on a kindergarten wall.

Now I've said that Hans is an ultraweenie, and that needs a little explanation. Somehow the modernist novel became a Petri dish for milquetoasty male protagonists, and some of the best novels have the biggest wimps: Marcel in *Remembrance of Things Past*, Stephen Dedalus in *A Portrait of the Artist as a Young Man* (but less so in *Ulysses*), and Hans Castorp in *The Magic Mountain*. You'll remember Marcel saying that he couldn't go to sleep unless his mama would kiss him goodnight; in Hans's case, "it went against his grain to eat butter served in the piece instead of in little fluted balls." And work, for Hans, "stood somewhat in the way of his unclouded enjoyment of his Maria Mancini [cigars]." That *is* the unfortunate thing about work, isn't it?

Unlike modern lit's other great weenies, however, Hans's role in the novel isn't actually so central, even though he sets the actions in motion. Mann calls him "mediocre" at one point and "simple" at another, and it's clear that he saves his philosophical and psychological insights for the mouths of other characters: Dr. Krokowski and his research into the "chemical illness" of love;

the sanitorium's Hofrat (director) and his hangman's humor; Hans's fellow patient and spiritual mentor, Settembrini, and his inspired, Enlightenment antagonism to disease, death, and renunciation (all the subjects of his great project the "encyclopedia of suffering"); the jaded intellectual Naphta's political/mystical radicalism, etc. Then there's the ever-ironic, ever-profound, somewhat detached and often very wry voice of the narrator, speculating on such things as the unaccountability of memory, the threshold between matter and nonmatter, the fact that the actual embodying of life out of immateriality is our first and fatal Fall, etc. If you go through *The Magic Mountain* underlining the ideas and insights that move you, there will be ink on almost every page.

But don't get me wrong; *The Magic Mountain* will also entertain. The most important chapter, "Snow," could actually be read as an all-time magnificent short story in itself (maybe not a bad idea if you want to test the Mannian *Wasser* a little). Caught in a snowstorm that threatens to kill him, Hans finally figures out what he thinks and feels, sorting from all the ideas and experiences he's been inundated with during his stay on the mountain. It's a culminating moment, both for Hans and the reader, though both humorously and tragically (as I mention in "The Buzz" on page 282), Hans the not-quite-hero immediately begins to forget most of what he learned. Oh well.

Eventually our mediocre, simple, but by-now beloved weenie will descend the mountain to fight in World War I, but even the critical decision to leave the sanitorium doesn't take his spirit as far as it travels in the snow. It's in the nature of the miracle he sees there, not unlike the flakes themselves that triggered it, to dissolve at the moment of grasping. Amid the falling white, a rainbow appears, and Hans recalls hearing an Italian tenor whose voice "gushed a glorious stream to witch the world with gracious art." I suspect that is what Mann set out to do as well, and *The Magic Mountain* is his singular, staggering, incomparable, witching triumph.

A note on the translation: Many people prefer the new Wood translation (Everyman Books), but I had already read the old Lowe-Porter version many times and know it so well, I couldn't make the switch. A good bookstore will probably have both, so you can compare a few passages and see which you prefer (try one of the long paragraphs in "Snow" as your test).

The Buzz: Mann famously advised anyone who wanted to understand *The Magic Mountain* to read it twice. I, of course, feel that if you're not going to read a book twice there's no point in reading it at all (unless it's a dishwasher installation manual or the like). Still, people do seem to get frustrated by what's called the "ambiguity" of the narration, meaning that you can't necessarily pin down which of the philosophical positions represented in the book the narrator or author adheres to. Big friggin whup, if you ask me. Yes, there's classicism, Enlightenment rationalism, Romanticism, hedonism, radicalism, and a brace of other isms convincingly articulated and/or demonstrated in *The Magic Mountain,* but to me, the fact that Mann's giving us a smorgasbord to choose from is an achievement not a defect. I could be biased, but Hans' Romantic epiphany in the snow felt like the strongest message of the book, underscored by the fact that, by that evening, the things he had thought and felt were "already fading from his mind." Hans can't hold on to the all-is-connected, all-is-beautiful sensation, but I think Mann is challenging us to try.

And, just to set the record straight, if you take your time, you won't feel like you *need* to read *The Magic Mountain* twice; you'll just feel like you're excited to.

What People Don't Know (But Should): "Phthisis and concupiscence go together" (try writing that without a spell-check!); in other words, illness and sexual desire are linked—a theme Mann takes up again in *Death in Venice*. In *The Magic Mountain*, the two twine around the various men's obsessions with Madam Chauchat (whom I will address further in "What's Sexy" on page 284) and anticipate and parallel elements of J. G. Ballard's outstanding novel *Crash*. Where Ballard brilliantly skewers postmodern society by making its eroticism center around technology—the characters come to need to crash their cars to get turned on, and forgo genitals to make love to each other's scars—Mann, half a century earlier, sexualizes illness. He has various characters speak of "the heightening and accentuation" of Madam Chauchat's "physical parts by disease." They call her "the lovely, contaminated creature" and fetishize the visible blue veins of her breasts and arms. At the end of the Walpurgisnacht party scene, Chauchat herself expresses to Hans (in French) the erotic connection: "Let me feel again the exhaling of your pores, destined for . . . the tomb, and let me die, my lips on yours" (my translation). In both *Crash* and *The Magic Mountain*, the libidinal cathexes are part metaphorical, part literal; they are meant to diagnose society's hidden obsessions, our fascination with the abject, as when the consumptive Frau Stöhr "began to talk about how fascinating it was to cough. . . . Sneezing was much the same thing. . . . That was the sort of pleasure life gave you free of charge." Once we see how far-reaching Mann's metaphor of illness is, the full effect of his novel can be felt.

Best Line: Although there are legion magnificent one-liners (Settembrini's "my great complaint is that it is my fate to spend my malice upon such insignificant objects," for a cheeky example), Mann reaches his stylistic crescendo with this discussion of the scientific basis of living.

What was life? No one knew. No one knew the actual point whence it sprang, where it kindled itself. Nothing in the domain of life seemed un-caused, or insufficiently caused, from that point on, but life seemed without antecedent. . . . Death was only the logical negation of life, but between life and inanimate nature yawned a gulf which research strove in vain to bridge. . . . What then was life? It was warmth, the warmth generated by a form-preserving instability, a fever of matter . . . too impossibly complicated, too impossibly ingenious in structure. It was the existence of the actually impossible-to-exist, of a half-sweet, half-painful balancing, or scarcely balancing, in this restricted and feverish process of decay and renewal upon the point of existence. It was not matter and it was not spirit, but something between the two . . . It was a secret and ardent stirring in the frozen chastity of the universal.

What's Sexy: Our young protagonist, at one point described as "not without all and any experience in the realm of the illicit" (nice litotes!), nonetheless is far from the ladies man. He does develop a crush on the fetching young Kirghiz-eyed Clavdia Chauchat (hottest name in literature?), who comes and goes from the dining room with the bang of the screen door that she lets slam and leaves a scent of orange blossoms everywhere. Both the smell and the sound eventually begin to evoke autonomic arousal from young Hans—the first literary use of Pavlovian erotic responses, to my knowledge.

In general, though, we get the sense that Herr Mann was not so big on the coital act. Early on, there's a pretty comical scene in which Hans hears some sounds that he seems to recognize from somewhere, "a struggling, a panting and giggling, the offensive nature of which could not long remain hidden to the young man." Then later, as Hans reads a book on micro-organic embryology, Mann quips that there is "no conceivable trick or absurdity it would not have pleased nature to commit by way of variation upon this fixed procedure." Ah, variations on the "fixed procedure"—now if that doesn't sum up the love dance, what would?

Quirky Fact: *The Magic Mountain* was first published in 1924 and is among the earliest novels to mention X-rays (which were in use by the turn of the century). At one point, Hans gets his chest examined and then is allowed to put his hand behind the screen (the device of the time) to see "what is hardly permitted man to see, and what he had never thought it would be vouchsafed for him to see: he looked into his own grave . . . the finely turned skeleton of his own hand . . . and for the first time in his life he understood that he would die." We are all used to X rays by now, but this helps us realize how odd it must have been for the early patients to see their own bones.

One other medical quirk stands out: There used to be a "treatment" for tuberculosis called "pleural shock," a zapping of the lungs with current. The uncannily bizarre feeling it elicited is described by one of the sanitorium's patients: "I heard myself laughing as it went off—not the way a human being laughs—it was the most indecent, ghastly kind of laughing I ever heard. Because, when they go over your pleura like that, I tell you what it is: it is as though you were being tickled—horribly, disgustingly tickled—that is just what the infernal torment of the pleura shock is like." Dude . . .

What to Skip: I find the scenes with Naphta overly pedantic and dry; if you wanted to skim or skip these, you could certainly live without the chapters "The New Comer" and "The City of God"—though read the last page of the latter for a summation of the ideas.

FRANZ KAFKA
(1883–1924)

ᏙᎪᏙ

The Trial
(1925)

In college, in my equally limited senses of humor and business acumen, I wanted to open a company: Godot's Pizza Delivery. Somehow I don't think our phones would have been ringing off the hook, but there's an interesting phenomenon behind the college-boy silliness: certain literary works are so familiar and iconic that they can be made into jokes, even if people barely read the sources anymore. And books that famous, especially if they're famous for only one thing, almost beg to be summarized instead of being read. If I told you that in Samuel Beckett's best-known play, *Waiting for Godot,* two guys sit around on a virtually empty stage doing just that—waiting for someone named Godot—and that Godot never comes, we know nothing about him, and that that's a metaphor for something or everything in modern life, you'd pretty much get the play, even if its finer points are lost in the encapsulation. Not many books can be summed up so easily, and most that can are just as easily dispensed with, but there's a select short list of literary greats that are nonetheless perceived to be one-chord wonders: *Don Quixote, The Trial, Moby Dick* to many people, perhaps even *Hamlet* or *Macbeth.* And even if close listening reveals polyphony, these books tend to remain famous for their most prominent trait. They risk being ignored in the shadow of their reputations.

Franz Kafka's *The Trial* might actually be foremost among these. Hallowed as the ultimate expression of modern bureaucratic and technological alienation and frustration, *The Trial* crafts a world that's the fictional equivalent of those automated "service" lines that snare you in their labyrinths and never get you where you want to go (Press 1 for this, Press 2 for that, Press 3 if you want to car-bomb company headquarters . . .). Kafka hadn't finished the novel when he died in 1924—it was edited to "completion" by his friend Max Brod a year later—yet the precision with which his descriptions fit myriad twenty-first-century situations becomes both an argument for reading it and something of a case for not having to. His message—that we're all trapped—is impressively clear and accurate, but in some ways, the book suffers because it's still so dead-on this many decades later.

The setup is simple: The protagonist, Josef K, wakes up and finds himself arrested—not arrested in the sense of being hauled off to prison, merely notified. Even more mysteriously, he's not told of his crime; he is simply told that he's under arrest, that the officers (who happen to look like ordinary people) don't know why, and that's that. At first K thinks it's a practical joke being played by his colleagues from the bank, but eventually he is given a court date (though no exact address or time), and he's forced to acknowledge that the arrest is real. From there, he struggles to figure out what's going on in his case (which everybody seems to know about), and though he is embroiled deeper and deeper, we never learn of what he's accused.

Start to finish, *The Trial* is an allegory, meaning that the elements of the story are symbolic and meant to be read for deeper significance. So when K has to go seek his courtroom on an out-of-the-way block that's dominated by a single structure but can find nothing official-seeming at all until he's finally in the attic rooms (it turns out almost all attics in *The Trial* contain court-rooms) and a washerwoman says he's been expected, it sounds absurd but is supposed to be telling (of the near impossibility of finding justice, of Big Brother always watching, of law being impersonal and obscure, of guilt being inescapable, etc). I honestly doubt that many of you are going to want to tease out the subtle meanings behind too many of Kafka's details, and truthfully, it probably wouldn't be worth it. The overriding allegory of being arrested without ever knowing why, of feeling guilt without overt cause, of being unable to make headway with or get answers from the system—that's what's important about *The Trial*. Like Kafka's famous short story "The Metamorphosis" (in which the protagonist awakens to discover that he has turned into a cockroach), the art and glory of *The Trial* is more in the setup than the execution. It's one of the few great novels that could work as a play—and Orson Welles' film adaptation isn't bad, either.

That said, there might never have been a novel to foretell the future so chillingly and accurately—and so far in advance. Though *The Trial* has passed its eightieth birthday, it still reads like it was written today. So if you want to be reminded of just how inhuman and alienating life can be, or if you can take comfort knowing that it felt that way in 1920s Europe as well, let *The Trial* impress you with its meticulous tableau.

The Buzz: Not much ambiguity here: everyone seems to know that *The Trial* is a parable of modern life, as described above. Thus the word "Kafkaesque" refers to inscrutably complex, confusing situations.

What People Don't Know (But Should): Kafka didn't finish the novel and wanted it destroyed, and its final section does seem rather abrupt and perhaps a little forced.

It is also perhaps the classic novel with the least emotion in it. At the beginning, K is frustrated with and perplexed by what's happening to him, and he responds with anger and impatience. As the novel progresses, however, he demonstrates less and less surprise at the oddities of his situation and eventually acquiesces to his fate without objection. Yes, it's an allegory, as we see Kafka's character become almost as inhuman as the forces that beleaguer him.

Best Line: These two parts of K's indignant speech in the court-room stand out: "What has happened to me is not just an isolated case . . . How are we to avoid those in office becoming deeply corrupt when everything is devoid of meaning?" I also love this summation by the all-knowing court painter: "They could replace the whole court with a single hangman."

What's Sexy: One of the foremost surprises of *The Trial* is just how racy it is. Sex keeps sneaking in again and again, as when K gets to take a look at what appeared to be a judge's manual, and it turns out to be a dirty novel with pictures: *What Grete Suffered from Her Husband.*

Yet more odd—or perhaps symbolic—is that most of the women in the book are downright trampy (which makes me wonder how *The Trial* continues to find its way into so many high school literature classes). The washerwoman who shows K the courtroom is quickly "lying on the floor with [a] student" in front of everyone. Later we discover that, though married, she's at the physical disposal of the lawyers and judges—and even offers herself to K.

Leni, the servant girl of the old lawyer who wants to help K, also throws herself at him with no provocation. She too has many lovers, as she "finds most of the accused attractive." Even the little girl at the painter's studio lifts her skirt to K before she runs off. Symbolic though it may be, it's hard to know what to make of the curious behavior of the women in Kafka's world.

Finally, I'd be remiss if I didn't mention this rather unfortunate description of K planting some decidedly wet ones on his neighbor: he "kissed her on the mouth and then over her whole face like a thirsty animal lapping with its tongue when it eventually finds water." Ick.

Quirky Fact: Kafka died at forty of starvation, as various illnesses made his throat so sore he couldn't swallow. That's awful.

What to Skip: Of the ten chapters, two can be skipped: Chapter 4 concerns goings-on in K's apartment building that aren't central to the story, and Chapter 5 has the three policemen who arrested K being whipped in the building's junk room because K has complained about them—it's overly absurd and unnecessary.

VIRGINIA WOOLF
(1882–1941)

❧

To the Lighthouse
(1927)

When life sank down for a moment, the range of experience
seemed limitless.

Some literature is necessary precisely because we don't and
can't scientifically understand our own brains. Yes, you'll tell
me, there's a field called neuroscience for that, but I just don't
buy the second half of the word. Science? Please. We're talking
about the brain here, not what keeps a skyscraper standing or
how to span the Hudson. We might know how it fires, how
trauma can deprive us of functionality, what sections light up
when we think about torrid sex or hot fudge sundaes, but how an
aggregate of molecules, responding to electric signals through
nervelike ganglia, can reason and err and invent and suffer and
remember and dream and long—no. No matter how clear the
MRIs are and how many electrodes they hook up, the magic of
what makes the meat conscious, capable of thinking and feeling—much less of loving—is going to remain obscure. By the
time man understands man, another organism will have taken
our place as the highest species in the known, and it won't understand itself either.

For this reason, Virginia Woolf deserves garlands for her

finest books, *To the Lighthouse* and *Mrs. Dalloway* (and, by the way, these two are *much* better than any of her others). Both novels show us thinking and feeling as they really are, allowing us to see their complexity and nuance more clearly than in any other literature—or perhaps any other books. Though Molly Bloom's interior monologue in *Ulysses* is supposed to be the apex of modernist stream-of-consciousness writing, to me it reads like someone representing thinking, not entirely like thinking itself. One can still sense Joyce's hand (and libido) behind the language. But with Woolf the illusion is stronger, more convincing, much more real. Somehow her disjointed choppiness and herky-jerk redirecting oddness (a kind of controlled stylistic epilepsy) seems more like the actual disjoint of our mental functions. Time and again I can't help but think, "Ooh, that's good. That's it. That's how it really is. How did she know that? How did she hear it that clearly, much less restate it?" To my mind no writer had as great an instinctive sense of the movement and fabric of consciousness as Woolf, placing us deftly inside the awesome aware pulp of her characters' minds and hearts.

We also feel her characters so strongly because they themselves feel so strongly. Here the puppeteer risks showing the strings as we see figure after figure with similar propensities probe and fret in deep, dark emotional waters. The novel centers around the Ramsays—he a philosopher of modest repute, she an entrancing, regal beauty—their eight children, and some of the guests at their summer house. But apart from the drama over whether they can and will make an excursion to the lighthouse (which represents, among other things, a self-sufficiency that few of the characters possess), the novel is really about the emotions of each individual as they struggle with themselves and one another. They are all deeply emotive: from Mr. Ramsay knowing he can think to the level Q but disconsolate that he can't reach R (see "Best Line" on page 294); to his wife who wants to esteem him but can't quite; to their children who must fight both to resist and to forgive the father's tyranny; to the communal bewitched fascination with Mrs. Ramsay; to the Ramsays' friend, the painter Lily Briscoe, her romantic fantasies and renunciations, and her fraught relationship with her art (the major theme of the novel's last section). You can't help but marvel at how much access we get to virtually everybody in *To the Lighthouse*.

Unfortunately, Woolf's unorthodox mode of representing her characters' thought and emotive processes can get annoying if you try to piece the sentences together logically. Don't bother; let the overall impressions leave their moth-wing traces on you and move on. The point is to get a sense, emotional and intellectual, of what's going on inside the character, not to get a pure understanding. What you're after is a feeling of communion, a little Vulcan mind-meld, as it were. Sometimes it's going to work, sometimes you're going to think that Woolf was batty or just jotting down words at random, but what she was after is elusive, not something one can make an exact science. Nor will we ever.

The Buzz: Virginia Woolf is rightfully held to be one of the pioneers and most important figures in the development of the so-called "modernist" novel. I'm not the biggest fan of that category since it's typically only negatively defined—novels that don't use traditional narrative, that aren't realist, naturalist, etc.—but at least it points to what otherwise might be called "experimental" writing, as if all writing isn't a kind of lab project. Historically, Woolf's technique was absolutely original, but practically it's just cool and challenging, and different from anything else you've probably ever read. (If I can recycle the neuroscience analogy, Woolf was effectively a self-taught surgeon who lets you stand in the operating room and watch.) As books in English go, Woolf's *To the Lighthouse* and *Mrs. Dalloway* are mentioned alongside

Joyce's *Ulysses* as the earliest and strongest developers of the interiority and "stream of consciousness" (which for Woolf isn't so flowing) that I talk about above.

What People Don't Know (But Should): In Part III of the novel, "The Lighthouse," it becomes clear that Lily Briscoe is in some ways the heroine of the novel and that her painting is as primary a metaphor as the lighthouse itself. Through that optic, we can see this line as a declaration of Woolf's intent to try to record both the particular thing and the majesty of all things (one of my favorite themes): "One wanted, she thought, dipping her brush deliberately, to be on a level with ordinary experience, to feel simply that's a chair, that's a table, and yet at the same time, It's a miracle, it's an ecstasy."

Best Line: Mr. Ramsay's Q/R problem (mentioned above), takes up the last five pages of section VI in Part I, "The Window," and is, I think, the single most impressive depiction of a man reflecting on his life in all literature (please, drop this book and go get hers!). Below is but a taste, but note how Woolf intermingles Ramsay focusing his thoughts, Ramsay being distracted, and some truly extraordinary narrative descriptions. And this is just a quarter of it!

> If thought is like . . . twenty-six letters all in order, then his splendid mind had no sort of difficulty in running over those letters one by one, firmly and accurately, until it had reached, say, the letter Q. He reached Q. Very few people in the whole of England ever reach Q. Here, stopping for a moment by the stone urn which held the geraniums, he saw, but now far, far away, like children picking up shells, divinely innocent and occupied with little trifles at their feet and somehow defence-

less against a doom which he perceived, his wife and son, together, in the window. They needed his protection; he gave it them. But after Q?

. . . He dug his heels in at Q. Q he was sure of. Q he could demonstrate. If Q, then is Q—R— Here he knocked his pipe out, with two or three resonant taps on the handle of the urn, and proceeded. "Then R . . ." He braced himself. He clenched himself.

Qualities that would have saved a ship's company exposed on a broiling sea with six biscuits and a flask of water—endurance and justice, foresight, devotion, skill, came to his help. R is then—what is R?

A shutter, like the leathern eyelid of a lizard, flickered over the intensity of his gaze and obscured the letter R. In that flash of darkness he heard people saying—he was a failure—that R was beyond him. He would never reach R.

What's Sexy: Throughout Part I, especially in section V, Mrs. Ramsay's radiance is described in some of the more original and funky ways since the French poet Lautréamont (in 1869) famously wrote that a boy was "beautiful like a chance encounter of a sewing machine and an umbrella on an operating table." The longer, more impressionistic of Woolf's descriptions you'll have to read for yourself, but here's one of the great compliments of all time, Mr. Bankes's Yeatsian comment to Mrs. Ramsay: "Nature has but little clay like that of which she moulded you."

Beyond this, there are some romantic leanings from various characters but nothing especially sexy, though Woolf does mention the "arid scimitar of the male." . . .

Quirky Fact: Woolf was born the same year, 1882, and died the same year, 1941, as her modernist rival, James Joyce.

What to Skip: The second part of *To the Lighthouse*, "Time Passes," seems almost intended to be skipped. It attempts to represent a chronological fast-forwarding of ten years with an extended, often seemingly confused and garbled description of wind moving through the summer house, noting in parenthetical asides SPOILER ALERT that Mrs. Ramsay and two of the children, Prue and Andrew, have died. This information is repeated in Part III, however, as if she knew we'd either skip Part II or nod off on the davenport trying to read it.

WILLIAM FAULKNER
(1897–1962)

∽∾∽

The Sound and the Fury
(1929)

American literature sounds its supreme crescendo with Faulkner. *Moby Dick* might be our finest novel, but Faulkner is our finest novelist. In the history of this rebels' nation, no writer took as many risks, had so many pay off, had as much style, was as elaborate in his language, or was as simultaneously difficult and rewarding as Faulkner. He's daunting, he's demanding, and he was often drunk off his rocker, but nobody thinks like him, nobody's dialogue is better (his only rivals, in my mind, are Joyce and Cormac McCarthy), nobody's characters are more vivid and original, and nobody but Dostoevsky plumbs as deep psychologically. He's utterly masterful with America's nuanced, complex post–Civil War race relations—managing to be sympathetic to both sides at once—but more than anything, he diagnoses and documents the insidious residuum of Appomattox, worked into the blood and sinew of generations of the South. There is no question that Faulkner is the foremost poet of the effects of losing the Civil War on the group psyche of the former Confederacy. His stories are of a people and a place, of the below-the-fold half of a country that, as a whole, acknowledges him among its most golden sons.

So who would have thought that the most famous novel by

the foremost American writer would be the one where he seemed the most hell-bent on pissing the reader off? I mean, who begins their novel with an appendix (don't those come at the end?), much less an appendix that makes very little sense but without which you can't really figure out what's going on in the book that follows? (It's a list of characters and their histories, but good luck making heads or tails till you read the rest.) And then there's the two-page-long sentence. *Two pages long? For no good reason?* Have mercy.

And in case that wasn't enough to have you repacking the Amazon mailer, *The Sound and the Fury* proper commences with a section told from the point of view of a seemingly autistic narrator that switches back and forth among multiple different times without really letting you know, and has two characters with the same name, one a male Harvard student, the other his sister's illegitimate daughter. I honestly love Faulkner, but to me that's unconscionable behavior. Joyce ticks me off enough with his shenanigans, but at least the crazy parts of *Ulysses* aren't central to your understanding of what's going on (*Finnegan's Wake* is another story—why even bother?). But with *The Sound and the Fury,* if you don't figure out the Benji-narrator and the time/name problems, the whole section is a wash.

Why would Faulkner go so far out of his way to ruffle our wisteria? The best I can figure is that he was thirty-two when he wrote it, not yet heralded, had a few much more straightforward novels under his belt *(Soldier's Pay, Mosquitos,* and *Sartoris),* was getting rattler-bit by an ego larger than Mississippi, and just said, "Screw it; I don't give a cat's ass. I'm doing what I want." Then he remembered the end of the "Out, out brief candle speech" speech in *Macbeth*—"a tale / Told by an idiot, full of sound and fury, / Signifying nothing"—and the light clicked. Since an idiot in Faulkner's era could mean someone mentally handicapped, it must have just hit him like this: "You're all so gee-dee impressed

by modernism? Well, I can top that. How's *this* for modernism?!"
And thus Benji the narrator, and thus our problem.

There's no question that Faulkner managed his narrator
deftly and with enormous originality (in fact, Benji shares a lot
of traits with the autistic protagonist of *The Curious Incident of
the Dog in the Night-Time*, even though autism wasn't diagnosed
as such until the late 1930s). But the sad truth is that, for most
readers, Benji only detracts from the pleasures of the rest of the
novel. Without the Benji section, *The Sound and the Fury* is utterly incredible—and somewhat understandable to boot—but a
lot of people get so lost in Benjispeak and the confusion of times
and names that they never find that out.

I'd recommend that you skip ahead to the Quentin section,
but if you choose to gut it out, here's a little schema I made to
help you understand the shifts and interconnectedness of both
the Benji section and the others:

1. Benji. April 7, 1928. Italics tend to signal shift in time. Both
   Quentins present. Shifts among four primary times: 1928,
   Benji with Luster at the golf course; 1902, Benji with Versh;
   1913, Benji with Dilsey and T. P.; 1898, Benji with Caddy and
   the brother Quentin. There are a few more time shifts but
   they're minor.

2. Quentin. June 2, 1910. Italics signal shift in speaker, flash-
   backs with mother/father. He's the only Quentin.

3. Jason. April 6, 1928. No italics to worry about. The only
   Quentin is Caddy's daughter.

4. Unnamed narrator. April 8, 1928. Straightforward.

The Sound and the Fury's first basic story line—which the appendix will "tell" you—is that Quentin the Harvard sophomore-
to-be is a bit overattached to his sister, Caddy. He can't get over

that she's been with other men (note his repeated, plaintive "Why did you have to?" to her and "Did you ever have a sister?" to his male friends), so he decides to relieve his angst by taking himself to the river with pockets full of flatirons. His chapter takes place on his last living day, and cuts back to scenes with Caddy in the past, including some riveting exchanges with one of Caddy's men. Faulkner's novels frequently contain a southern gallant or two, and no one, I mean no one, makes swashbuckling studs like he does. This section is poignant in the extreme. Quentin slides back and forth on the razor-limen between protective brotherhood and incestuous desire until you're appalled, transfixed, and ultimately wrenched. Quentin is writ tragic—tragic in an ancient Greek, doomed, problematic hero kind of way. You'll feel it.

The last two sections are Jason and the younger Quentin's story. Faulkner downshifts a gear and gives us a different kind of drama: that of the neglected, unspoiled younger brother who grows up hard and hardening and then takes it out on the world at large. Jason is Caddy, Benji, and Quentin (the male's) flinty, machinating, no-B.S. younger brother, a trapdoor spider to Quentin's monarch in chrysalis. The only sibling left after Quentin dies, Benji is shipped off, and Caddy runs away; he supports his feeble mother and terrorizes his niece, Quentin—Caddy's teenage daughter whose revenge arcs the plot of these sections. Jason is Faulkner's way of showing how he handles the other end of the male spectrum: the man with no privilege, the mercantile Machiavel skimping and scheming himself into the power he couldn't inherit. It's one of Faulkner's fascinations, played out best perhaps in the Snopes novels (see "What People Don't Know" on the opposite page), but Jason is still a triumph of the type.

The Sound and the Fury, then, is something of a Faulkner sampler. With a few of his great character types, a lot—maybe too many—of his writerly chops, and a strong embodiment of the general themes that run through the rest of his novels (love, race, the South, power, privilege, family, etc.), it can stand in for his work as a whole. As one of his toughest books, though, it might not make the best intro to the oeuvre, but if you want to jump into the deep end of a pool, you won't find one deeper than Faulkner's.

The Buzz: For better or—most likely—for worse, people remember the Benji section of *The Sound and the Fury*, probably because they read three pages of it and got no further, and don't realize or remember that Caddy, Jason, and both Quentins are the real protagonists. Apart from being the narrator of the first section, Benji is really only a bit character. People also talk about the two-page sentence in the appendix, but Faulkner's longest sentence actually occurs in *Absalom, Absalom,* coming in at over one thousand words. And, of course, the hint of potential incest doesn't go unnoticed by people who do make it to Quentin.

What People Don't Know (But Should): For some reason, people are often introduced to Faulkner's novels with *The Sound and the Fury* or his great but exceedingly challenging *Absalom, Absalom.* To be honest, I think it's crazy; these books are just too confusing and risk sending you away from Faulkner forever (unless you follow my advice above). The ideal way to approach Faulkner is this: Read the novella "The Bear"—it's softly, deeply moving, and presents no especial challenges to the reader. Then read either the agonizingly disastrous story of trying to move and bury the dead mother told in *As I Lay Dying* or the very quirky and utterly hysterical first volume of the Snopes trilogy, *The Hamlet. As I Lay Dying* is the easier read and is tremendous, but *The Hamlet* is among Faulkner's all-time best. Once you've got those down, you're probably familiar enough with him—and a big enough fan—to tackle *The Sound and the Fury* and

Absalom, Absalom, the latter being my personal favorite (though I recommend that you turn from the last page back to the first and read it twice straight through to figure out what's going on).

Best Line: Before you read this, know that the "that" in the first bit is Quentin saying to himself "when will it stop, when will it stop?" and the honeysuckle he refers to is the smell that reminds him of his sister knocking boots al fresco:

> "Sometimes I could put myself to sleep saying that over and over until after the honeysuckle got all mixed up in it the whole thing came to symbolize night and unrest I seemed to be lying neither asleep nor awake looking down a long corridor of halflight where all stable things had become shadowy paradoxical all I had done shadows all I had felt suffered taking visible form antic and perverse mocking without relevance inherent themselves with the denial of the significance they should have affirmed thinking I was I was not who was not was not who."

What's Sexy: Early in Quentin's section, the mother of his Harvard classmate Gerald (another of Faulkner's dashing young men) says to her son, "What a shame that you should have a mouth like that it should be on a girl's face," to which he replies, "Mother, it often is."

That's an isolated moment, but Caddy's and her daughter Quentin's licentiousness runs through the whole book. It's most directly (and painfully) expressed in this passage where Caddy confesses to Quentin that she never had to be coerced into doing it, and says that if he tells, she'll say that she and he had also been together. (Note that the speaker changes back and forth midline—Quentin is the one saying I'll tell Father and I was in the house. And, yes, that's how it's punctuated and spelled.)

"It was a crime we did a terrible crime it cannot be hid you think it can but wait Poor Quentin youve never done that have you and I'll tell you how it was I'll tell Father then itll have to be because you love Father then we'll have to go away amid the pointing and the horror the clean flame I'll make you say we did I'm stronger than you I'll make you know we did you thought it was them but it was me listen I fooled you all the time it was me you thought I was in the house where that damn honeysuckle trying not to think the swing the cedars the secret surges the breathing locked drinking the wild breath the yes Yes Yes yes."

Quirky Fact: Jason insists that Benji be "gelded." Faulkner clearly had some ideas about the libidos of the autistic, as another of his "idiot" characters, Ike Snopes, gets himself in some romantic trouble with a barnyard cud-chewer in the Trilogy.

What to Skip: The Benji section (the first one after the appendix) isn't worth the hassle, and the rest of the novel works just fine without it. Read the full-frontal appendix for what it's worth; then start with the second section, "June 2, 1910," where Quentin the Harvard student is the narrator. From there, you'll want to read the rest.

ERNEST HEMINGWAY
(1899–1961)

༺☙༻

A Farewell to Arms
(1929)

It might be that no writer since the author of Genesis has been so terse and yet so powerful as Ernest Hemingway. He is the undisputed master of the simple sentence, the polar opposite of Proust and Henry James (both in prose and in testosterone), and, I long thought, the sworn enemy of the comma. But it's not that; Hemingway uses commas—though probably fewer than anyone this side of e. e. cummings—he simply saves them for effect, for fireworks, when he is going to let a sentence run and damn well you're going to know it.

Now that I see what he's up to, I love it when Papa goes for the haymaker instead of the jab. Take this sentence for an example:

> I loved to take her hair down and she sat on the bed and kept very still, except suddenly she would dip down to kiss me while I was doing it, and I would take out the pins and lay them on the sheet and it would be loose and I would watch her while she kept very still and then take out the last two pins and it would all come down and she would drop her head and we would both be inside of it, and it was the feeling of inside a tent or behind a falls.

Beneath her hair? Like being behind a falls? The studmo Hemingway we normally think of would never write such a sentence (he wrote *Men Without Women,* after all), but it can't be denied, it's gorgeous and extremely poetic. (See, ladies, you can actually like Hemingway!) That's why I think *A Farewell to Arms,* his tale of Frederic Henry, an American serving as an ambulance driver for Italy in World War I, and his affair with Catherine Barkley, a Scottish army nurse, is Hemingway's finest novel: it's his most feeling, most romantic, and even most tragic. (I always cry at the end—the last two times at a Philly bar and on the New York subway, respectively. I guess that puts me in the Proust/James testosterone camp.)

Florid passages like this don't come very frequently, so to appreciate Hemingway fully you have to realize that the simplicity of most of his writing is like the simplicity of Italian or Japanese cuisine: yes, it seems effortless, but when you try to re-create it, your version doesn't carry as much flavor. Like Plato, Aristotle, or Thomas Aquinas, Hemingway knows that to come across simply is not to be simple; there's an art to confecting clarity, and one only creates the illusion of simplicity with bonsai-tree pruning.

One of his mottoes was "the first draft of anything is shit," and he subjected his prose to such merciless shears because he was striving for something very particular: a certain "it" that he refers to in many of his books. (In his tour-de-force story "The Snows of Kilimanjaro," the dying protagonist thinks of life: "He had been in it and he had watched it and it was his duty to write of it; but now he never would. . . . There wasn't time, of course, but it seemed as though it telescoped so that you might put it all into one paragraph if you could get it right.") Hemingway's "it" is the reality deep in the story, that thing that language at its best hopes to point to but can't corral. Many writers speak of this (remember Dante's "so from the fact the telling doesn't differ"?), but it's not just representation that Hemingway is after. There's also a deep, grave, majestic essence to reality—a capital-b Being—that is gestured toward in all of his best work. Hemingway lived a restless, migratory, self-ended, daredevil's life, but I'm not convinced it was adventure he was after; I think it was this "it" that captivated and drove him. He knew it when he saw it, he knew it probably couldn't be expressed, but he knew also that there was no point in expressing anything else.

Hemingway's "it" lurks behind *A Farewell to Arms* as well, haunting the protagonist, turning both him and the novel as a whole into a study in ambivalence: ambivalence to love, to the war, even to thinking itself. Each of these three things can and should contain the it, so when they don't, the lack of profundity echoes all the louder. With war, as you'll see in "Best Line" on the opposite page, the dates and sites of military battles have "dignity" for Hemingway, but terms like "glory" or "courage" or "winning" ("Perhaps wars weren't won anymore. Maybe they went on forever") or "victory" ("I don't believe in victory any more . . . but I don't believe in defeat. Though it may be better") are hollow. What might appear on the surface to be an antiwar novel is actually just an insistence that the it of war, the poignant agonizing essence, not be lost in the rhetoric.

The authenticity of love, too, is in perpetual doubt in *A Farewell to Arms.* Toward the priest and his fellow ambulance driver Rinaldi, Frederic's love is palpable and uncomplicated, but toward Catherine, the reader must decide. Most of the time, Frederic stays guarded: "Have you ever loved anyone?" "No." Later: "You are sweet." "No, I'm not." Then: "You did say you loved me, didn't you?" " 'Yes,' " I lied. I had not said it before . . . I knew I did not love Catherine Barkley nor had any idea of loving her. This was a game, like bridge, in which you said things instead of playing cards." But then you read the scene in "What's Sexy" on page 308 or remember the hair quote from above, and it's hard to believe that Frederic isn't putting up a smokescreen. To my eye, his relationship to Catherine is similar to the affair late in Cormac McCarthy's *Suttree* (one of my all-time favorite novels): it's one of the few times these ultramacho writers take women and relationships seriously, allowing real sentiment to sneak through their chain-link, but then quickly closing the gate behind.

Watching the modulations of feeling in *A Farewell to Arms* is fascinating and gives us a dimension both of Hemingway and his "it" rarely seen in his work. And for that reason, I think it is his supreme achievement.

The Buzz: Like his protagonist, Hemingway himself served as an ambulance driver in the Italian army in World War I, giving him much of the material for the novel. *A Farewell to Arms* is sometimes called the best war novel ever written; I'd have to save that accolade for *War and Peace,* but it's definitely among the top, a maximum-poignancy testament to the camaraderie and gravity of war, and to a soldier's perpetual fight against the feeling of futility (see "Best Line" below).

What People Don't Know (But Should): When most people think of Hemingway, they think of his first full-length novel, *The Sun Also Rises,* but in my opinion that's actually not among his best books. *A Farewell to Arms* is obviously my favorite, but his short stories are also outstanding—and Hemingway was originally renowned for them among other writers. My favorite original collection is *The Snows of Kilimanjaro and Other Stories,* an all-time classic.

Best Line: Let this sink in: "I did not say anything. I was always embarrassed by the words sacred, glorious, and sacrifice and the expression in vain. We had heard them, sometimes standing in the rain almost out of earshot, so that only the shouted words came through, and had read them, on proclamations, now for a long time, and I had seen nothing sacred, and the things that were glorious had no glory and the sacrifices were like the stock-yards at Chicago if nothing was done with the meat except to bury it. There were many words that you could not stand to hear and finally only the names of places had dignity. Certain numbers were the same way and certain dates and these with the names of the places were all you could say and have them mean anything. Abstract words such as glory, honor, courage, or hallow were obscene beside the concrete names of villages, the numbers of roads, the names of rivers, the numbers of regiment and the dates."

What's Sexy: *A Farewell to Arms* contains a perfect Hemingway sex scene—our laconic author outdoes even himself:

> "You mustn't," she said. "You're not well enough."
>
> "Yes, I am. Come on."
>
> "No. You're not strong enough."
>
> "Yes. I am. Yes. Please."
>
> "You do love me?"
>
> "I really love you. I'm crazy about you. Come on please."
>
> "Feel our hearts beating."
>
> "I don't care about our hearts. I want you. I'm just mad about you."
>
> "You really love me?"
>
> "Don't keep saying that. Come on. Please. Please, Catherine."
>
> "All right but only for a minute."
>
> "All right," I said. "Shut the door."
>
> "You can't. You shouldn't."
>
> "Come on. Don't talk. Please come on."

Quirky Fact: After numerous previous attempts, Hemingway succeeded in committing suicide in 1961 at the age of sixty-one. Placing the butt of his double-barreled shotgun on the ground, he pressed the barrels to his forehead and discharged both at once. Sadly, it seems that a death wish might have been part of his genetic legacy; his father and two of his siblings also killed themselves.

What to Skip: *A Farewell to Arms* is short and straightforward; you'll have no trouble gliding through it. By now you can probably guess that I'd advise you to skip *The Sun Also Rises* and instead read *For Whom the Bell Tolls* or the short stories or go back over *Farewell* again (and again).

HENRY MILLER
(1891–1980)

༺⁓⁓༻

Tropic of Cancer
(1934)

Though apparently philosophers spend a lot of time debating it, it might just be that the point of life is to be alive. Growing up, my idol was my great-grandfather Pete; he was a man's man, knew how to live, liked everyone, ate everything, butchered whole pigs in his basement and used every last bit—tail to snout, blood and all. It's that process of extracting everything, of getting it all, fully exemplified in his ninety-three-year life that eventually registered for me as the only way to go. Having fled from impoverished Hungary alone at fourteen, he appreciated the whole and all of what came his way in the New World. I don't think there was a drop of wine or a crumb of bread he wasn't thankful for and enthusiastic about.

That kind of gusto-filled infatuation with life is the hallmark of a strain of great American writers—and it's part of why we associate them with America. Melville, Whitman, Thoreau, and Henry Miller: it's hard not to think of Grandpa Pete when I read them. Their message is the same all around: embrace! Sure, you can eat chicken with a knife and fork, but what's the point? Pick up that drumstick, dirty your fingers, let the sauce drip down your chin. Theirs is a mode of living hitched to the axis of Yes, which is to say, it's a mode of *living*.

Of that group, Miller was clearly the weakest writer, his reveler's prose at times tottering drunkenly toward the Bukowski-esque (don't get me wrong, there's a charm to the barfly, but let's say he could have used an editor). Miller has much of Bukowski's grunge but a lot more insight and élan. It's true that compared with any other great writer (even France's poster-boy of argot, Céline), Miller clearly lacks some Lemon Pledge, but ultimately it's his imperfection itself that one comes to appreciate—with reservations. Miller unbuttons himself in his novels as he would in the men's, with the same ease and unabashedness, and out he flops: stark, abscess-ridden, hard to look at, but real—real in a way you'll be hard-pressed to find in many other authors of his stature.

In that sense, Miller's best work, *Tropic of Cancer,* might be the most flawed classic ever written. Early on, speaking of the Paris where the book was penned, Miller says, "Everything is raised to apotheosis." Well, he was certainly correct in his novel's case, as *Tropic of Cancer* is the apotheosis of male adolescence—pimpled, strident, egoistic, naive, fearless, caustic, overreaching, often artless but continually resonant. Hank's tale of his penniless expatriate existence in Paris in the early 1930s might as well be shelved in autobiography, though one suspects that Miller trumped up his story a bit for the benefit of the "novel." Intended to be a "bomb up the asshole of creation," its first word is "I" and it is, by its own admission, "colossal in its pretentiousness." But it's also colossal in its courage, jumping up on the bar and belting out its barrelhouse ditty. Miller wanted to write what he hadn't found in other books, and that he did: the bathroom-stall sex, the false-limbed whores, the lice, the hunger, the slime and sewers of Paris, but ultimately, the ecstatic human spirit—spurting as awkward and enthusiastic as a premature ejaculation.

At a certain point in the book, one of Miller's friends says that he's nothing but "cancer and delirium." And in that we have a

summary both of Miller and his best work. His favorite word is
"ecstasy," but he lives and sings from dreck. And he *wants* to go
hoarse, to overdo it, to sing himself out. It's both his ethos and his
aesthetic. His idols are Villon, Rabelais, and Rimbaud—all mas-
ters of excess—and our own homegrown Whitman, for whom
he holds a special place: "Whitman, that lone figure which America has produced in the course of her brief life, her past and her
future her birth and her death. Whatever there is of value in
America Whitman has expressed, and there is nothing more to be
said. . . . There is no equivalent in the languages of Europe for
the spirit which he immortalized. Europe is saturated with art
and her soil is full of dead bones and her museums are bursting
with plundered treasures, but what Europe has never had is a
free, healthy spirit, what might be called a MAN." Whitman,
Miller, Grandpa Pete: there is something compelling to the type;
they can make us feel a little tame, a lot reserved, and inspire us
to bloom.

So follow old Hank around town; have a drink or ten with
him; do some skanky fucking; flick off a louse or a cockroach;
meet his reprobate friends; forgive him his sexism, his anti-
Semitism, his vulgarity, his gutter mouth; dance a jig; bum a
smoke, raise your glass again and let him ramble on about God
knows what—some of it will jump out at you as inspired, and all
of it will say Yes.

"Art," he says, "consists in going the full length." So, Miller
teaches us, does life.

The Buzz: *Tropic of Cancer* is most famous for its sexual content
(see page 314) and for having been banned in the States from
its first publication (in Paris) in 1934 until 1961 when Grove
Press fought and won in court for the ability to publish "obscene"
literature—Miller and D. H. Lawrence included.

What People Don't Know (But Should): Relatively early on in *Tropic of Cancer,* Miller says that he intends not to edit his work: "I have made a silent compact with myself not to change a line of what I write." Who knows if this is braggadocio or actually the M.O. for Miller and the Beat poets whom he inspired? Of their lines, I can simply say, borrowing from Ben Jonson's quip on Shakespeare, would that they had changed many.

Best Line: It's not hard to find a quote that's saturated with Miller's vitality and philosophy. Here's perhaps my favorite:

> I am almost tempted to say: "Show me a man who over-elaborates and I will show you a great man!" What is called their "over-elaboration" is my meat: it is the sign of struggle, it is struggle itself with all the fibers clinging to it, the very aura and ambiance of the discordant spirit. And when you show me a man who expresses himself perfectly I will not say that he is not great but I will say that I am unattracted. . . . I miss the cloying qualities. When I reflect that the task which the artist implicitly sets himself is to overthrow existing values, to make of the chaos about him an order which is his own, to sow strife and ferment so that by the emotional release those who are dead may be restored to life, than it is that I run with joy to the great and imperfect ones, their confusion nourishes me, their stuttering is like divine music to my ears. I see in the beautifully bloated pages that follow the interruptions the erasure of petty intrusions, of the dirty footprints, as it were, of cowards, liars, thieves, vandals, calumniators. I see in the swollen muscles of their lyric throats the staggering effort that must be made to turn the wheel over, to pick up the pace where one has left off. I see that behind the daily annoyances and intrusions, behind the cheap, glittering

malice of the feeble and inert, there stands the symbol of life's frustrating power.

What's Sexy: As most of you are already aware, *Tropic of Cancer* is pretty famous as a dirty book. And by the end of page 5, it's already delivered the excellent line, "Tania, I'm going to fuck you so you stay fucked." Now the rest of that passage—and the one on the next page—are pretty ludicrous, so, as I say in "What to Skip," you might just fast-forward a bit. You'll find some halfway decent raunch every few pages—and in Miller's other novels, too (especially *Sexus*). If that's all you want to read of the novel, get a library copy; it will no doubt be dog-eared on all the hottest pages.

Quirky Fact: Henry Miller might be the only author in this collection who'd be acutely offended by being called a classic—and with my idea of wanting us to revisit the great books in general. In his words, "Every man with a bellyful of the classics is an enemy to the human race." Don't read another page, you would-be scourge!

What to Skip: Much as it pains me to say it, everything in the first thirty-three pages gets said again and with less boyish bravado later. Yes, a few of the women's names change, but Miller's women can barely be distinguished from each other anyway, so it's hardly important. Skipping these early pages, you won't be put off by his overblown claims and occasional anti-Semitism; if you do read them, give him the benefit of the doubt and keep going.

RICHARD WRIGHT
(1908–60)

Native Son
(1940)

I didn't know we were so far apart until that night.

As I write this, Barack Obama has been nominated as the Democratic candidate for president, and as you're reading this, he is already in the Oval Office; it would seem that race relations in America have really come a long way. And they have—for some, at times. But why is it then that most white people still feel so uncomfortable reading *Native Son*? Why, on this my third time through, did it again feel like a knee to my solar plexus and a smack to the face? Why did the psychology of Bigger Thomas seem like it might very well apply to a still-staggering number of underprivileged urban black youths—and many white ones too?

Native Son was a wake-up call to me and, depending on your background, it might well be a wake-up call for you too. It forces home, in clinical detail, the psychology of hopelessness and the long-term effects of oppression—on black people or on anyone. But Wright's insight goes further, to realize how, despite the oppression, the spirit of life emphatically *has* to exist, to pick another direction, to find something, anything, to become, and won't be stopped just because there are obstacles in its way. With eminent sophistication, Wright diagnoses the causes behind black people's struggles in this country, but his wisdom allows him to diagnose whites as well. His theory is simply that white America wants—perhaps even expects—black America to be more like them, and that's what gets called "race relations." He dares his white readers to ask themselves if they genuinely accept black America on its own terms, to ask if they're not still both guilty and afraid (he is magnificent on fear), and if they don't do many things that appear like "helping" but really are just attempts to atone for those same feelings of guilt and fear. If you can read *Native Son* and not have to rethink racial interactions in this country, then maybe you're more advanced than I am. But I challenge you to try.

Reading *Native Son,* if you didn't already know better, you'd probably be next to positive that it was written in the late '60s, part of the foment and frustration of that watershed era. But no—it was written in 1940. That in itself should make people feel a little queasy when they realize how true it still holds today. Almost seventy years have gone by, and the psychological characterizations that Wright makes and their real-world effects remain completely valid (if in some what less of a vise-grip)—so much for any smug conclusions that we've done so well. *Native Son* has been a quietly steady and insistent voice, broadcasting America's shame, damning us for decades.

If you've never read *Native Son* or don't remember its plot, it's easy to bring you up to speed. Through an outreach program, Bigger Thomas, a black twenty-year-old, is hired by a privileged liberal white family as a driver for their teenage daughter, Mary. She is a communist, and instead of having Bigger take her to school, she has him take her and her boyfriend, Jan, to "a *real* place . . . one of those places where colored people eat, not one of those show places." They go, and the three of them end up drinking a lot. Bigger drops off Jan and then carries the passed-out Mary up to her room. While he is putting her to bed, her blind mother hears something and comes into the room. SPOILER ALERT. Panicking, Bigger puts his hand over Mary's mouth to keep her quiet, hoping the blind woman will suspect nothing and go away. She does, but he inadvertently suffocates Mary in the process. Knowing just how bad the situation would look, he takes her body down to the incinerator, decapitates her with a hatchet (grisly), and pushes the body into the furnace. Her bones are discovered anyway, so he tries to pin the murder on Jan, but eventually the snare tightens, and Bigger is caught and charged with murder and rape. The book ends with Bigger's trial, where he is defended by Max, a communist lawyer sent by Jan, and Bigger being sentenced to death.

In the novel's final scenes, when Max is addressing the judge, his voice is clearly that of Wright addressing the reader. Didactic as his speeches are ("the mere act of understanding Bigger Thomas will be a thawing out of icebound impulses, a dragging of the sprawling forms of dread out of the night of fear . . . an unveiling of the unconscious ritual of death in which we, like sleep-walkers, have participated so dreamlike and thoughtlessly"), they are beautifully executed, so much so that they could be taught as philosophical/psychological documents in themselves ("They're mad because deep down in them they believe that they made you do it"). Most contemporary editions of *Native Son* contain a prefatory essay by Wright called "How Bigger Was Born"; it's an erudite and personal history of race relations in America, but it's also an unnecessary explanation of that which he already dramatized with such power in the novel. There are times in the book where Wright needs to be direct, and he's not afraid of putting his characters on soapboxes. But one of the stronger compliments one can pay *Native Son* is to say that no amount of commentary by the author or anyone else is going to add very much to the book. What *Native Son* sets out to achieve, it achieves: it is socio-political drama of the first order.

I've tried in writing this book not to strike strident chords too frequently, but *Native Son* leaves me no choice. It is precisely one's intense, emphatic, deeply personal response to the novel that makes it so great—and so necessary. It's not always subtle, and I tend to prefer books that show rather than tell, but that's not Wright's method. From a stylistic sense, *Native Son* would not stand out among the books in this volume, yet it has one element few of the others can match: consistent political and emotional relevance. If we read in order to feel and to learn, then *Native Son* becomes mandatory for anyone unwilling to remain ignorant of the realities of the America of the last century and this one. It tells a story we still need to hear, and though we might think we've been told it again and again by books much newer and hipper, *Native Son* tells it as intelligently, poignantly, and beautifully as literature ever has. As Wright says, "Multiply Bigger Thomas twelve million times."

The Buzz: The buzz around *Native Son* typically is that Bigger got a raw deal, railroaded for a crime he didn't intend to commit, and was a victim of his circumstance, not of inner weakness. Technically, that's not quite right. Wright preferred the word "product" to "victim," and in Bigger, he was attempting to show how society creates this product: a young, underprivileged, urban black male exemplar. He succeeded.

What People Don't Know (But Should): As much as *Native Son* is a study in race relations it's also a study in class conflict. Wright crafts several prominent, exceptionally sympathetic communist characters, especially Jan and Max. Wright was a communist in his early adult life (even editing a Party newspaper and a literary magazine) and, before his disillusionment with the movement, saw class equality as the revolution that would unify all people, including blacks and whites. His arguments remain convincing to this day.

Best Line: Apart from Max's defense of Bigger toward the end of the book (which is masterful in the extreme but too long to quote here—plus I'd ruin the buildup), my favorite lines are these:

> Having been thrown by an accidental murder into a position where he sensed a possible order and meaning in his relations with the people about him; having accepted the moral guilt and responsibility for that murder because it had made him feel free for the first time in his life; having felt in his heart some obscure need to be at home with people and having demanded ransom money to enable him to do it—having done all this and failed, he chose not to struggle any more. With a supreme act of will springing from the essence of his being, he turned away from his life and the long train of disastrous consequences that had flowed from it and looked wistfully upon the dark face of ancient waters upon which some spirit had breathed and created him, the dark face of the waters from which he had been first made in the image of a man with a man's obscure need and urge; feeling that he wanted to sink back into those waters and rest eternally.

What's Sexy: There is a palpable—and highly vexed—sexuality when Bigger takes the drunk Mary up to her bedroom just before the tragedy, but the more overtly sexy scene is later between Bigger and his girlfriend, Bessie: "He felt two soft palms holding his face tenderly and the thought and image of the whole blind world which had made him ashamed and afraid fell away as he felt her as a fallow field beneath him stretching out under a cloudy sky waiting for rain, and he floated on a wild tide, rising and sinking with the ebb and flow of her blood, being willingly dragged into a warm night sea to rise renewed to the surface to face a world he hated and wanted to blot out of existence, clinging close to a fountain whose warm waters washed and cleaned his senses, cooled them, made them strong and keen again to see and smell and touch and taste and hear, cleared them to end the tiredness and to reforge in him a new sense of time and space;—after he had been tossed to dry upon a warm sunlit rock under a white sky he lifted his hand slowly and heavily and touched Bessie's lips with his fingers."

Quirky Fact: In a *New York Times* article from the '80s, James Baldwin, referring to the time he spent with Wright in Paris, says: "Richard was much, much better than a lot of the company he kept. I mean, the French existentialists. I didn't think that Simone de Beauvoir or Jean-Paul Sartre—to say nothing of the American colony—had any right whatsoever to patronize that man. It revolted me and made me furious." That is some kind of compliment, but having read a lot of Wright, Sartre, and de Beauvoir, I can't say I'm surprised.

What to Skip: The plot of *Native Son* moves along briskly enough, but if what you're really interested in is the psychology (as I am), then you can afford to skip the middle section, "Flight," the less-probing narration of Bigger's attempts to avoid conviction (but do read "Best Line" on page 319, which comes at the beginning). Then in the last section, the trial scenes go on a bit too long. You'll want to read the speeches of Max, Bigger's lawyer, but the prosecutor's can be skimmed.

ROBERT MUSIL
(1880–1942)

∽∾∽

The Man Without Qualities
(1942)

Acertain breed of man is haunted by the word "impossible";
for him, the precise challenge itself matters little compared
to the challenge *of* challenge: the degree of difficulty, the scale of
the mountain (and the frostbite, the winds, the difficulty in finding a translator). Men have climbed Everest without oxygen tanks
or with only one God-given leg; lord, men have climbed Everest
repeatedly carrying other people's luggage (convenient for the
beneficiary, thus the translator issue). History has proven again
and again that the unthinkable eventually becomes doable, and
humanity rests easy.

For those of us who wear more cerebral than steely ice cram-
pons, there are analogous challenges, the much-touted, veritable
Everests for the reader: Aquinas' *Summa Theologica* (our version
of the Tour de France), Spenser's *Faerie Queene* (the hundred-
mile supermarathon), Flaubert's *Bouvard and Pécuchet* (reading
the encylopedia), Proust's *Remembrance of Things Past* (glazing a
cathedral window), Joyce's *Ulysses* (deciphering ancient Greek),
or his *Finnegan's Wake* (deciphering jibberish), Pound's *Cantos*
(learning Mandarin), Pynchon's *Gravity's Rainbow* (reuniting
with your ex, just back from the asylum), or Gaddis' *The Recognitions* (mastering go), and, yes, you guessed it, Robert Musil's

The Man Without Qualities, perhaps the intellectual version of the Nathan's hot-dog-eating contest every year in Coney Island, if Coney Island was *entre guerre* Austria and the wieners (lower case, no pun intended) were social criticism, and the buns dunked in glasses of water were . . . Never mind, you get the drift.

The Man Without Qualities: its two volumes sit obese but, after twenty-plus years of its author's endeavor, still not completed— and for this we take a communal sigh of relief. Still, if you include the intended but draft-form posthumous papers (the bulk of Volume II of the English printing), Musil's madness runs to over half a Proust in length. And *The Man Without Qualities* is easily half as crazy as *Gravity's Rainbow* (which is a lot), half as experimental as *The Recognitions* (quite), and half as ironic as *Ulysses* (yes, very). The amalgam is certainly a novel like no other, one that I recommend if you thought *The Magic Mountain* was a little light and tend to enjoy itches that aren't entirely scratchable.

If Musil was going to have a champion stateside (where our days seem shorter than Europeans' and our attention spans shorter still), it would have to be William Gass, essayist extraordinaire and author of a knotted-pearl-necklace novel of his own, *The Tunnel. The Man Without Qualities* is a—perhaps *the*— novel William Gass would have written, a Pierre Menard to Musil's Cervantes, had Musil not beaten him to it. And thus Gass' praise is as extreme as it is acute; he calls *The Man Without Qualities* "seventeen hundred pages of the most intelligent and unflagging scrutiny modern life has ever had to bear—described with fondness by François Peyret as a *Foltermaschine*—a torture machine."

I'm not sure about "most intelligent," but a torture machine, described with fondness—that pretty much sums up *The Man Without Qualities* for me as well. The story itself isn't so torturous, apart from its length. It follows the not exactly qualityless protagonist, Ulrich (see "The Buzz" on page 324) as he comes to be obsessed with, for about one "part" each, an animalistic murderer named Musbrugger, the political identity of Austria, and his long-lost sister with whom he reunites (to say the least). The third part is my favorite (naughty!), but throughout the novel I found myself mumbling, "German, German" over and over even though Musil, technically, is Austrian. That's where the torture comes in; it's as if the philosophers Nietzsche (from his later years) and Wittgenstein (from his earlier) teamed up to write a novel and adopted the joint nom de plume Robert Musil.

Musil had in fact done a Ph.D. in philosophy prior to taking up fiction, and this is both the book's boon and bane. Reading *The Man Without Qualities,* one feels the cumulative force of the Germanic intellectual *Geist* tearing itself out of Musil's crepe-paper literary packaging, incinerating his cardboard characters, bulldozing his toy-train-set narrative, begging, begging to be reshelved far from fiction's glitzy artifice and instead amid the immaculate theoretical artifacts of the relentless Teutonic drive. Up from the vast seas of Musil's mind bob tremendous philosophical observations (for example, the hysterical and brilliant discussion of the soul that's five paragraphs into I, 45), but regrettably one has to navigate much novelistic flotsam to get to them. How torturous you'll find this flotsam, or how easily you'll forgive it, I'm not sure, but as with the wiener-eating contest in Coney Island, no matter how far you make it through, you'll be left with both pride and perhaps a bit of a stomachache, knowing that you tried.

One side note of interest: Despite the Germanic feel to the novel (and the crest of the Austro-Hungarian Empire on the cover of the first English translation), Musil was no nationalist and had to flee with his Jewish wife when the Nazis came to power. They banned *The Man Without Qualities* in both Austria and Germany and he lived in penury from that point forward. I thought I'd better mention it before you come across these lines: "A conscious human essayism would find itself confronted with something like the task of transforming the world's haphazard state of consciousness into a single will. And many individual lines of development indicate that this may happen soon" (Wilkins and Kaiser translation). Ah, the gods or irony—you'd think the brownshirts would have licked their chops at that one.

The Buzz: *The Man Without Qualities* is a translation of the German *Der Mann ohne Eigenschaften,* literally something a little closer to "man without characteristics" but meaning, to Musil, the man who commits to nothing, who adheres to nothing, who is, in the early-decades-of-the-twentieth-century-in-Europe sense, modern. "Nothing is stable for him. Everything is fluctuating, a part of a whole, among innumerable wholes that presumably are part of a superwhole, which, however, he doesn't know the slightest thing about. So every one of his answers is a part-answer, every one of his feelings only a point of view, and whatever a thing is, it doesn't matter to him what it is, it's only some accompanying 'way in which it is,' some addition or other, that matters to him." Ulrich, the fellow in question, is both a Musil stand-in and a vehicle for his critique of the modern consciousness and state of man.

What People Don't Know (But Should): Although *The Man Without Qualities* is a supremely intellectual novel, it is also surprisingly engaged with physicality and sport. Ulrich, the protagonist, among his various nonqualities, is an accomplished boxer, and early on after he's gotten into a scrape, Musil writes, "A brawl always leaves a bad taste in the mouth, a taste, so to speak, of over-hasty intimacy." Awesome.

Best Line: Note the almost tragic struggle of the philosopher attempting to get to the base of things, only to have to confront the failure of language and the ultimate indescribability of feeling:

> What he was thinking of was how to find a magical formula, a lever that one might be able to get a hold of, the real mind of the mind, the missing, perhaps very small, bit that would close the broken circle . . . Ulrich had no words at his disposal. Words leap like monkeys from tree to tree; but in the dark realm where a man is rooted he lacks their friendly mediation. The ground streamed away under his feet. He could hardly open his eyes. Can a feeling blow like a storm and yet not be a stormy feeling at all?

What's Sexy: From a book that reminds us that "a flea favors the same areas as a lover," there's a surprising amount of (admittedly not particularly sexy) lasciviousness in *The Man Without Qualities*. Clearly, Ulrich is a man who hasn't quite figured out what sex is for (say, emotional intimacy), as at one point he says, "The woman is a nymphomaniac and I find that irresistible," and at another, "I'm convinced most people would be glad if this connection between an epidermic itch and the entire personality could be revoked."

Another line suggests what I believe are the author's true sentiments. After an account of a peeping Tom watching a woman and her lover without knowing that he's being watched by both her husband and Ulrich, the lover utters this summation, "We attach far too much importance to sex." Musil didn't seem to be able to feel good about it, but he certainly couldn't leave it out, either (though in seventeen hundred pages, not many things do end up being left out).

Quirky Fact: You can easily gloss over the implications of a lit-tle phrase like "the pain and triumph of the misunderstood," but then you find out that Musil's former schoolmates apparently wouldn't talk to his biographer "out of bitterness." Sounds like maybe the young Musil felt a tad too much triumph and a tad too little sadness when he realized he was misunderstood. I hope no one ever tries to write my biography, right Centennial High?

What to Skip: The whole damn thing—just kidding. I think the first and third parts are more compelling, both narratively and intellectually, than the more political (and dated) middle section. If you want to be more thorough, read all three but leave out the supplemental "posthumous papers"—working matter he was supposedly going to put in but died before doing so. And re-member, even Musil didn't finish *The Man Without Qualities,* so don't be too upset if you don't either.

VLADIMIR NABOKOV
(1899–1977)

❧❧❧

Lolita
(1955)

*L*olita, Nabokov's ultrascandalous tale of a twelve-year-old nymphet and her degenerate adult admirer, needs next to no introduction. It's rightfully famous and beloved and has one of the greatest first thirds of any novel in any language, so the fact that the second two-thirds are repetitive and lackluster shouldn't bother us all that much, right? Though I fear the gods of literature might be training lightning bolts on my mortal skull as I type this, I can't not say it: I think Nabokov is overrated, and I think people forget how much *Lolita* falls off after the breathtaking beginning. And of his work in general, I simply want to suggest that one wee thing is missing, almost across the board: flow. Lexically, Nabokov's a kestrel, eying and striking the precise word with exceptional grace, but at the level of the sentence— like his fellow Ur-aesthete Henry James—he's almost flightless: the accumulated weight grounding whatever dirigible he was trying to send up. Granted, Nabokov was born in Russia and only immigrated (first to Britain, later to America) when he was twenty, but somehow he's still widely regarded as one of English's foremost stylists. Apart from *Lolita*, I don't buy it. One of my most literary friends told me that Nabokov's novel *Ada* is among her favorite books, so I "read" it, if pedaling the square-wheeled trike of his prose can be called reading. And I said to her, "You really liked this book? What about the 'rhythm'? Didn't it clunk and stagger like a besotted Cossack?" "I guess you're right," she said. "I just liked it for the incest."

Trust me, I've tried to love Nabokov, I really have, and shouldn't I be his ideal reader? I'm a calcified pedant too; I overwrite my sentences cripplingly; I'm not immune to the lures of females (though of my own age and from outside my family, preferably). But in none of his novels (apart from *Lolita*) did I ever feel like I was really feeling. Thinking, yes. Being impressed, yes. Laughing, often. Acknowledging Nabokov's virtuosity, certainly. But communing? No way. So maybe there's another wee thing missing across the board: sentiment. And without that, how deep can you go? How meaningful can you be? Read Nabokov next to a writer like Gabriel García Márquez and all the Russian's Kasparovian feints and stratagems become mere waterbug dances on the surface of things.

Which is why one should jump straight to Nabokov's masterpiece and read *Lolita* and love *Lolita* and tell me to shut it, since the very first paragraph contradicts everything I said above about flow and feeling (granted, he's talking about a twelve-year-old). Assuming you're not put off by the subject matter—and you probably wouldn't be reading this if you were—you'll find *Lolita* fabulous, regardless if it's the first time through or you're paying a repeat visit. Yes, Humbert Humbert is another demented professor protagonist (and how many of his books have them? *Bend Sinister, Pale Fire, Pnin,* etc.) and yes, he speaks Nabokovian Stilt-ese, but somehow it's nice coming from the dirty old mandarin. It's a felicitous combination: Humbert's rarified discourse and aesthete's discernment twist the warm knife of perversion. He is all the more compelling, and thus all the more monstrous, because he employs the language of an oenophile to describe the decanting of a particularly immature vintage.

For the first third, that is. After that—eh. The novel's true wonder, the ostrega on the tongue that must be savored to the utmost, is the tension of the early pages: Humbert fighting his own impulses, Humbert failing to conquer his own impulses, Humbert trying to glean what he can of looks and brushes and strokes and sittings on the lap without getting caught, Humbert plotting, Humbert ploying, Humbert spidering. Tauter and tauter, tenser and tenser, the web he weaves, the sexual energy, the suspense—perhaps this is why *Lolita,* like the majority of erotic novels (and, ahem, a certain gender in general) has a hard time sustaining itself. Once Sputnik launched, everything had to go a little earthward.

One final thing should be said on Nabokov and *Lolita*'s behalf: it was published in 1955 (in Paris, 1958 in the States), while Vlad was a literature professor at Cornell. That he had the audacity to come out with that book then and in that context is almost unimaginable—and laudable in the extreme. I've been a little concerned that this book might get me fired from my teaching job (he wants his students to *enjoy* books!)—imagine coming out with one where the prof seduces and runs away with a twelve-year-old. To do that, whew. We always knew Nabokov was cranially heavy; now we know he had a little ballast below the belt to keep him upright.

The Buzz: Let's see, what *do* people say about *Lolita*? Apart from those oft-linked responses, outrage and titillation, that one always hears about, the novel's opening lines, especially "light of my life, fire of my loins," tend to get trotted out with some regularity—at least by me.

What People Don't Know (But Should): The original film version of *Lolita* was done by Stanley Kubrick in 1962 (so there was proof he was a perv thirty-seven years before the laughable *Eyes Wide Shut*) and is better than the *fromager* Adrian Lyne's 1997 version, primarily because Peter Sellers made such a creepy Quilty in Kubrick's. But if you're thinking of taking the celluloid way out, don't bother; not only can Humbert not sound like himself on screen (even though Nabokov assisted Kubrick with the screenplay), but the glib visual arousal is a cheap stand-in for the complicated enticement/guilt/horror experience of reading it. Some books should never be made into movies—much less twice.

Best Line: Buckle up:

> With perfect simplicity, the impudent child extended her legs across my lap. By this time I was in a state of excitement bordering on insanity, but I also had the cunning of the insane. Sitting there, on the sofa, I managed to attune, by a series of stealthy movements, my masked lust to her guileless limbs . . . All the while keeping my maniac's inner eye on my distant golden goal, I cautiously increased the magic friction that was doing away, in an illusional, if not factual, sense, with the physically irremovable, but psychologically very friable texture of the material divide between the weight of two sunburned legs, resting athwart in my lap, and the hidden tumor of my unspeakable passion. . . . Every movement she made, every shuffle and ripple, helped me to conceal and to improve the secret system of tactile correspondence between beast and beauty—between my gagged, bursting beast and the beauty of her dimpled body in its innocent cotton frock. . . . Because of her very perfunctory underthings, there seemed to be nothing to prevent my muscular thumb from reaching the hot hollow of her groin. . . . She wriggled, and squirmed, and threw her head back . . . and my moaning mouth, gentlemen of the jury,

almost reached her bare neck, while I crushed out against her left buttock the last throb of the longest ecstasy man or monster had ever known.

What's Sexy: Duh.

Quirky Fact: Nabokov is famous for having been a lepidopterist (butterfly collector), but he apparently had an especial knack. A staff writer at the Harvard Museum of Natural History has said that Nabokov "actually did quite a good job at distinguishing species that you would not think were different—by looking at their genitalia under a microscope six hours a day, seven days a week, until his eyesight was permanently impaired." It's a full-time job, examining those butterfly genitalia!

What to Skip: As I argue—or at least assert—above, once Humbert and his nymphet leave the motel and hit the road, the novel doesn't live up to what preceded. It's not bad, but it's certainly not transcendent.

JAMES BALDWIN
(1924–87)

∾∾

Giovanni's Room
(1956)

James Baldwin is a historian of pain and a tactician of delicacy. Like a blind man's fingers telling a scar, he reads the history of injury with a touch so gentle, so noble, you can forget it's agony that he's tracing out. But when Baldwin whispers, thundering quietly, it is agony, always agony, the frustration and despair of an inner self at complete odds with outer circumstance. A black American from Harlem who was more at home in the cafés of Paris, a gay man who couldn't make peace with his own desires, Baldwin was forever in conflict, and his novels give character and voice to these turmoils, to the wrenching caused by life moving one way while the spirit moves the other. It's a cliché to compare an artist to an oyster that generates the pearl because it can't assimilate the foreign, unwelcome presence of grit within its shell, but James Baldwin truly was such an oyster, forever struggling with impulses he couldn't escape, but forging them into beauty at the cost of his own contentment.

Of his great novels—*Go Tell It on the Mountain, Giovanni's Room, Another Country*—*Giovanni's Room* is, to my mind, the most regal and perhaps the most intimate. Taking its epigraph from Whitman—"I am the man. I suffered. I was there."—it tells of David the narrator's affair in France with the "insolent and dark and leonine" barman Giovanni. When the novel begins, David is alone drinking in a house in the south of France, his fiancée, Hella, has just left him, and Giovanni is awaiting execution for murder (the reasons for which we won't learn till later). The events are loosely based on Baldwin's affair with a young Frenchman, Lucien Happsberger, to whom the book is dedicated, but things don't turn out exactly as they did in life (see "Quirky Fact" on page 335). It's clear that David loves Giovanni as Baldwin loved Happsberger, but it's also clear that, even before Giovanni's imprisonment, these men who thought they had found each other will instead find severance before solace.

Reading *Giovanni's Room* this time, the diverse feelings it elicited made me think of that wonder of mélange, the estuary, where an ocean—in this case the still, stately beauty of Baldwin's narration—is met by a foaming expiring river—the inner anguish and outer tragedy of each of the novel's characters. Whether pain or beauty predominates, it's hard to say. Both are so fully present, so intricately enmeshed, one can't tell whether to take hope in humanity's ability to feel and express as beautifully as Baldwin does, or to despair that so many lives are careering off the rails. What you eventually remember is the oceanic feeling, with Baldwin's aesthetic grace like hints of sandalwood in the air, but while reading one feels the blows and fists, the back and forth of engagement and retreat, desire and despondency, where no ecstasy goes untainted by shame.

What makes *Giovanni's Room* truly incredible is the main character David's "discovery," if you will, of his homosexuality, first in as nuanced, lucid, and tortured a moment of sexual awakening as you will ever read (in the childhood scene with his friend Joey, see "What's Sexy" on page 334) and later in his slow, inexorable but resisting capitulation to Giovanni's seduction. From there, the novel asks a simply phrased, excruciating-to-answer question: how do you walk away from love? In Baldwin's answer, we have one of the absolute finest of American novels.

The Buzz: *Giovanni's Room* is famous both for being as explicit a gay novel as it was for the time and for Baldwin choosing to have all his characters be white. I agree that it's pretty shockingly explicit, but not because of the actual physical details (which are graphic—*sans* the porno prefix), but in the precision of the psychological picture. We enter numerous minds (and bodies) in conflict, and we enter them deeply.

What People Don't Know (But Should): In addition to its explorations of homosexuality, *Giovanni's Room* contains an exceptionally pained and strained both-sides-know-it's-a-one-night-stand heterosexual encounter. When David, trying desperately to unconvince himself that he's gay, makes "love" to his friend Sue—egads. As he's leaving, she says, "Maybe you'll be lonely again" (wearing a smile the description of which will devastate you). He walks out the door saying only, "Keep a candle in the window." Ouch.

Best Line: My favorite single line is: "My crime, in some odd way, is in being a man and she knows all about this already." For my favorite paragraph, keep reading.

What's Sexy: Here, as the adolescent David wrestles with his friend Joey, is the decisive moment in his sexual awareness:

> When I touched him something happened in him and in me which made this touch different from any touch either of us had ever known. And he did not resist, as he usually did, but lay where I had pulled him, against my chest. And I realized

that my heart was beating in an awful way and that Joey was trembling against me and the light in the room was very bright and hot. I started to move and to make some kind of joke but Joey mumbled something and I put my head down to hear. Joey raised his head as I lowered mine and we kissed, as it were, by accident. Then, for the first time in my life, I was really aware of another person's body, of another person's smell. We had our arms around each other. It was like holding in my hand some rare, exhausted, nearly doomed bird which I had miraculously happened to find. I was very frightened, I am sure he was frightened too, and we shut our eyes. To remember it so clearly, so painfully tonight tells me that I have never for an instant truly forgotten it. I feel in myself now a faint, a dreadful stirring of what so overwhelmingly stirred in me then, great thirsty heat, and trembling, and tenderness so painful I thought my heart would burst. But out of this astounding, intolerable pain came joy, we gave each other joy that night. It seemed, then, that a lifetime would not be enough for me to act with Joey the act of love.

But Joey is a boy.

Quirky Fact: Yes, the novel is based on Baldwin's affair with Lucien Happsberger, but the truth of the matter is that Happsberger wasn't executed, technically—he simply married a woman! I guess Baldwin didn't attend the wedding.

What to Skip: *Giovanni's Room* is short; it'll only take you an afternoon to read. And trust me, there's nothing to skip.

GABRIEL GARCÍA MÁRQUEZ
(1928–)

⌒⌒⌒

One Hundred Years of Solitude
(1967)

If you've read the book you're holding straight through, you've heard me compliment a lot of different authors for a lot of different things; what you haven't heard me say is that one of them wrote the greatest novel of our era. That's because Gabriel García Márquez, with the hand of God or of an angel or perhaps simply by carrying within him a bison's heart, a burro's cojones, and the wisdom of a row of palmists, extended to the world the singular masterpiece of the second half of the 20th century— or perhaps of any half of any century—the novel that arches above and beyond all others, covering them in its eclipse like a sequoia does a sapling.

But the fact that it's the "best" novel barely makes a difference compared to the effect that this one book will have on you, the humanity it incarnates, the wisdom, love, humor, imagination, joy, and sex that it contains, its ability to strum you like a zither and make your heart sing out beautiful.

When I read, I hope the book will reach me in at least one of three places: where I zip, where I button a shirt, and where I put on a hat. Into these, all three, *One Hundred Years of Solitude* makes its mark; all the way down, to the bone, to the blood, etched in the tubes that hold the marrow and the channels that pump the platelets; there is nowhere in you it won't plumb and no nerve it won't twang.

What is it that makes a book great? You make your list, I'll make mine, and it doesn't matter what you've got on there, you will find it in *One Hundred Years of Solitude*. I've read Gabo's great triumph at least a dozen times, and I'm convinced there's no book that can teach us more. It doesn't merely tell, nor at times even show, it *embodies*, instantiating not only all the glory that's in there, but making us realize the staggering fact that a human being could write such a work, could make something with that much feeling, something so full of everything that makes our lives fuller. To know that such a man was out there and that he could give us such a work restores hope to even the most jaded among us.

For two years after college, I gave up on all other books; I simply read, over and over, *One Hundred Years of Solitude* and his other Everest, the tragically neglected *Autumn of the Patriarch* (not to be confused with the far inferior *The General in His Labyrinth*; see "What People Don't Know" on page 338). I read one, then the other, then back, on and on until each line I came upon prompted in my memory the words that were about to follow, as if I was an actor refreshing his lines or an author editing his own work. I honestly had no desire to read anything else; that's how much I loved them, that's how much I got out of each read-through. Even now, if my library went up in flames, and I escaped with only a copy of *One Hundred Years* or *Autumn* to sustain me for the second half of my life, I'd still thrive.

There are people who struggle with *One Hundred Years*, and I can see why. It has as involuted and imaginative a story line as virtually any in history, out-Tolstoying even Tolstoy in chronicling seven generations of the majestic Buendía family in Macondo, the village they founded in a Latin American hinterland. The plot is jungle-dense and jungle-teeming, and the characters are as simultaneously real and improbable as your own family. But the real problem is the names—especially three boy names: José, Aurelíano, and Arcadio—that in one combination or another seem to make up all the male characters of the book. Most editions will have a genealogical chart in the front that you can consult as you go, but you might want to annotate it a little so you can remember which José Aurelíano Arcadio is which.

Apart from that, just realize that *One Hundred Years of Solitude* is a feast. Eat slow, eat lots, taste everything, relish it all, then go back to the buffet as many times as you can. It's a standard question to ask someone what book, if they were shipwrecked, they'd want to have with them. Read it once and you'll know: *One Hundred Years of Solitude* is what you'd want in your back pocket as you swam for the sandy shore.

The Buzz: Forget magic realism. Right now. If I hear you say the words, I'll sneak up behind you with a piano-wire garrote; I'm not kidding. Yes, Gabriel García Márquez is associated with that dimwit's category (lumping him with the epigone Isabel Allende and other charlatans), but his imaginative leaps *are the least important thing about this book*. To reduce García Márquez's narrative genius to such an infantilizing pseudoconcept as magic realism is high treason in itself, but to allow that academic manure to be what people talk about regarding this novel, as if humanity doesn't need to be sat down, as a whole, at grandpa Gabo's knee and told what's really important, *that* is utterly inexcusable. Literature classes have a sacred book on their hands and they make it sound like the trip journals of a peyote fiend. For shame.

What People Don't Know (But Should): *One Hundred Years of Solitude* is often hailed as Gabo's singular achievement (although people who prefer Literature Lite lean toward *Love in the Time of Cholera*), but García Márquez has a hidden masterpiece in the novel that followed *One Hundred Years*: the astounding *Autumn of the Patriarch*. Shorter, but in some ways both stylistically more ambitious and harder to read, it revs itself up to three-page-long sentences (some of which change speaker midway) and forty-page paragraphs. It sounds like a gimmick but it isn't; the narrative and voices actually need to come out that way. Unfortunately, *Autumn of the Patriarch*'s perceived difficulty has resulted in a kind of gulag-ing of the book to all but a few rapt devotees (me being one). Having read and loved *One Hundred Years of Solitude,* one might think there's nowhere to go but down; *Autumn of the Patriarch* is more like a lateral move, getting more of Gabo at his very best.

Best Line: Where to begin? I feel like God is asking me, *Mortal, which is the most beautiful jonquil in the meadow?* Can't I say I love them all? *But only one will fit in your buttonhole.* Good point, Lord. Though my favorite lines are in the passage in "What's Sexy" on page 340, there's a bit that, for me, is a metaphor of living in this world and reading men's books and growing sad and despairing and then suddenly finding Gabriel García Márquez. The setup is this: José Arcadio Buendía (the patriarch) has been leading a group of men from the village through the jungle ("a universe of grief") in search of the sea. They've found nothing, the path they cut with their machetes grows closed behind them, and they finally take a break to hang their hammocks and sleep properly for the first time in weeks. When they wake, in a clearing in the dense flora far from the sea, they see a wonder: a beached Spanish galleon. "The whole structure seemed to occupy its own space, one of solitude and oblivion, protected from the vices of time and the habits of birds. Inside, where the expeditionaries explored with careful intent, there was nothing but a thick forest of flowers." A galleon filled with flowers with no clue how it got there: such is the miracle of *One Hundred Years of Solitude.*

What's Sexy: My lovelies, I have good news: *One Hundred Years of Solitude* has sex, good sex, convincing sex, Latin sex, and no small amount of it. There's José Arcadio's enormous tool, covered in tattoos; there's Aurelíano Segundo and his concubine making so much love that his livestock starts breeding out of control ("Cease, cows, life is short!"); there's the girl prostitute that Aurelíano visits (who reappears in Márquez's short stories); there's Aurelíano José discovering his aunt's nipples; there's Remedios the beautiful being so gorgeous that when they shave her head and dress her in a burlap sack she looks that much better, causing every man who sees her to be forever miserable. But there's also one of the great losing-virginity scenes in all of literature. Here's just a sample:

> That night, in his burning bed, he understood that he had to go see her, even if he was not capable. He got dressed by feel, listening in the dark to his brother's calm breathing, the dry cough of his father in the next room, the asthma of the hens in the courtyard, the buzz of the mosquitoes, the beating of his heart, and the inordinate bustle of a world that he had not noticed until then, and he went out into the sleeping street. With all his heart he wanted the door to be barred and not just closed as she had promised him. But it was open . . . [and] he let himself be led to a shapeless place where his clothes were taken off and he was heaved about like a sack of potatoes and thrown from one side to the other in a bottomless darkness in which his arms were useless, where it no longer smelled of woman but of ammonia, and where he tried to re-

member her face and found before him the face of [his mother] Úrsula, confusedly aware that he was doing something that for a very long time he had wanted to do but that he had imagined could really never be done, not knowing what he was doing because he did not know where his feet were or where his head was, or whose feet or whose head, and feeling . . . the bewildered anxiety to flee and at the same time stay forever in that exasperated silence and that fearful solitude.

Quirky Fact: Among the innumerable tiny bits of quirky wonder poppyseeding *One Hundred Years of Solitude,* one of the most imaginative is the blind old matriarch Úrsula's ability to find things that people have lost. The reason is that she notices when they've deviated from their normal patterns; they look for the thing along the accustomed routes of their daily lives— without even realizing it—so if they lost the thing during a lapse in routine, they'll never find it. But she remembers the lapse, so she can go right to the place it was waylaid.

What to Skip: Skip the rest of printed matter, skip church, skip a date, skip eating, but please don't skip a moment of *One Hundred Years of Solitude.*

THOMAS PYNCHON
(1937–)

⌒⌒⌒

Gravity's Rainbow
(1973)

To read *Gravity's Rainbow* is to submit yourself to a psycho-logical experiment, but how you read it will dictate which experiment you get. Read it the way we normally consume liter-ature—ten or thirty pages before bed, another fifteen on the sub-way—and *Gravity's Rainbow* will subject you to an enormous and seemingly endless exercise in confusion and frustration. Very few people make it very far in Pynchon's double-wide master-piece, and there's a good reason: it's a near-impenetrable man-grove of interconnected elements, sprawling and expanding, almost metastasizing, to the point where unless you're keeping notes on a graph-paper wall board, you're almost sure to lose your bearings.

The alternative is one I stumbled upon by accident while bedridden on vacation with a nasty cold and *Gravity's Rainbow* as my only book: I did nothing but read the bugger for four straight days; then, the second I finished, I turned from the last page to the first (as I recommend you do with Faulkner's *Absa-lom, Absalom* too) and read the whole thing again. Only that way could I keep the gajillion pieces of the mosaic together; only that way could I follow the obsessive, brilliant, paranoid mind of one of the most reclusive writers in America, Thomas Pynchon.

Now I said that you get a psychological experiment any way you go about it, and the problem is that if you've put in the sustained immobility to read the whole thing twice through consecutively, then you actually get it, I mean really get it, which means that you find yourself fully participating in Pynchon's paranoia and demented Weltanschaaung. You'll stand up from your sickbed, take a look around, and start to feel reality pushing in on you, everything in concert, everything part of something larger, unseen hands intimating themselves everywhere. Other than Aquinas' *Summa Theologica* or Hegel's *The Phenomenology of the Spirit,* no other books so involve you in their own process as to alter, at least temporarily, the modalities of your thinking and your experience of the world. Give Pynchon credit; he might well be crazy, but he can make us crazy right alongside him.

Gravity's Rainbow might contain not only the most paranoid, but the most hyperactive plotline in all literature. Set during World War II, it's a fictional account of Britain's responses to the German V-2 supersonic missiles detonating around London seemingly from out of nowhere. Though he doesn't discuss this in the book, I think Pynchon became obsessed with the V-2 because, as the first supersonic missile used against England, it didn't announce itself with the usual incoming warning sounds. In fact, until the Germans issued a report of their new technology three weeks after they started the bombing, *the Brits didn't even know they were being bombed.* First an explosion, *then* "a screaming came across the sky" (*Gravity's Rainbow*'s famous first line), but no one ever knew where it was coming from. Talk about mass-induced paranoia—and a perfect metaphor for Pynchon's worldview. (A side note: my 1990s German textbook had us translate—no joke—"The V-2 was a retaliatory weapon." Who are they kidding? Still trying to make that claim fifty years later—and in a textbook!)

That's the base metaphor of *Gravity's Rainbow*, but the story itself reticulates so exponentially, it's vital not to miss the primary thing that makes it worth holding on to: humor. The comedic trajectory of the book plays out in its main character, Tyrone Slothrop, an American officer serving in Britain. Slothrop is a perfect cross between Leopold Bloom and his Dublin bumblings in *Ulysses* and the ever-watched but ever-unaware misadventures of Jim Carrey in the film *The Truman Show*. Due to some experiments he was subjected to as a child (perhaps), Slothrop gets a hard-on when the German bombs are coming, so the forces that be think that they can somehow use Slothrop to anticipate where they will fall.

They decide to tail and manipulate and monitor and get Slothrop tail, but the connections and interconnections and attenuations—involving chem labs, rocket cartels, plastics, the Masons, a rocket-worshiping African tribe, a secret SS squad, and a very baroque masturbation fantasy (among many other things)—just get more and more inscrutable for both the reader, the watchers, and Slothrop himself. At one point in the novel, Pynchon quips about the "derangement of aim" behind the design of Gothic cathedrals, but clearly a similar mania undergirds *Gravity's Rainbow*. Time and again, Pynchon pens the words "everything fits" or "everything is connected"—this is his worldview, this is his novel's ambition—but he clearly has a lot of anxiety as to whether the reader of *Gravity's Rainbow* can, as he says, "make it all fit."

I'm not sure anyone can make it all fit, but I'm not sure it matters, either. Like Spenser's *Faerie Queene*, *Gravity's Rainbow* is not a book to try to commit to memory or to hope to be able to summarize. If you can feel the intelligence and frenzied paranoia linking up everything, if you can take a stroll in Pynchon's amphitheatric mind for nine hundred pages or so—and appreciate the switchblade wit and rampant depravity mentioned below—then you've gotten the *Rainbow* experience. Your brain might hurt, your eyes might ache, your vision will swim, and you will definitely start wondering who's watching, who's listening, and why you have a Krups coffeemaker, but you'll be able to say that you entered into Pynchon's great Habitrail and came out the other end.

The Buzz: "A screaming came across the sky"—one of the most famous and oft-quoted first lines of a modern novel. But next time you hear someone quote it, ask him (it will almost certainly be a him) about the bananas (which occur on page 4). Don't be surprised when he has no idea what you're talking about.

What People Don't Know (But Should): The title and the first line both refer to the trajectory or sound of the German V-2 bombs coming across the horizon toward London. And if you knew that already, did you know about Slothrop's outfits? Here's the order (I think I got them all) of the duds Slothrop wears over the course of the novel. I'm willing to bet it's the kookiest and widest-ranging of any character in classic lit:

American Army office-wear

A Hawaiian shirt so aggressive it pains his friends

A purple sheet

An English, taken-to-be-Nazi uniform

A green-and-purple pimp suit, fedora, and spectators

A white (perhaps an error?) zoot suit

Workman's clothes, shoes get stolen

Overalls streaked in paint

The Rocketman outfit: a green velvet cape, helmet with
    Viking horns, and buckskin trousers

A tux, later with a "Kick Me" sign written in Low Pomeran-
    ian stuck on his back

A pink pig suit

A dungaree shirt and trousers

Best Line: *Gravity's Rainbow* starts off with a bang and then
keeps chocking up great lines. Here are a few of my brief favorites
(and because there are no chapter markers, I'm including page
references to the Bantam paperback edition): "Ruins he goes
daily to look in are each a sermon on vanity" (28); "the yellow
sun being teased apart by a thousand chimneys breathing" (29);
"a *star,* that anal/sadistic emblem of classroom success which so
permeates elementary education in America" (98); "all you feel
like listening to Beethoven is going out and invading Poland"
(513); "consumers need to feel a sense of sin" (758); and, for those
of you who like to know the point of it all: "the object of life is to
make sure you die a weird death. To make sure that however it
finds you, it will find you under very weird circumstances. To live
that kind of life" (866).

What's Sexy: With *Ulysses, Gravity's Rainbow* has to be the most
explicit and encyclopedic raunch-fest in highbrow lit. When it
begins, we find out that Slothrop has a map of London in his office with stars stuck all around representing different women he's
diddled (and, as we discover, also marking where German bombs
are hitting) and it just continues from there. So here are references to some of the better, more prolonged, or just plain skanky
scenes: the wartime lovers Roger and Jessica (43–45 and 140–

41), "together they are a long skin interface"; pedophilia (58–59); the sex slaves Katje and Gottfried kneeling before Captain Blicero in his superkink Inquisitor drag with the bladed mirkin—oh my (109–11); Slothrop and Katje—"Slothrop undoing belt, buttons, shoelaces, hopping one foot at a time, oboy, oboy, but the moonlight only whitens her back." (228–29); the geriatric Brigadier Pudding's S/M and scat scene—the most disturbing sex in any classic novel ever (268–75); "Tannhäuserism" (348); on stockings (461); the orgy a-sea and Slothrop being "inside his own cock" (539–48); on snuff S/M (781–82); the Chiquita banana-lady fantasy (790); and Gottfried as "an erotic category, hallucinated out of that blue violence, for purposes of self-arousal" (885).

Quirky Fact: I love it when Osbie Feel cooks up the amanita mushrooms to make himself hallucinogenic cigarettes (who knew?) and was fascinated/horrified by the story of the Dutch explorer committing genocide on the dodoes on Mauritius simply because they wouldn't fly away. Better still, though, is the "Disgusting English Candy Drill" when Slothrop is forced to eat deathly "prewar" bonbons by an old British woman—"the Meggezone is like being belted in the head with a Swiss alp"(138). But the weirdest moment has to be the cameo appearance of Mickey Rooney sharing a mutual befuddled stare with Slothrop who's still in his Rocketman outfit (444–45). Remind me to work Mickey Rooney and Viking horns into my next novel.

What to Skip: I'm afraid there's not much you can miss if you want to have any idea of what's going on in the rest. That said, you can certainly skim Slothrop following the mouth harp down the jazz club toilet (71–81)—it's racist and utterly baffling (though it prefigures Ewan McGregor's character diving for the suppositories in *Trainspotting*). Also skim Roger's disjointed and uninteresting thoughts during the choir (151–59). And, I hate to say it, but skim or skip the above-mentioned orgy scene, which, unless you're especially into that sort of thing or want to laugh along at its slapstick execution, is by far the least literary (and downright clumsy) part of the book. Oh, and that crazy banana scene at the beginning—what's that about?

CORMAC McCARTHY
(1933–)

❦

Blood Meridian
(1985)

If man is to undo man, if the apocalypse is to come and it is we who have set it afoot, then Cormac McCarthy has been its prophet. In his novel *The Road*, the worst has already taken place; what's left of humanity cannibalizes itself, and a father seeks to rescue his son with no greater plan than simply to lead him into the unknown. In *Blood Meridian*, the apocalypse has also arrived, but it lies within. Written as if with a jagged bottleneck inked in the flow of a jugular, McCarthy's riveting portrayal of the Glanton gang, a band of mercenaries paid to exterminate Indians along the Texas-Mexico border in the middle of the 19th century, shows a human heart as black and unyielding as obsidian. One of McCarthy's early novels is entitled *Outer Dark*, and it's a description he uses often, believing that there is no end to the darkness, no limit to the horror humans will inflict on each other. The unshuttered eye will know that he's correct, though tragically this is a lesson learned more often from the stories of fact, not fiction.

Perhaps then it's not surprising that McCarthy's tale is based in part on truth, taking its departure from the Indian-hunter Samuel Chamberlain's *My Confession*, a purportedly accurate account of the author's time in the Mexican-American war.

Chamberlain's story is bloody and bleak, but McCarthy's is far more so, whetting the historical details of the actual Glanton gang into tools for his fictional slaughteryard. No novel has ever been as unremittingly, unrepentantly violent as *Blood Meridian,* but few novels have ever been more entrancing or gripping either. To read *Blood Meridian* is to walk rapt through a Shiloh of the dead and mutilated. You read and squirm and your lunch sits unsteadily in your stomach, but McCarthy's fascination doesn't waver. And at the end—for it will keep you spellbound all the way through—you will know you've been shown a truth that few writers have dared to depict: humanity at its most gruesome, most damned and self-damning. There is an outer dark, and McCarthy shows us that the place where it resides still pumps and beats and covets.

Shocking, gruesome, and pessimistic as *Blood Meridian* is, it's also a stunning stylistic triumph. Cormac McCarthy is my favorite living American writer, and both here and in his preceding novel, *Suttree,* he shows an English more ornate and original than any since Faulkner's. Alternating between filigreed constructions of mesmerizing complexity (see "Best Line" on page 352) and stark, studly, Memorex dialogue, McCarthy turns the American novel into a diamond drill: sharp, precise, but almost limitless in force. What he manages is breathtaking and completely unrivaled; no current writer in English comes close. *Blood Meridian* is his most ambitious effort, and the most shocking; like the fabled tapestry of Arachne, the level of atrocity is matched only by the art of its presentation. After the first time I read it, dumbstruck, I summed it up to a friend just as I would do today: *Blood Meridian* is like something released from the fist of an angry god.

A final note: I'm including *Blood Meridian* here because the literary powers that be have already dubbed it McCarthy's masterpiece and, after Toni Morrison's *Beloved*, the best novel of the last twenty-five years. But there's actually a different novel that I think is better, and McCarthy happened to write that one too. It's *Suttree*, the novel just before *Blood Meridian* and that McCarthy supposedly spent twenty or thirty years finishing. Though less pyrotechnic than the book that followed, *Suttree* is actually both richer and more accessible. Of all McCarthy's novels, it's the most autobiographical, the most human, and the most wise, funny, and sublimely poignant. Many McCarthy devotees consider *Suttree* his greatest, and it's quite simply among my favorite books ever. I've reread it at least ten times now, and I can honestly say that no single American novel has better dialogue and characters (though Faulkner's oeuvre as a whole still takes the cake), and none is more moving. Sadly, *Suttree* hasn't yet gotten the accolades and cinematic fanfare that the later novels have; critics and directors seem to have arrived a little late to the McCarthy party.

The Buzz: All readers are in agreement: *Blood Meridian* is the most violent thing they've ever read. From a tree Christmas-strung with murdered babies to the scalp-tonsuring of still-live skulls (by both Indians and whites), *Blood Meridian* is as lurid and un-Novocained as a battlefield suture. It's also as imaginative as anything anyone has ever read, and as vivid. There is literally no novel remotely like it; turn the pages and let it axe itself into you.

What People Don't Know (But Should): The character of the judge is based on Glanton's second-in-command, but from the mortal man McCarthy stretched the very envelope of myth. More sinister than Iago, more biblical than Ahab, as jaded and godless as the Grand Inquisitor, the judge might be literature's most originally conceived avatar of evil. Huge, white, bloated, and hairless, he looks like an upright manatee, but he's a nimble dancer, a dead-eye shot, a mordant sage, and an obliterating, consuming Kali. Whether he's to be taken as the devil himself I'll leave up to you, but this quote will give you a small sense of his deep-space coldness. He's been filling his rifle with cactus seeds and gunning down songbirds, so one of his fellow reprobates asks him why. The judge's response: "Whatever exists in creation without my knowledge exists without my consent. . . . Nothing must be permitted to occur . . . save by my dispensation. . . . The freedom of birds is an insult to me." Damn!

Best Line: Every description of the Indians appearing is utterly stupefying. Early in the book, Comanches ride down the mercenaries while piping flutes of human bone, dressed in garish theater garb and carrying shields besprinkled with mirror bits that cast light beams everywhere. The scene is unbelievably intense: all the horses are painted, the men are painted, arrows are whizzing everywhere, the white men are surrounded, ridden down, speared through, and scalped. A more harrowing three pages you'll never find. But for a few sentences of McCarthy at his most dense and dazzling, this description of horsemen becoming visible in the distance, shimmering and reflected on the glassy desert floor, left me literally wide-eyed:

> The riders were beginning to appear far out on the lake bed, a thin frieze of mounted archers that trembled and veered in the rising heat. They crossed before the sun and vanished one by one and reappeared again and they were black in the sun and they rode out of that vanished sea like burnt phantoms with the legs of the animals kicking up the spume that was not real and they were lost in the sun and lost in the lake and they shimmered and slurred together and separated again and they augmented by planes in lurid avatars and began to coa-

lesce and there began to appear above them in the dawn-broached sky a hellish likeness of their ranks riding huge and inverted and the horses' legs incredibly elongate trampling down the high thin cirrus and the howling antiwarriors pendant from their mounts immense and chimeric and the high wild cries carrying that flat and barren pan like the cries of souls broke through some misweave in the weft of things into the world below.

What's Sexy: The sex in *Blood Meridian* is as grim as everything else. The band visit prostitutes at various points, but nothing is especially sexy. At one point, the judge is found with an imbecile and a twelve-year-old girl, all naked. That doesn't bode well. Nor does the very end, but I don't want to spoil that for you. . . .

Quirky Fact: On a volcano surrounded by Apaches and the entire band out of gunpowder, the judge leads the men to the rim of the crater and starts scraping the sulfurous rock with his knife. Eventually he mixes in nitre and charcoal (not quite sure where he got those), then has all his men tinkle into it, spreads it out on the rock to dry, crumbles and cuts it with his knife—and lo, they have gunpowder. Keep that in mind next time your horn is empty and the indigenes are closing in.

What to Skip: You won't want to skip anything—unless the bloodshed gets to you, in which case you might want to skip it all and go read *Suttree*. One thing to note, though: as with most of Cormac McCarthy's novels, the vocabulary of *Blood Meridian* can be a little over-the-top, especially when he's doing static descriptions of things. If you can't understand his unabridged Webstering—or his untranslated Spanish—well, don't worry too much; the rest of the novel will make up for it.

One last consideration, especially for aficionados who want a little more C. McC. Don't be fooled by fame and accolades; McCarthy's prize winners aren't his best. *All the Pretty Horses* won the National Book Award but lacks the depth of character of *Suttree* or the imaginative scope of *Blood Meridian*. *The Road* won the Pulitzer but is McCarthy's lightest novel, and *No Country for Old Men* (whose film version won Academy Awards for Best Picture, Director, and Adapted Screenplay—the holy trifecta for cinematic renderings of books) almost feels like he was on autopilot (*il s'est cliche*, if we can invent a French verb). Read *Blood Meridian*, read *Suttree*, repeat.

TONI MORRISON
(1931–)

❦

Beloved
(1987)

Beloved is one of those—and there are few—extraordinary, rapturous, spin-you-round-its-finger books. It's an every-sense novel, smelltouchtasteseefeel writing, an all-the-heart/all-the-mind journey, a world you prance in, a dream that doesn't wake you, a path where there is no path through the tall corn, your hand being held, led by fingertip there where you can't see anything at all above the tassels and the pale green neckties, but your guide is sure. We open Morrison's book and we are taken.

You can't not feel the love and history and strength behind *Beloved,* and you can't not feel the tragedy and grace of its characters. It's an amazing human document, attesting to wisdom and sensitivity and deep raw sadness where light's hard to shine but Morrison manages to shine it there. *Beloved* feels like a porch swing—ready, smooth, and weight suspending—moving in a motion almost perpetual, almost effortless.

It's a novel to give yourself over to. It will confuse you, but you just have to sit tight; eventually it will tell you what you need to know. It will disturb you and it wants to and that's good. It has ghosts and superstitions but don't even think the words "magic realism" and don't worry if you don't believe—you'll believe here. It's experimental and not all the experiments work but that doesn't matter either. Because even when they don't, you'll still feel the power of Morrison's incantation, gumming your eyelids in search of another seeing.

Beloved takes its story from actual facts about erstwhile slaves in the years after their freedom, freedom either paid for or run for. Its title is taken from the lone word, body-bought, on the gravestone of a one-year-old, as well as from a sphinxy visitor who arrives seemingly from the aether, calling herself just Beloved. How the two are connected we will have to learn, but the ghost of the baby haunts the house of her mother, Sethe, forms a bond with her sister but scares off her two brothers. It is a novel of enormous emotional layering and complexity. There are deep, troubled protagonists in Sethe and Paul D., the man who comes and finds her. There are deep, real heroes in Sethe's mother, the cornfield preacher Baby Suggs (holy, as she is called), in the runaway-slave-sheltering ferryman, Stamp Paid, and in the insuppressible rebel, Sixo. There are good whites and a lot more bad whites. There is horror everywhere because there was horror everywhere. There are blackberry pies too but even these don't turn out like you'd expect. Stamp Paid had to slide full-weight through bramble to get the berries, but your way won't be so thorny.

Wrapped in its beauty, in the enormity of its feeling, *Beloved* will ultimately tell a tale of the deepest fear and anguish human beings can face. What slavery led Sethe to, led Sixo to, led Stamp Paid and Paul D. to, are human acts as tender, tragic, and noble as the causes were obscene. The reality that Morrison paints is a truth more horrific than the imagination could conjure, but her characters, fired in the kiln of suffering, emerge as large, rich, lovely, and real as literature has ever made.

Beloved is simply a novel to cherish, to curl and dog-ear, to underline and read out loud, and to give to everyone you know.

You won't need my help to get through, just pay good attention and don't worry if something doesn't make sense; there is a hand holding you, and she will steer you to the clearing. And you will know that you've gotten there.

The Buzz: Morrison first won the Pulitzer Prize for *Beloved* in 1987 and then the Nobel Prize in Literature in 1993. She has become the most famous and iconic black writer in America, and this is the most celebrated and important slavery novel since *Uncle Tom's Cabin.* To all this I just say that whatever social, political, feminist, African-American, American, or other role anyone wants to attribute to her (many of which she might actually choose to represent) or to *Beloved,* the novel would have been lauded as a classic even if Morrison had had to invent the entire background of slavery and race in America. That *Beloved* is based not only on this country's history but on true events only widens the prism of its meaning and shines brighter its necessity.

What People Don't Know (But Should): In her acceptance address to the Nobel Committee, Morrison tells a fable of a group of boys going to an old blind black woman, asking her if the bird they are holding is alive or dead. Morrison gives this story various outcomes and interprets it in various ways. Eventually she concludes that the bird stands for language, but then imagines that they aren't holding a bird at all. They have no bird, they have nothing, and they want the woman to give them what they lack. They say, "Make up a story. Narrative is radical, creating us at the very moment it is being created. We will not blame you if your reach exceeds your grasp; if love so ignites your words they go down in flames and nothing is left but their scald. Or if, with the reticence of a surgeon's hands, your words suture only the places where blood might flow. We know you can never do it properly—once and for all. Passion is never enough; neither is skill. But try." It's not hard to read between Morrison's lines: that's what *Beloved* was. The woman spoke.

Best Line: Sadly, the statutes of fair use won't let me transcribe all the great lines I'd love to, so I'm going to stick with one outstanding passage. Here's most of the sermon of Baby Suggs, holy:

> We flesh; flesh that weeps, laughs; flesh that dances on bare feet in grass. Love it. Love it hard. Yonder they do not love your flesh. They despise it. No more do they love the skin on your back. Yonder they flay it. And O my people they do not love your hands. Those they only use, tie, bind, chop off and leave empty. Love your hands! Love them. Raise them up and kiss them. Touch others with them, path them together, stroke them on your face 'cause they don't love that either. *You* got to love it, *you*! . . . This is flesh I'm talking about here. Flesh that needs to be loved. Feet that need to rest and to dance; backs that need support; shoulders that need arms, strong arms I'm telling you. And O my people, out yonder, hear me, they do not love your neck unnoosed and straight. So love your neck; put a hand on it, grace it, stroke it, and hold it up. And all your inside parts that they'd just as soon slop for hogs, you got to love them. The dark, dark liver—love it, love it, and the beat and the beating heart, love that too. More than eyes or feet. More than lungs that have yet to draw free air. More than your life-holding womb and your life-giving private parts, hear me now, love your heart. For this is the prize.

What's Sexy: There are three very sexy scenes in *Beloved,* and only one involves turtles doing the loving. The first is right at the end of the book's second section, involving Sethe and Halle in a cornfield, thinking no one can tell, while the other guys hear the rustle and see the corn tops swaying back and forth—fabulous. Later, when Paul D. comes to Sethe's house at 124, he touches Sethe from behind and she feels "the weight and angle of him; the true-to-life beard hair on him; arched back, educated hands." Love that. The third one, like I said, is turtles. Don't underestimate . . .

Quirky Fact: The explanation of how Baby Suggs got her name is both goofy and very tender. One day, she asks her owner, Mr. Garner, why he calls her Jenny. "Ain't that your name? What you call yourself?" "I don't call myself nothing . . . Suggs is my name, sir. From my husband. He didn't call me Jenny." "What he call you?" "Baby." So Baby Suggs it is.

What to Skip: Pains me as it does to say it, I don't think the final chapter works at all. My first time through, I actually thought the book was done, then turned the leaf to find two more pages, read 'em and wished it had been done. Also both (but especially the first) non-narrative, "I Am Beloved" chapters will grate on a lot of readers and genuinely don't make much sense. Don't feel bad if you rush through.

Tips on Reading Classics—
and Good Books in General

1. Use a pen.

In the act of taking notes, you're really *taking note*. Pick books that are worth the effort and underline, star, and write in the margins. Meaning is everywhere; profundity is everywhere; humor, irony, eros, and wisdom are everywhere, in books as in life. Don't just let meaning hit you—go find it.

2. Read slowly.

Don't ever let a sentence go by without fully processing it. Too often we drift through paragraphs, sometimes focusing, sometimes not, but still letting our eyes run down the page. With books that merit the attention, slow-read every sentence, all the time. If you miss a line, turn around. Don't let anything escape.

3. Reread.

Don't have literary one-night stands. Go back again and again; the really good ones get better and better. Instead of there being a lot of books out there that you barely know, pick a few and love them well.

4. Seek out wisdom, one-liners, aphorisms, and life-quotes.

This is the stuff that makes great books great. And the more you're on the lookout for lines that relate to your life, the more you'll find stuff you can treasure—and quote—later.

5. Watch for irony, humor, puns, turns of phrase, rhythm, etc.

Great writers pack a lot into every page. If you strive to notice, they're sure to deliver.

6. But don't miss the little things either: vocabulary, Scrabble words, crossword answers.

If you're going to read tough literature, you might as well get some of the fringe benefits: impress your friends and kick butt on the Sunday crossword.

7. Don't worry about what you don't understand.

Even if you pay close attention to each sentence, you can't understand everything. Give the tough ones a second look, but then move on. The point is to derive as much as one can from reading; no one can get it all.

8. Keep a "commonplace" book and use the backs of your books as crib sheets/indices.

Have a notebook or journal where you write down observations, favorite quotes, etc. If you keep it with you, you'll reap the full benefit of everything you've read.

9. Pick the right edition.

Choose versions with useful but not overly specialized footnotes. And always pick footnotes over endnotes; endnotes are annoying to flip back and forth to, so you're unlikely to use them.

10. Pick the right translation.

Go to the bookstore and compare lines from different translations and pick which one sounds good to you. Sometimes the newest ones aren't the best.

11. Avoid online translations.

Almost all online translations are uncopyrighted, i.e., severely out of date. The last thing you want is a 19th-century translation of Boccaccio that you don't even know was bowdlerized.

12. Don't watch the movies first.

The linguistic beauty and subtlety of great books can't be appreciated at the speed dialogue goes by. Most movies end up infantilizing the classics. Best not to watch them—at least until you've read the original.

13. Above all, engage.

Put yourself in dialogue with some of the most brilliant minds, sensitive hearts, quick wits, vivacious spirits, and wise teachers the world has ever created. The greatest men and women of all of history are speaking to you—and you can hear them.

A Note on the Selections

When I decided to get down on paper what's great about the greats, I started by reading everything again, asking myself all the while, "What is outstanding, vital, pleasurable, or compelling here, and how can I get people to see it?" Eight years and a few hundred thousand pages later, I had the answers, but there was still a wee dilemma: how to reduce the Western Canon (for the East, I confess, is beyond me) to a manageable number of books. How could I pick not only my favorites, but also the most influential, famous, must-read, and iconic books of all time? It was clearly an impossible task, and no matter what I chose, it still felt like taking spoonsful out of an ocean.

More than anything I wanted to feature books that people felt they had missed: that they either never read or never enjoyed and still felt kind of bad about. So I asked around a lot, and the responses I got ended up accounting for most of my selections. As it turns out, there's a lot of lingering curiosity—and guilt—about *The Iliad*, the Old and New Testaments, *Hamlet*, *Moby Dick*, *Ulysses*, *Remembrance of Things Past*, and many others. Almost everyone I spoke with said there was something they felt they *should* have read, so communal remorse dictated my first list.

Then I added a bunch of titles to try to patch the holes left in literary history: Ovid's *Metamorphoses,* Spenser's *Faerie Queene,* Fielding's *Tom Jones,* Musil's *Man Without Qualities.* Even though they don't blip on many radars anymore, critics and scholars still consider these books to be among literature's finest achievements, and one can see why. That accounted for most of my remaining picks.

Finally, I added a few more—and here's where the accounting gets a little shady. A handful of books on my list aren't universally considered classics (*Tropic of Cancer, Giovanni's Room, A Farewell to Arms,* to name three) but they are, in my opinion, not only magnificent achievements, but also carve out corners of literature that no one else occupies (Miller with his lusty exuberance, Baldwin with pained homosexuality, and Hemingway with elegant understatement). They might not make everyone's lists, but mine wouldn't feel complete without them.

Hard as the selection was, I take a lot of comfort in the fact that all of the books here, given the chance, will do a good job speaking for themselves.

As to the so-called Great Books debate, i.e., whether we teach the dead white guys or keep opening up "his"-story to other voices, call me a conscientious objector. Yes, I think these fifty classics (and many others) are great—if they're read with the right care and counsel—but that doesn't mean that other books aren't great too. What's my definition? If it's great for you, then it's great—simple as that. I just want people to connect with books—and with life.

But that doesn't resolve the practical question of what gets taught. Here a dose of reality helps clarify things. In college wasn't it ultimately less important what books your professor had you read and more important whether he or she made them meaningful to you? I have no doubt the right teacher could make a course on comic books as significant as a course on Shakespeare, but I also have no doubt that the right teacher could make students like *Macbeth* as much as they like *The Watchmen*. Instead of worrying so much about what we teach, let's worry about how.

Acknowledgments

And of my swynke yet blered is myn ye
—Chaucer

I was never good at getting help; this book changed that. Gratitude too is a new thing, but perhaps that makes me that much more thankful for all the people who've shown their love and care in this jog-26-miles-then-sprint-the-last-385-yards process. Courtney Nichols and Jay Greenberg spurred me to move from my Causobon-esque "taking notes" phase to the rather more dynamic "selling the proposal" phase, one at a considerably higher hourly rate. My agent, Beth Vesel, teamed up with my editor, Lucinda Bartley, to soothe my various panicked episodes and give good advice. Rufus Griscom reeled in a few of my grad-student indulgences and gave some sobering feedback on my early working titles, as did my dad. Alisa Volkman Griscom and her mother Dolores conspired to house me in paradise for the sprint portion of the writing—mahalo. Professor Andrew Cole, "a man of greet auctoritee," was my Yank mole at the Bodleian. Jyl Kutsche provided inspired encouragement and good tea. Hunter Argeri helped me catch some of my mistakes. Mike Moore, always my guardian angel reader, came through again with early drafts, as did Lisa Moro, the planet's best-read bombshell. But mostly I have to thank Sarah—for the edits, the support, the nurturing I had never known before. At a time when I didn't think I could be happy, you made me smile more than ever.

Works Cited

Alighieri, Dante. *Inferno.* Translated by Allen Mandelbaum. New York: Bantam Books, 1981.

———. *Paradiso.* Translated by Allen Mandelbaum. New York: Bantam Books, 1981.

Anonymous. *Beowulf.* New York: W. W. Norton & Co., 1975.

Austen, Jane. *Pride and Prejudice.* New York: New American Library, 1980.

Baldwin, James. *Giovanni's Room.* New York: The Dial Press, 1962.

de Balzac, Honore. *Père Goriot.* Translated Burton Raffel. New York: W. W. Norton & Co., 1994.

The Bible: Authorized King James Version. Oxford, U.K.: Oxford University Press, 2008.

Boccaccio, Giovanni. *The Decameron.* Translated by G. H. McWilliam. New York: Penguin Books, 1987.

Brontë, Charlotte. *Jane Eyre.* New York: Tom Dougherty Associates, 1994.

Brontë, Emily. *Wuthering Heights.* New York: New American Library 1959.

de Cervantes, Miguel. *Don Quixote of La Mancha.* Translated by Walter Starkie. New York: New American Library, 1979.

Chaucer, Geoffrey. *The Riverside Chaucer,* 3rd ed. Oxford, U.K.: Oxford University Press, 1988.

Dickens, Charles. *Bleak House.* Oxford, U.K.: Oxford University Press, 2008.

———. *Great Expectations.* New York: Penguin Classics, 1996.

Dostoevsky, Fyodor. *The Brothers Karamazov.* Translated by Constance Garnett. New York: The Modern Library, 1982.

———. *Crime and Punishment.* Translated Jessie Senior Coulson. New York: W. W. Norton & Co., 1975.

Eliot, George. *Middlemarch.* New York: Signet, 1964.

Faulkner, William. *The Sound and the Fury.* New York: Vintage Books, 1991.

Fielding, Henry. *The History of Tom Jones, a Foundling.* Middletown, Conn.: Wesleyan University Press, 1975.

Flaubert, Gustave. *Madame Bovary.* Translated by Paul de Man. New York: W. W. Norton & Co., 1965.

García Márquez, Gabriel. *One Hundred Years of Solitude.* Translated by Gregory Rabassa. New York: Harper Perennial Modern Classics, 2006.

von Goethe, Johannes Wolfgang. *Faust.* Translated by Walter Kaufmann. Garden City, N.Y.: Anchor Books, 1963.

———. *Faust Part II.* Translated by Philip Wayne. New York: Penguin Books, 1959.

Hemingway, Ernest. *A Farewell to Arms.* New York: Collier Books, 1986.

Homer. *The Iliad.* Translated by Richmond Lattimore. Chicago: University of Chicago Press, 1961.

———. *The Odyssey.* Translated by Albert S. Cook. New York: W. W. Norton & Co., 1993.

James, Henry. *The Wings of the Dove.* New York: Penguin Classics, 1986.

Joyce, James. *Ulysses.* New York: Vintage Books, 1986.

Kafka, Franz. *The Trial.* Translated by David Wyllie. Kindle Books, 2008.

Mann, Thomas. *The Magic Mountain.* Translated by H. T. Lowe-Porter. New York: The Modern Library, 1952.

McCarthy, Cormac. *Blood Meridian.* New York: Vintage International, 1992.

Melville, Herman. *Moby Dick.* New York: W. W. Norton & Co., 2001.

Miller, Henry. *Tropic of Cancer.* New York: Grove Press, 1961.

Milton, John. *Selections.* Edited by Stephen Orgel and Jonathan Goldberg. Oxford, U.K.: Oxford University Press, 1990.

Morrison, Toni. *Beloved.* New York: Plume, 1988.

Musil, Robert. *The Man Without Qualities.* Translated by Burton Pike. 2 vols. New York: Vintage International, 1996.

———. *The Man Without Qualities: Volume 1.* Translated by Eithne Wilkins and Ernst Kaiser. New York: Capricorn Books, 1965.

Nabokov, Vladimir. *Lolita.* New York: Everyman's Library, 1993.

Ovid. *Metamporphoses.* Translated by Mary M. Innes. New York: Penguin Books, 1977.

Proust, Marcel. *Remembrance of Things Past.* Translated by C. K. Scott-Moncrieff and Terence Kilmartin. 3 vols. New York: Vintage Books, 1982.

Pushkin, Alexander. *Eugene Onegin.* Translated by John Bayley. New York: Penguin Books, 1979.

Pynchon, Thomas. *Gravity's Rainbow.* New York: Bantam Books, 1976.

Shakespeare, William. *The Riverside Shakespeare.* New York: Heinle, 1996.

Spenser, Edmund. *The Faerie Queene.* New York: Penguin Classics, 1979.

Tolstoy, Leo. *Anna Karenina.* Translated by David Magarshack. New York: New American Library, 1961.

———. *War and Peace.* Translated by Rosemary Edmonds. New York: Penguin Books, 1982.

Virgil. *The Aeneid.* Translated by Allen Mandelbaum. New York: Bantam Books, 1981.

Woolf, Virginia. *To the Lighthouse.* New York: Harcourt Brace Jovanovich, 1927.

Wright, Richard. *Native Son.* New York: Harper and Row, 1966.

Index